VASILY OSIPOVICH KLYUCHEVSKY

# Modern Russian Historiography

*by*

## ANATOLE G. MAZOUR

*Professor of History*
*Stanford University*

## SECOND EDITION

### D. VAN NOSTRAND CO., INC.

PRINCETON, NEW JERSEY

TORONTO          LONDON

NEW YORK

## D. VAN NOSTRAND COMPANY, INC.

120 Alexander St., Princeton, New Jersey (*Principal office*)
257 Fourth Avenue, New York 10, New York

### D. VAN NOSTRAND COMPANY, LTD.

358, Kensington High Street, London, W.14, England

### D. VAN NOSTRAND COMPANY (Canada), LTD.

25 Hollinger Road, Toronto 16, Canada

PRINTED IN THE UNITED STATES OF AMERICA

TO MY STUDENTS
PAST AND PRESENT

# Preface

Twenty years have passed since the appearance of the first edition of *Modern Russian Historiography*. The book has long been out of print. During these two decades an increased interest has made a new and revised edition more compelling and long overdue. The student of Russian history today finds it more rewarding to seek information that pertains to the recent period; the further back he looks, the less material he is liable to find on Russian historiography. This is a regrettable situation, even if understandable, for hardly any country produced a richer historical literature prior to 1917 than Russia. The general disregard of the prerevolutionary period and the disproportionate bulk of writings devoted to the "Stalinist Era" gives one a distorted picture of Russian historiography. Furthermore, laboring within a limited scope of time seriously curbs a writer's field of historical vision and thereby deprives him of proper historical perspective. Writing in a tense atmosphere of what came to be known euphemistically as the "cold war," a writer exposes himself to further perils of seriously testing his nonpartisanship. Yet this generation cannot rest on its oars and wait for "historical perspective"; it must seek to chart the stormy seas into which it has been tossed, lest it surrender to aimless drifting and be carried to unknown shores.

In undertaking the present work I have tried conscientiously to present in fair proportion the historiographic development in Russia prior to 1917 and after. I still adhere to the determination of some twenty years ago, for reasons cited in my first preface, "to deal with Russian historians of Russian history only." Furthermore, I continue to adhere to the original decision of supplying English-speaking students with only the basic writings of Russian history in Russia.

Many reviews, personal letters, and advice from colleagues of my profession motivated my revision, and to them I acknowledge my gratitude. Twenty years of teaching experience must not be discounted either. All together, these have led me in the present edition to make revisions, additions, and several retreats from former views, which I recognize in all humility. Whether these changes enhance the value of this study I shall leave to the fair judgment of the reader.

Once again, as in the earlier edition, I must express my thanks to the University of Chicago Press and the editors of the *Journal of Modern History* for allowing me to incorporate with minor changes an article which appeared under the joint authorship of Professor Herman E. Bateman, University of Arizona, and myself in the *Journal* for March, 1952. It is my genuine pleasure to acknowledge my profound indebtedness to my colleague and coauthor for graciously consenting to let me utilize the published article in the present study.

A.G.M.

*Stanford, California*
*June, 1958*

# Preface to the First Edition

This study was undertaken at the suggestion of a number of professional colleagues. Upon commencing it, I found at once so great a number of writers to discuss or at least to mention—lest I be accused of ignorance of them—that for awhile I wondered if I should not abandon the project, and the difficulty of presenting many of the problems to readers who lack acquaintance with Russia only made me hesitate the more. However, I decided to keep on; and to facilitate the task, I determined to deal with Russian historians of Russian history only, leaving out the contributions which a legion of scholars of that country have made to ancient, Byzantine, and modern history. From the first sentence to the last, I have borne in mind that this work is designed merely as a guide for students who wish to acquaint themselves with Russian historiography. The degree of success attained in this endeavor is to be judged by others than the author.

I take pleasure in expressing gratitude to Professors Robert J. Kerner of the University of California, George Vernadsky of Yale, and Michael Karpovich of Harvard for their readiness not only to accept the laborious task of reading the manuscript in its original form, but particularly for sparing neither time nor effort in gathering bibliographical data and correcting errors. I also wish to express my thanks to the University of Chicago Press and the editors of the *Journal of Modern History* for allowing me to reprint parts of this outline which appeared as an article in the *Journal* for June, 1937.

A.G.M.

*Berkeley, California*
*April, 1938*

# Contents

# Annalistic Literature

*AMONG* the earliest sources of Russian history the chronicles occupy a most prominent place.[1] There is hardly another country which possesses a richer stockpile of annalistic literature than Russia. During the Middle Ages cultural development centered in a number of principalities, among them Kiev, Novgorod, Vladimir, Rostov, Pskov, Pereyaslavl, Volyn, Ryazan, Suzdal, Tver, and Moscow. In each of these principalities chroniclers connected with either the princely court or a monastic institution kept a record of events, copied former accounts of the past, and added comments, often reinterpreting or altering the narrative to favor the local prince or to touch

[1] Among the numerous studies of Russian annalistic literature the following references may be suggested as the most helpful: *Povest' vremennykh lyet* [Tale of Bygone Years], text prepared by D. S. Likhachev, tr. into modern Russian by D. S. Likhachev and B. A. Romanov, 2 vols., Moscow, Academy of Sciences, 1950; A. A. Shakhmatov, *Povest' vremennykh lyet* [Tale of Bygone Years], Petrograd, 1916 (see particularly the introduction and annotations to the text); A. A. Shakhmatov, *Obozreniye russkikh letopisnykh svodov XIV-XVI v.v.* [A Survey of Russian Chronicles of the XIV-XVI Centuries], Moscow-Leningrad, Academy of Sciences USSR, 1938; D. S. Likhachev, *Russkiye letopisi i ikh kulturno-istoricheskoye znacheniye* [The Russian Chronicles and Their Historical Significance], Moscow, 1947; M. D. Priselkov, *Istoriya russkogo lyetopisaniya XI-XV v.v.* [A History of Russian Chronicle Writings of the XI-XV Centuries], Leningrad, 1940; and *Istoriya russkoy literatury do XIX vyeka* [A History of Russian Literature until the Nineteenth Century], ed. by A. E. Gruzinsky, Moscow, 1916 (note particularly the part contributed by A. E. Presnyakov).

Also A. E. Presnyakov, *Lektsii po russkoy istorii* [Lectures on Russian History], Moscow, 1938; M. O. Koyalovich, *Istoriya russkogo samosoznaniya* [A History of Russian Self-Realization], St. Petersburg, 1884; and V. S. Ikonnikov, *Opyt russkoy istoriografi* [A Study of Russian Historiography], Kiev, 1908 (see especially Vol. II, Part I).

1

up the story with local color. Expert students, after examining many of these chronicles, have shown how each of these additions or "layers" reflects the peculiar environmental conditions or reveals the cultural atmosphere of the time the particular part was added.

The year-by-year accounts show that some periods were colorless, others were notable for more dramatic developments. The chronicles vary in style and content: while some are devoid of literary grace, others show noticeable talent and even display poetic genius. For this reason some of the chronicles may be rightly considered not only of historic but also of pure literary value. The spirit with which a record is imbued often indicates the prevailing political atmosphere of the time it was compiled. As the influence of Kiev began to fade, particularism became more pronounced. Yet three factors served, even though faintly, to hold the principalities together: a common faith, common memories of former unity, and a common language. For this reason each chronicler could safely start with the Primary story and then go on to embellish it with local bias.

It was quite common to change the names or even the locality to fit the narrative to this or that principality or to please the local prince. Yet one fact remained vital: by his dependence upon the Primary Chronicle each writer started with the *Tale of Bygone Years* and with the traditional version concerning the origin of the Russian people and the early formation of the state. This became the traditional beginning and standard interpretation of virtually every medieval chronicler. After the chronicler copied his predecessor's text, he considered that he had a perfect right to attach his own name to the completed assignment, often without even mentioning the former author. He regarded it as his further right to handle the text quite

freely and to expand, abridge, or alter entirely the previous version. It is for this reason that many of the chronicles reaching us today display so many textual "layers" and call for such caution, knowledge, and ingenuity in dissecting them according to date, author, or location.

In some chronicles the prevailing theme was the story of the endless wars in which the particular principality had been engaged. In others the stress was on bitter social strife or on the protracted struggle against oppressive rule. The striking feature, however, remained the same: the traditional desire to record faithfully and sometimes fancifully all past events for posterity. In most cases the chroniclers proved themselves well-informed persons not only about local conditions but also about their relations with the outside world. Virtually all the earlier writers made their appearance with the year 862 A.D., the year the Varangians were "invited" to rule the Slavs.

The extensive annalistic literature has been the subject of intensive study by a legion of eminent Russian scholars for over two centuries. Suffice it to mention such names as Tatishchev, Karamzin, Bestuzhev-Ryumin, Sreznevsky, Sukhomlinov, Shakhmatov, Priselkov, Nasonov, Grekov, Lavrov, Andreyev, Cherepnin, Bakhrushin, and Tikhomirov. To the historian the chronicles represent a source of special interest since on many occasions the authors made earnest efforts not only to record year-by-year accounts but also to present a broad historical synthesis. Furthermore, the distinguishing characteristic of all medieval writings in Russia was an extraordinary quality of historicalness put before entertainment.

One of the most striking illustrations is the Primary Chronicle, which is commonly attributed to Nestor and hence is known more popularly as the Nestor Chronicle. (Modern scholarship has conclusively proved that Nestor had only a share in the authorship of the Primary Chronicle.) The very beginning of this chronicle states clearly the purpose of the original author: "These are the narratives of bygone years regarding the origin of the land of Rus', the first princes of Kiev, and from what source the land of Rus' had its beginning."[2]

A large part of the chronicle, as has been proved by eminent scholars, is of compilatory character: it incorporates colorful folklore, local traditions, legendary tales, hearsay, and quotations from earlier records of Arabic, Byzantine, and Bulgarian origin. All these were skillfully woven into the general pattern of the narrative that made a composite story of "bygone years." Later it required a great deal of knowledge and archeological, paleographical, and historical ingenuity to dissect each component and trace it to its original source. Scholars of the last century have convincingly proved that the so-called Nestor Chronicle was not the work of a single man but a compilation of writings originating in much earlier periods.

*Tale of Bygone Years* (*Povest' vremennykh lyet*) is one of the best preserved written sources from earliest Russian history. This chronicle includes the versions of Sylvester, Prior of St. Michael's Monastery of Kiev, and the redaction by Nestor, the monk of the Crypt Monastery. The Nestor compilation dates to 1113 and is the nearest version of the Primary Chronicle that has reached modern historians.

Of the numerous chronicles only two have come down to us in their original form. Under careful, scholarly scrutiny they have been identified as the most authoritative ones: the Laurentian and the Hypatian. The first bears the name of its last author, the monk Laurence, who copied it in 1377 from an

[2] *The Russian Primary Chronicle. Laurentian Text*, tr. and ed. by Samuel H. Cross and Olgerd P. Sherbowitz-Wetzor, Cambridge, Mass., The Medieval Academy of America, 1953.

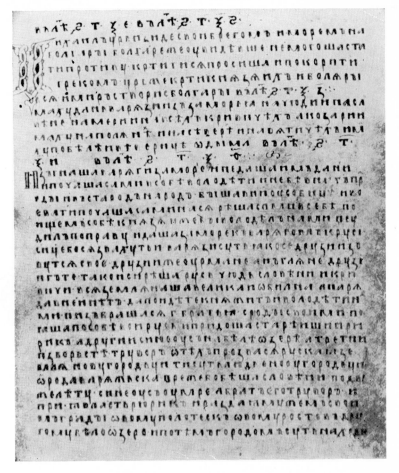

FROM THE LAURENTIAN CHRONICLE

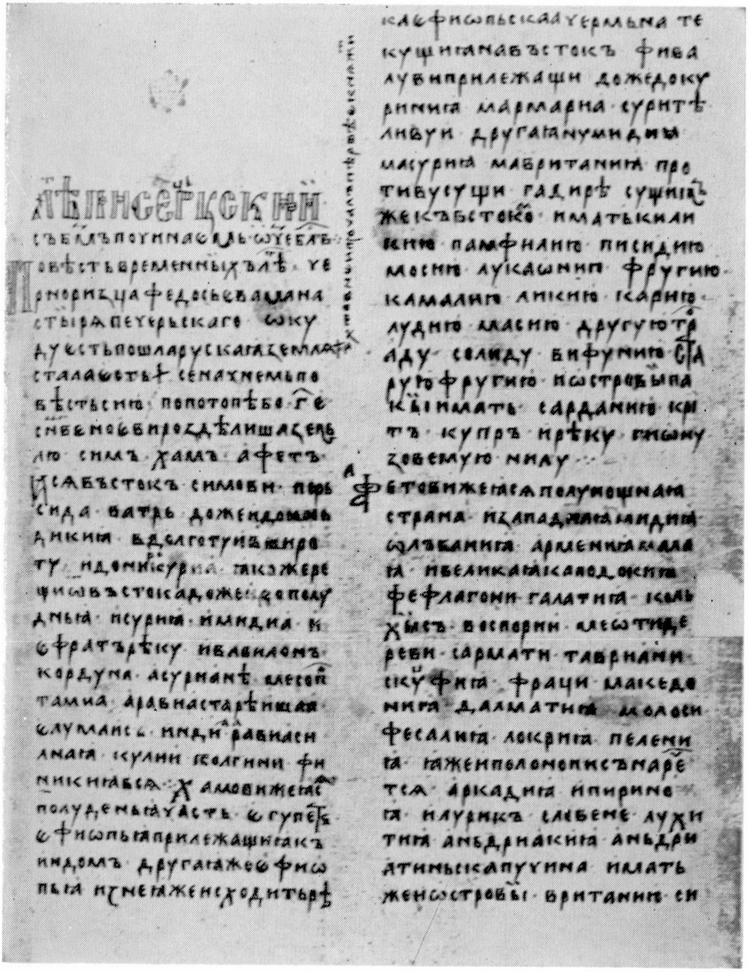

FROM THE HYPTIAN CHRONICLE

earlier manuscript for the prince of Suzdal. Only a single copy of this chronicle is known to be in existence; the original has never been found. In 1792 the document came into the possession of the eminent collector of antiquities, A. I. Musin-Pushkin, and eventually landed in the Leningrad Public Library, where it remains to this day. The period covered by the Laurentian Chronicle is from 852 to 1305. The first complete text to appear in printed form was published in 1846; it was not, however, until 1926 that a complete scholarly edition made its appearance. The Hypatian Chronicle is so named because it was found in the Ipatievsk Monastery in Kostroma. It was copied from the original sometime during the early part of the fourteenth century and brought the narrative to the year 1292. At present the copy is owned by the Soviet Academy of Sciences. The Hypatian Chronicle is a lengthy record of over six hundred sheets and consists of two parts: the first is the *Tale of Bygone Years;* the second, a copy of a Galich-Volyn' chronicle of the thirteenth century. This chronicle was first published in 1843; the latest scholarly edition appeared in 1923.

In the case of the Moscow chronicles, which date to a later period, the striking theme is the struggle of the Muscovite grand princes for national unification. The struggle as described was of a dual nature: against the Mongolian domination and against cantankerous local princelings for national unification. The centripetal force of Moscow is a recurring theme drawn against a background of local color and with an obvious Muscovite bias. As time went on, the chronicles came increasingly to serve the court, and their authors became ardent champions of their respective governments. In most instances the chronicle writer was not merely a pious hermit, consciously dedicating his life to Clio; he was a down-to-earth man motivated by political passions and mundane interests.

Chronicle recording in Russia continued for nearly seven hundred years until almost the eighteenth century, and altogether there are several hundred chronicles. The claims to territories which the Muscovite princes were continually setting forth were usually justified by citations from the chronicles. Their references to disputed lands later served the tsars most conveniently. To judge by the frequency of reference and accuracy of citations, the Muscovite princes must have known the textual contents by heart. They kept insisting upon title to their old "patrimonies" of Kiev, Chernigov, Smolensk, Polotsk, Tver, Novgorod, or Suzdal, "as cited in the chronicles." Whenever occasion called for it, whether in time of peace or war, in diplomatic pronouncements or personal correspondence, there was the ever-existing "absolute proof" of legality to "formerly owned lands" as stated in the chronicles. The centuries-long rivalries between Moscow and Poland and between Moscow and Lithuania invariably involved lengthy references to chronicles which conveniently supported territorial claims. Is it any wonder that local princes competed for men of learning who would be in charge of copying or of compiling data from the medieval chronicles? Indirectly the annalistic literature proved instrumental in the growth of an extensive though at times conflicting amount of interpretative writing. Yet it came to express the basic aspirations of the Muscovite state and the moving national force that proved instrumental in the building of the modern Russian state. For this reason any historical study of the origins of the Russian state is inconceivable without a thorough familiarity with the chronicles of Russia.

As in the case of belles-lettres, so in historical writing, Russia demonstrated an amazing outburst of vigorous talent and productive scholarship. Yet it would be remiss to bypass a century which has left a legacy that no student can possibly afford to overlook. The eighteenth century assured later historians of convenient access to formerly unknown archival material; it was a period of the *Geschichtssammler,* to use the term of Schlözer, which enabled the nineteenth-century *Geschichtserzähler* to exploit more effectively the work of their predecessors. It is chiefly for this reason that any conscientious work on modern Russian historiography must first pay due tribute to the pioneers of the eighteenth century.

The writing of history in Russia began not with the universities or learned societies, but with amateurs. Not until the nineteenth century did history become an organized subject, approached in a systematized fashion and transferred from private study rooms to university seminars, where the teaching and writing of history became the profession of men who devoted themselves exclusively to it. However, those amateurs who had begun to write history in the eighteenth century must not be sneered at. Confronting them was a problem of enormous difficulty—that of sifting through all legendary, unauthenticated material and placing the study on an entirely new and scientific basis, turning back for this purpose to the original documents in order to reconstruct the true story. Formerly, Biblical legends had not only been the chief sources for a national interpretation of the earlier time; they had also served as a patriotic justification for the assumed origin of the national state as well as of the "glorious past" of the Slavs. The earlier writers on Russian beginnings had to liberate themselves from medieval influences, particularly that of the Polish chronicles. The historians of the latter half of the eighteenth century faced a still more difficult task; they had to undertake a study of the increasing volume of documentary materials gathered by a legion of pioneering students. Newly discovered chronicles required not only a re-evaluation of former writings but also knowledge to read the texts correctly. The old canvas on which writers freely embellished their narratives with fanciful additions had to be cast overboard and the story of the past entirely rewritten. One can imagine the nature of the struggle in which the modern historian found himself engaged during the eighteenth century. We may well begin with the writings of Tatishchev as the representative of this early modern period in Russian historiography.

# The Eighteenth Century

## Tatishchev (1686-1750)

*THE* father of modern Russian historiography was Vasily Nikitich Tatishchev. He was the first to conceive Russian history on a large scale—a scale not even imagined by any previous writer; he was the pioneer in endeavoring to construct a pragmatic narrative of the Russian past.[1] A true son of the age of Peter the Great and an ardent admirer of his reforms, Tatishchev naturally turned westward—not to forsake the past, but to understand it more rationally. Under the direct encouragement of Peter himself, he set out to demonstrate to the Western world that Russia, too, had a history of which her people might well be proud. Tatishchev began his career in the army, like most men of his time, and participated in the famous battles of Narva and Poltava. Later, as a product of the Petrine epoch, he became a mining engineer and in this capacity was commissioned on several occasions to assume administrative responsibilities. In 1724 he was sent to Sweden to meet mining engineers and entice them to come to Russia

[1] N. A. Popov, "Ucheniye i literaturniye trudy V. N. Tatishcheva [Scientific and Literary Works of V. N. Tatishchev]," *Zhurnal Ministerstva Narodonogo Prosveshcheniya,* June 1886; separate edition, St. Petersburg, 1886; N. A. Popov, *Tatishchev i ego vremya* [Tatishchev and his Time], Moscow, 1861; P. N. Milyukov, *Glavniye techeniya russkoy istoricheskoy mysli* [Main Currents of Russian Historical Thought], Moscow, 1897; M. Tikhomirov, "Vasily Nikitich Tatishchev," *Istorik Marksist,* No. 6, 1940, 43-56. Valuable references may also be found in P. P. Pekarsky, *Istoriya Imp. Akademii Nauk* [A History of the Imperial Academy of Sciences], 2 vols., St. Petersburg, 1870.

to lend their skill and talent. Here for the first time he came
in contact with the West and was able to observe closely economic and political life abroad. Still later, he held a number
of responsible government positions in the Ural districts and
was appointed governor of Astrakhan Province in 1742, three
years before his retirement.[2]

For Tatishchev history was a sort of by-product; his main
interest was economic development of national resources. But
in pursuing his studies on this subject, he came to realize the
utilitarian advantage of historical knowledge in general.[3]
While he studied the national economic wealth, he was also
impressed by the abundance of documentary historical sources
scattered throughout the country. Tatishchev soon began to
collect these from various parts of the vast Empire and later
extended his search throughout foreign countries, where he
employed special copyists. His final aim was not merely to
compile but also to master the sources thoroughly and ex-
haustively and to write an interpretative history; he sensed
intuitively the presence of some pattern in history, which he
saw as something more than a chain of unrelated accidents.
His great ambition was to free Russian history from the current Germanic interpretation, particularly concerning the origin of the Slavs. It was for this reason that he emphasized
the early history of the Republic of Novgorod. While on his
mission to Sweden he had met many scholars of that country,
authorities on the early relations between Sweden and Novgorod.[4] Unfortunately his work was handicapped by his preoccupation with politics, while his utter lack of literary style

[2] A. N. Pypin, *Istoriya russkoy literatury* [History of Russian Literature], St. Petersburg, 1911, Vol. III, 369-70.
[3] *Russky biografichesky slovar* [Russian Bibliographical Dictionary], XX, 342-43.
[4] P. P. Pekarsky, *Noviye izvestiya o V. N. Tatishcheve* [New Information Concerning V. N. Tatishchev], St. Petersburg, 1864.

and inability to read Greek and Latin prevented him from personally familiarizing himself with important sources at home and abroad.

In 1738 Tatishchev submitted to the Russian Academy of Sciences two documents he came upon in his work: the texts of the medieval code of law (*Russkaya Pravda*) and the code of 1550 (*Sudebnik*), accompanied by extensive commentary notes. In this manner two of the most valuable sources of earlier Russian history appeared for the first time. Despite the errors which Tatishchev committed in interpretation, basically his approach and commentary notes proved surprisingly sound. While endeavoring to interpret the earlier period of history, he determined to put aside the so-called "Norman theory," the thesis concerning the origins of the Russian state. Tatishchev came to view the current "Norman" thesis as a product of the German members of the Academy of Sciences, who professed neither respect for nor understanding of Russia's past and therefore were liable to distort it.

A year later, in 1739, Tatishchev presented his *magnum opus* to the august body of the Academy, his *Russian History from Earliest Times,* consisting of five parts.[5] These included a history of the Scythians and early Slavic peoples prior to 860, followed by developments leading up to 1557; the period after that date reaches us in fragmentary form. This bulky undertaking was motivated by strong patriotic sentiments, and the author, with candid pride, stated that he did it in order to acquaint western Europe with Russian history. His work, he hoped, would dispel the calumnies and misunderstandings caused by German, Polish, and other unfriendly writers and prove that Russia

[5] V. N. Tatishchev, *Istoriya rossiyskaya s samykh drevneyshikh vremyen* [Russian History from Earliest Times], 5 vols., Moscow, 1768-1848. The five volumes were published posthumously and, as can be seen from the dates of publication, at considerable intervals.

had a great past of her own. Tatishchev ignored Biblical legends, basing his interpretations on "man's achievements only." Three factors, according to Tatishchev, played a most important part in the development of Russia as elsewhere: the art of writing, the Christian faith, and the art of printing. In this pronouncement it is not too difficult to detect the dawn of the Era of Enlightenment.

The monarchical form of government, according to Tatishchev, came about as a result of a contract, a theory which he evidently borrowed from Locke. Of the three forms of government—monarchy, oligarchy, and democracy—Tatishchev considered the first to be the most appropriate for his country. Oligarchy, he argued, prevailed in countries well-protected by natural boundaries such as mountains or seas, like Sweden or England. Democracy prevailed only in small countries and where cities played a predominant part in national life. In Russia, a country of vast and poorly protected territories where the masses were inadequately enlightened, monarchy was the only effective government. Tatishchev did not believe in a national destiny but in a social order best suited to the country and in the highest caliber of leadership the state could produce.

The amazing thing about Tatishchev's work was the enormous body of sources which he utilized for the first time. He consulted all the writings then available: chronicles, diplomatic correspondence, the letters exchanged between Prince Kurbsky and Ivan IV, and widely-scattered archival materials found at Moscow, Perm, Astrakhan, Kazan, and other localities throughout Russia; he also sought and on many occasions obtained copies of documents related to Russian history that were to be found in foreign archives. In 1725 he wrote to the University of Uppsala, Sweden, ordering all "useful books" and sources. Tatishchev was unable to organize properly or to evaluate critically the bulk of his gathered sources. Yet, taking into consideration the general cultural atmosphere in which the author labored and his lack of training as a student of history, it is surprising how much he did manage to accomplish.

When at last the manuscript was submitted to the Academy of Sciences, the learned dignitaries looked at it askance and severely censured it because of its forbidding size, dubious conclusions, and stylistic defects.[6] The author was compelled to undertake a revision of his thesis in order to suit the views of the German members of the Academy. Death caught Tatishchev while he was in the midst of revising his manuscript. Later other complications occurred when a fire destroyed a good portion of the writings. The entire work had to be reproduced from copies in the possession of Tatishchev's colleagues. Thanks particularly to Gerhard Friedrich Müller the work of Tatishchev was saved from complete loss.[7] Notwithstanding well-deserved criticism, Tatishchev was one of the first historians in Russia with a vision broad enough to realize the relationships among the various factors which collectively account for national life. It is only by embracing all phenomena that one is able to comprehend and reconstruct a nation's past as well as arrive at a philosophy of history. Tatishchev keenly appreciated the relationship to history of such sciences as geography, ethnography, and economics.[8] If his attempt proved unsuccessful, he at least gave impetus to others and served to presage a more enlightened method in the art of historical writing.

[6] Pypin, op. cit., III, 372.
[7] Sbornik II otd. russkogo yazyka i slovesnosti Imperatorskoy Akademii Nauk, XXX (1883), 51-53; N. A. Popov, Tatishchev i ego vremya [Tatishchev and His Time], 591-98.
[8] K. N. Bestuzhev-Ryumin, Biografii i kharakteristiki [Biographical Essays], St. Petersburg, 1882, 141, 145-47.

## Bayer (1694-1738)

Although feelings against the German members of the academic family in Russia were not always friendly, the antagonism derived from an emotional rather than a rational source. With a few exceptions the Germans invited to membership in the Academy, initiated in 1725, proved of inestimable cultural value to Russia, the German members serving as links between Russia and western Europe. Prominent among these was Gottlieb Siegfried Bayer, who, at the invitation of Empress Anna and her notorious favorite, the Duke of Kurland, Ernst Johann Biron, arrived in St. Petersburg from Königsberg. Hardly thirty-six years of age, Bayer had already proved himself a distinguished scholar in the fields of philology and history. A superb linguist and research student, he was among the pioneer academicians to bring to Russia the traditional ideals of Western scholarship. One of Bayer's main principles of research was his insistence upon the historian's meticulous examination of sources to establish authenticity before determining conclusions.

Even before arriving at the Russian capital, Bayer had an impressive list of publications, which he lengthened further while at the Academy. Of these, some monographs were devoted to various aspects of ancient Scythia, others to such subjects as Kievan geography (*Geographia Russica ex Constantino Porphyrogenito*), or to the Varangians (*De Varagis*), or to the origins of Rus' (*Origines Russicae*), or to the earliest Russian campaign against the Byzantine Empire (*De Russorum prima expeditone Constantinopolitana*).[9] Bayer has been justly considered the founder of the so-called "Norman school," which expounded the theory that the Russian state was of Scandinavian origin. The decade 1730-1740 in Russian history

---

[9] See also G. S. Bayer, *Auszug der älteren Staatsgeschichte,* St. Petersburg, 1728.

is notorious for the ascendancy of the German party at the court of St. Petersburg. In the light of what took place during those years it seems understandable how some observers might have deduced the Norman theory. The thesis was destined to touch off a fierce debate which continues to recur in historical literature to this day.

As an excellent linguist Bayer arrived at his deductions largely by means of comparative philology, collating names and terms in the Russian and Scandinavian languages. Though of speculative nature and vulnerable to much criticism, as any hypothesis is apt to be, the Norman theory led in some cases to such allegations as that anything constructive to be found in the formative process of the Russian state was due entirely to invited Normans. This armed some with convenient political weapons and instilled others with patriotic indignation. In the end the debates recurred with increasing heat and diminishing light on a subject stubbornly cloaked in the mists of the past. What seemed a purely historical issue was quickly to be converted into a battleground on which a questionable hypothesis and an injured national pride were to clash. One wonders if Bayer himself would not have experienced melancholy thoughts over the subsequent disputes.

The eight-year sojourn of Bayer in Russia was the cause not only of initiating a debatable hypothesis but also of stimulating an opposition that was forced to study the past and thereby encourage historical research. During his last four years, Bayer assumed the editorship of the historical journal of the Academy of Sciences.[10] Constant friction among the members often distressed him to such a degree that he would often decide to sever his relations with the Academy and return to his native

[10] *Sammlung Russischer Geschichte,* 9 vols., St. Petersburg, 1732-64. A posthumous volume, the tenth, was published in 1816 in Dorpat.

city of Königsberg. He failed to carry out his last decision, for he suddenly died in the prime of his career at hardly forty-four years of age. Behind him he left a profound influence upon standards of scholarship, for which the Academy became universally noted, and an interpretative philosophy concerning the origin of the Russian state that still divides the historians into the "Norman" and "Anti-Norman" camps.

## Müller (1705-1783)

Despite the tension that prevailed between native and German feelings, much constructive work was accomplished by the Academy, as subsequent developments will show. We must begin with the name of another member of that group, Gerhard Friedrich Müller, the phenomenally prodigious worker who was instrumental in opening up to students of Russian history forgotten or unsuspected archival wealth.[11] A successor of Bayer and one of the first German historians to settle in St. Petersburg, Müller emulated Bayer's diligence, though not his erudition. "I do not demand," wrote Müller on one occasion, "that the historian must narrate everything he knows, nor even everything that is genuine, for there are things that could not be told or that are not interesting enough to be narrated to the public; but whatever the historian does state must be strictly true and never should he give any cause for suspicion to be directed toward himself."[12]

Müller was only twenty years of age when he arrived in

---

[11] G. F. Müller, *Opisaniye Sibirskogo tsarstva* [A Description of the Siberian Kingdom], 2 vols., St. Petersburg, 1750; a later ed., Moscow, 1937-41; *Sammlung Russischev Geschichte,* 9 vols., St. Petersburg, 1732-64; a posthumous volume, the tenth, was published in 1816 in Dorpat; A. N. Pypin, *Istoriya russkoy etnografii* [A History of Russian Ethnography], St. Petersburg, 1892 (See chapter on Siberia in Vol. IV.).

[12] P. P. Pekarsky, *Istoriya Imp. Akademii Nauk* [History of the Imperial Academy of Sciences], I, 381.

the Russian capital from Leipzig in 1725. "In those days," wrote one German observer, "there was a popular movement from Germany to Russia, particularly among the students. These fools thought that nowhere was one likely to strike fortune more easily than in Russia. Everyone had in mind the student of theology expelled from the University of Jena, [Baron, later Count, Johann Friedrich] Ostermann [son of a Westphalian priest], who subsequently became Russian State Chancellor." Müller might have been one of those "foolish" young men whose high hopes for rapid advancement soon proved to be illusory. For a while he served in the capacity of an instructor at a gymnasium (i.e., high school) where he was compelled to teach whatever was assigned to him. Among the subjects he taught, besides history, were geography, Latin, elocution, and even the "art of letter writing."

After eight years of residence in the Russian capital with no definite assurance of a position, Müller decided to join Behring's second expedition to Siberia. The trip, for Müller a mere escape from material insecurity, proved of such consequence as eventually to place him among the notable pioneers in the field of historical research in his adopted country. The purpose of the expedition, further exploration of Siberia and the coast of Kamchatka, called also for a study of "the various subjects related to science." Müller assumed the responsibility of exploring "the geography of the earth, antiquities, customs, usages of the various natives." Above all, the government expected more pragmatic results: it wished to learn about the potential natural wealth of Siberia, its possible exploitation, and the possible commercial opportunities in the East; it wished to know whether Asia and America were separate continents. All data gathered, the government instructed, were to be kept secret so as to avoid the attention of foreign nations.

Though an historian by training and remote from the sciences called for by the assignment given to him, Müller extended his research to widely scattered fields of knowledge. He explored possible locations of mineral resources; he gathered information on local mines and home industries; he compiled *Notes on Siberian Commerce,* which aroused particular interest among the authorities in the capital. In the field of history Müller's travels in the East resulted in a two-volume study which represents a remarkable achievement. The work not only devotes many pages to the history of that little-known eastern domain but includes accounts of Russian relations with Asian countries. It is based on original documents uncovered throughout Siberia and in many instances in various local languages. It contains ethnographic, geographic, and diplomatic data, as well as local folklore revealed for the first time in historical literature.

It is difficult to imagine the obstacles which Müller had to overcome while collecting his source material. He examined some twenty archives in widely scattered localities of Siberia. Many documents, as he describes them, were in a deplorable state, carelessly cast in piles, the papers often chewed away by mice or stained by the dampness. The sorting out of these huge piles required the patience of a man who dedicates himself to a cause. Müller interviewed many people, especially the oldest survivors among the natives, to confirm local legends. Together with his compatriot, Johann Georg Gmelin (1709-1755), he made some archeological explorations, visited caves where stone figures and inscriptions were copied and legendary burial places searched, and came into possession of many Tartar chronicles.

The first volume of Müller's *History of Siberia* appeared in 1750. The publication called for an even greater strain than the Siberian expedition, for numerous difficulties had to be overcome before the author could see his laborious manuscript in print. A special commission appointed by the Academy to subject the manuscript to minute scrutiny resulted in endless disputes with Müller. The work had to be translated from German into Russian, and to this project a certain Golubtsov was assigned. He proved to be a drunkard and engaged in frequent bouts with Müller, who bitterly complained to the authorities against not only Golubtsov's drinking habits, but also his stealing of valuable paper and of the quills entrusted to him. The translated text was another source of friction. In desperation Müller wrote to the Academy authorities that his translator would lead him prematurely to his grave.

As one examines the materials amassed by Müller, one must conclude that he was not in the true sense a scholar, but a first-rate compiler—a fact for which we can be grateful, since no ambitious writer could have performed the valuable spade work which he did. With typical German diligence and persistence, he set out to copy voluminous collections of government records in the distant towns of Siberia. He combed the towns of western and eastern Siberia, visited many natives, sailed along various rivers, and located the "Siberian Chronicle" of Remezov; he copied and examined voluminous records, took many with him, and shipped others to St. Petersburg; he also discovered many sources that pertain to the Time of Troubles, charters issued by Boris Godunov, Prince Shuisky, and others. Altogether the ten years of labor (1733-43) resulted in his being able to hand over to the Archeographical Commission a mass of material which the Commission continued to publish for the next century and a half. Though begun incidentally, the collection of manuscripts gathered from Siberian archives and known as "Müller's Portfolios" (thirty-eight in all and for the most part still unpublished) opened a mine of sources from which students of Russian history, particularly of Russian eastward expansion, draw material to this day.[13] The originals of many of these documents are no longer available, so that the "Portfolios" remain the only valuable records of Siberian history.

Until the work of Müller appeared, almost all the historians had based their studies chiefly if not solely upon the only chronicles known to them. Müller's material, which makes up the larger part of the later supplements to documents published by the Archeographical Commission,[14] revealed new and more authentic sources, including numerous government decrees, orders, charters, and official correspondence. His papers contained extracts from the chronicles of the early seventeenth century, various statistical data, sources pertaining to Siberian ethnography and geography, and descriptions of the more important expeditions and personal adventures in eastern Siberia.[15] Besides offering these new documents, Müller was the first to direct attention to totally unknown Tartar and Mongolian sources; he interrogated natives and recorded their versions of bygone events, explored Siberian tumuli, and collected archeological, linguistic, and genealogical data. His discoveries led to an increasing interest in further search for archival material as well as in historical writing, particularly concerning later

[13] N. N. Golitsyn, *Portfeli G. F. Millera* [The Portfolios of G. F. Müller], Moscow, 1899. See particularly the more up-to-date account of N. Baklanova, and A. Andreyev, "Obzor rukopisey G. F. Millera po istorii, geografii, etnografii i yazykam narodov Sibiri, khranyashchikhsya v Moskovskikh i Leningradskikh arkhivakh i bibliotekakh [A Survey of G. F. Müller's Manuscripts on History, Geography, Ethnography, and Languages of Siberian Peoples, Kept in the Moscow and Leningrad Libraries]," in 1937 edition of Müller's *History of Siberia*, Vol. I, 543-69.

[14] *Akty istoricheskiye, sobranniye i izdanniye arkhograficheskoyu kommissieyu* [Historical Documents, Collected and Published by the Archeographical Commission], 5 vols., St. Petersburg, 1841-42. *Dopolneniya* [Supplements], 12 vols., 1846-72.

[15] P. P. Pekarsky, *Istoriya Imp. Akademii Nauk* [History of the Imperial Academy of Sciences], Vol. I, 418-24.

periods of Russian history. Moreover, they gave an insight into Moscow's eastward expansion and Siberian colonization—a subject barely touched at that time and one still awaiting due appreciation in Western historical literature. Müller's publication in German of the *Sammlung russischer Geschichte* further attracted the attention of Western scholars—among them Schlözer—to Russian sources; and Müller's *History of Siberia,* though a lifeless account, remains to this day a source to which students make frequent reference.[16]

The investigation of Siberian archives was followed by similar study of documentary evidence located in western Russia, especially in the archives of Moscow, which the government was long unwilling to open to curious scholars. In 1748 Müller was so carried away by his enthusiasm for his work (and to a degree by the animosity in academic circles) that he consented to abandon his Prussian allegiance (after twenty-three years of residence in Russia!) and become a Russian subject. Eventually he decided even to change his name to Feodor Ivanovich Meeller. There is good reason to believe that his frequent quarrels in the Academy were, in part at least, responsible for his decision to abandon his former citizenship. Anti-German feeling was rising, and frequent attacks by Lomonosov and other Russian members of the Academy who suspected Müller as "politically unreliable" motivated him to prove his loyalty. Personal experience, the fate of some of his compatriots in Russia, and particularly the conduct of Gmelin, who while on leave for a year decided never to return to Russia, made the position of Müller even more vulnerable to criticism. In 1752 Gmelin published his *Travels in Siberia* abroad without obtaining permission of the Russian government. As years passed by, Müller

---

[16] The reader is referred to an excellent essay, "Müller as an Historian," by S. V. Bakhrushin, in the latest edition of Müller's *History of Siberia,* Moscow, 1937, Vol. I, 5-55.

mellowed, became more sensitive and cautious, and finally surrendered to his fate. In 1764 he settled down permanently in Moscow, where two years later Catherine II appointed him to the superintendency of the Russian archives, a post Müller had long craved and which he held for the rest of his life. His departure from St. Petersburg ended the publication of the journal *Sammlung russischer Geschichte* and the monthly Russian publication *Yezhemesyachniye sochineniya*. The two journals contain much valuable historical material in both German and Russian.

Russian historiography is considerably indebted to Müller for having Tatishchev's *History* edited before its publication. Müller regarded this work as one of the outstanding achievements in Russian historical writings. Müller also edited the code of 1550, the *Sudebnik,* including the commentaries by Tatishchev, and several other sources of value to later scholars. In 1748 Müller requested that the Academy acquire the entire collection of materials painstakingly gathered by Tatishchev; he urged similar requests concerning other private libraries and collections of sources. He published the letters of Peter I to Sheremetev and was instrumental in the publication of a second edition of Krasheninnikov's *History of Kamchatka* (referred to below) not to mention numerous other documentary collections and historical accounts. Finally, Müller was the pioneering figure in the fields of Russian archeology and Siberian ethnography. Simultaneously he continued the compilation of all the sources, state-owned and privately owned, upon which he could possibly lay his hands. His toil was compensated by the fruitful research of later scholars, who began to exploit the material he had so meticulously gathered. More he had not expected. Realizing that his age permitted no ambitious literary undertaking and that archival work demanded unremitting attention, he sought younger men to continue his work, at first among his compatriots—like Schlözer—and later among the rising Russian generation represented by men like N. N. Bantysh-Kamensky, who succeeded Müller as director of the Moscow archive, or A. F. Malinovsky, who was later followed by such eminent archivists as K. F. Kalaydovich and P. M. Stroyev.

One more name must be mentioned in connection with Müller, that of Stepan P. Krasheninnikov (1711-1755). This man went east with the second expedition of Behring and under the direction of Müller and Gmelin explored the Kamchatka peninsula. The result of this ten-year investigation, thanks to the guidance of the two senior scholars, was that Krasheninnikov produced a monumental study of Kamchatka.[17] The two-volume study constitutes an excellent companion to Müller's two-volume *History of Siberia*. Historically speaking, Krasheninnikov's achievement is also significant in marking the beginning of the rise of a new generation of native intellect and talent that was soon to challenge effectively the cultural preponderance of the German elements among the ranks of the Russian Academy of Sciences during the eighteenth century.

### Schlözer (1735-1809)

There are four kinds of historians, according to August Ludwig von Schlözer: the collector (*Geschichtssammler*), the analyst (*Geschichtsforscher*), the writer (*Geschichtsschreiber*), and the artist (*Geschichtsmaler*). If Müller can be classified as the outstanding collector, Schlözer was without doubt one of the most distinguished analyst historians.[18] The two other kinds of historians were yet to appear in Russian historiography.

---

[17] S. P. Krasheninnikov, *Opisaniye zemli Kamchatki* [A History of Kamchatka], 2 vols., St. Petersburg, 1755; new ed., 1939; English ed., tr. by James Grieve, London, 1764).

[18] *Obshchestvennaya i chastnaya zhizn Avgusta Ludviga Shletsera, im samim*

# 24    MODERN RUSSIAN HISTORIOGRAPHY

A former student of oriental languages and theology and later of medicine, Schlözer eventually decided to devote himself to history. Already, while temporarily residing in Sweden (1755-1758), he had written an *Essay on the General History of Trade and of Seafaring in the most Ancient Times.* He soon came to extend his interest beyond the subject of trade, realizing that there was a need for widening the field of history.

Müller had already visualized the historian as a man "without a fatherland, without a religion, without a sovereign." Schlözer went further: he maintained that history must be universal, embracing more than mere political development, and that the historian must abandon his academic isolation for a closer acquaintance with the wide world of reality.[19] He was among the first to urge a scientific systematization of all sources upon which critical historical writing might be based. Whatever source material the historian finds, Schlözer insisted, must be analyzed objectively: historical writing was to be founded on sources that are without doubt authentic and the narrative based on these must be absolutely unbiased, regardless of racial or national affiliation of the author. "The first law of

---

*opisannaya* [The Social and Private Life of August Ludwig Schlözer described by Himself], tr. by V. Kenevich, St. Petersburg, 1809-19; A. L. Schlözer, *Allgemeine nordische Geschichte,* Halle, 1771; *Histoire universelle,* Tübingen, 1781; *Neuverändertes Russland, oder Leben Catharina der Zweyten,* Riga, 1771-72; *Probe russischer Annalen,* Bremen, 1768; *Nestor. Russische Annalen in ihrer slavonischen Grundsprache verglichen, übersetzt und erklärt von A. L. Schlözer,* 4 vols., Göttingen, 1802-05; *Geschichte von Russland,* Vol. I, 1768; *Tableaux de l'Histoire de Russie,* 1769. A Russian translation of *Nestor* appeared in St. Petersburg, 1809-19.

On Schlözer see the following: V. S. Ikonnikov, *A. G. Schlözer. Istoriko-biograficheskÿ ocherk* [A. G. Schlözer. An Historico-Biographical Sketch], Kiev, 1911; Bestuzhev-Ryumin, *op. cit.,* 177-203; P. N. Milyukov, *Glavniye techeniya russkoy istoricheskoy mysli* [Main Currents of Russian Historical Thought], 63-73; S. M. Solovyev, *Sobraniye sochineny* [Collected Works], 1539-1616; N. L. Rubinstein, *Russkaya istoriografiya* [Russian Historiography], Moscow, 1941, 150-66; Herbert Butterfield, *Man on His Past,* Cambridge Univ. Press, 1955, 52-59.

[19] It is interesting to note that Schlözer emphasized the significance of statistics, which he named *eine stillstehende Geschichte. Russky biograficheskÿ slovar,* XXIII, 342.

history," declared Schlözer in a famous utterance, "is to state nothing false; it is better to remain ignorant than to be deceived." The arts of writing history and of writing novels must never be confused; in the former there is no place for fancy, dreams, or invention. This new expostulation was delivered at a time when discord between German and Russian members of the Academy of Sciences was at its boiling point. The debates between Lomonosov and Müller over the "Norman" concept of history came to pose the question of what was the first and foremost purpose of the historian.

Schlözer found himself in Russia at the invitation of Müller in 1761. Here he hoped to find employment which would enable him to proceed with his studies and to travel in the Near East; while in Russia he found his interest aroused by the abundance of medieval sources of his patron, Müller. The reason the latter extended his hospitality to the young scholar was that he hoped he might gain his cooperation in examining the gathered sources.[20] With Schlözer's assistance Müller hoped to make use of the documents he brought from Siberia and write an extensive history.[21] The cherished scheme was based on more than mere seniority, as some writers seem to assume. Schlözer came to Russia as an intellectually mature person, carrying with him an air of erudition which Müller realized he himself sadly lacked. Schlözer, on the other hand, resentfully sensed his patron's scheme. With a degree of ill-concealed disdain he observed how poorly trained Müller was, largely because of his prolonged absence from western Europe. Of Russian historians, with the exception of Tatishchev and to some degree Shcherbatov and Boltin, he thought even less. Therefore a sharp disa-

---

[20] *Sbornik II otd. russkogo yazyka i slovesnosti Imperatorskoy Akademii Nauk,* XXX (1883), 1-3, 25, 30, 44.

[21] Pekarsky, *op. cit.,* I, 378.

greement between the two men was a foregone conclusion. Relations were further strained by the fact that Müller jealously guarded all the sources which Schlözer was eager to examine. After several years of hopes and disillusionments Schlözer left Russia in 1769. Presumably his departure was of a temporary nature; in fact, it proved to be for good, since Schlözer accepted an invitation extended by the University of Göttingen.

The impression Schlözer carried away about the state of scholarship in Russia was a strongly negative one. The most serious handicap, he felt, was the lack of proper training and familiarity with Byzantine and northern European history. Another reason explaining the academic backwardness was poor linguistic preparation among Russian historians. Even Bayer he regarded as an unsuitable scholar since he never managed to learn adequately the Slavic languages. As to his opinion of Müller, Schlözer considered him as a superb day-by-day worker. Realizing quickly the importance of linguistic equipment to the historian, Schlözer came to master Russian as few foreign scholars ever did. With the aid of the native tongue he soon extended his study from history into other fields, economics and ethnography particularly, both of which Schlözer came to regard as indispensable to history. It is to be regretted that Schlözer left Russia without ever familiarizing himself with the nature of the documentary material in Müller's possession. Though arrangements were made for a wide exchange of sources between the Academy of Sciences and the University of Göttingen, still much remained beyond Schlözer's reach. Without the knowledge of the content or general nature of many of the sources, he was bound to follow the outmoded method, relying almost entirely on the chronicles rather than on the more recently uncovered records in the east. Still it must be said that Schlözer felt intuitively that other documentary materials must be sought before a well-rounded history could be written.

The periodization of Russian history Schlözer outlined in his *Probe russischer Annalen* and in the *Tableaux de l'histoire de Russie* shows a surprising lack of originality. The first period begins with the orthodox invitation to the Varangians and ends with the death of Vladimir, 862-1015; he labels it *Russia nascens.* The second period, 1015-1216, Schlözer names *Russia divisa.* It deals with the process of Kievan decline and the rise of the appanage system. The third, *Russia oppressa,* 1216-1462, is marked by Mongolian ascendancy and ends with the death of Basil II. The fourth is named *Russia victrix,* 1462-1696. Finally, the climactic period begins with the ascendancy of Peter the Great and ends with the ascendancy of Catherine II, 1696-1762, which Schlözer exultingly entitles *Neuverändertes Russland* (Ressurrected Russia).

The writing of a complete Russian history, Schlözer believed, was a premature undertaking unless (1) all national sources (*studium monumentorum domesticorum*) and (2) those to be found in foreign archives (*studium monumentorum extrariorum*) had first been gathered and properly edited. While at the University of Göttingen he began to prepare materials for such a forthcoming collection. In 1768 he published his *Probe russischer Annalen* to be followed shortly after by other works such as *Allgemeine nordische Geschichte* and *Neuverändertes Russland.* Finally in 1802 Schlözer published the first volume of his monumental work, the study of that "old sage, Nestor." This work stands out as a unique accomplishment for its time, even in German historical literature. This labor of love Schlözer dedicated to Alexander I. In his preface the author expressed his hope that the work might inspire others to write a history of Russia with the *Gründlichkeit* of Maskow, the *Geschmack* of Robertson, the *Unbefangenheit* of Giannone, and the *Anmuth* of Voltaire.

Long before he published the Nestor Chronicle, Schlözer, with keen perception, outlined the preliminary work necessary to establish the authenticity of the Primary text. This called for a careful collection of all annalistic literature and an analytic study of each chronicle. It involved a minute comparative study in order to determine the influence of one chronicler upon another and detect through the borrowed textual parts the time each was recorded. The analysis would necessitate further a comparative study of Scandinavian, Byzantine, Arabic, and other eastern sources from which, most likely, some Russian chronicles must have borrowed parts of the texts for their own accounts. When such a *Corpus historiae russicae* was accomplished, only then could scholarship hope to attain its goal. This was the pious hope of many Russian scholars for over a century and a half and is far from fulfillment to this day.

Schlözer's method of tracing the genuine Primary text and weeding out the spurious parts demonstrated an astounding erudition and originality. This method was to become the basis of subsequent research throughout most of the nineteenth century. Though Schlözer was inclined to accept the "Norman" theory, he did so with some provisions. Thus he pointed out that within two centuries after the arrival of the Normans there was hardly a trace left of Scandinavian linguistic influence upon the Russian tongue, which led him to the conclusion that the Normans who descended upon the Slavs must have been numerically very few and therefore quickly absorbed. This interpretation was not challenged, and it even pleased the nationalist and Slavophile elements.

But Schlözer also maintained that prior to the arrival of the

Normans the Russians lived in a state of barbarism. This led to later accusations that Schlözer's Germanic loyalties were stronger than the historical methods which he advocated, that in effect what he endeavored to show was that the Normans (later to be considered Germans) were instrumental in civilizing the Slavs. The Slavophiles in particular were militantly opposed to such a contention, since they were most sensitive on this issue. They disregarded the fact that Schlözer also stressed the high literary standard which, prior to the arrival of the Normans, obviously prevailed among the Slavs, enabling them to create a rich annalistic literature. However, this consideration was overlooked by the nationalists; Slavophile nerves proved too taut to respond at any but the sore points, to pressure on which they reacted violently.

Objective judgment did not entirely depart from the ranks of scholars, and Schlözer even during his lifetime was recognized for his contribution to Russian historiography. His analytical study of the Nestor Chronicle was soon acknowledged as an outstanding accomplishment, and a request was made that it be translated from German into Russian. In recognition of his scholarship he was elected honorary member of the Society of Russian History and Antiquities. Schlözer's research convinced Russian scholars of the necessity for publishing all available chronicles and other documentary sources (a subject to be discussed in detail elsewhere). A more recent evaluation by Herbert Butterfield characterizes Schlözer thus: "There are defects in his critical practice. . . . It is not even true to say of him that he was a mind of the first rank; though he is certainly the most interesting figure in the Göttingen story, and the range of his activities is astonishing." [22]

Though Schlözer left Russia to escape the enervating squab-

[22] Butterfield, op. cit., 58-59.

bles within the academic family, he did not find the peace he sought in his native country either. At Göttingen he was annoyed by other experiences, mainly resulting from his utterances of personal views. He insisted, for example, that the historian must keep his faith apart from the institution of the church when dealing with the latter in history, that one must also dissociate from historical truth the superstitions accumulated over the centuries. Being an admirer of Voltaire, Mably, and other thinkers of the Era of Enlightenment, Schlözer came to be regarded by his colleagues as an atheist; for expressing approval of the execution of Charles I, Schlözer was labeled a dangerous radical who favored regicide and therefore should be watched with suspicion.[23] The path of Schlözer, like the path of many historians, was not always a smooth one, and it was only his devotion to historical truth that made the treading endurable.

### Lomonosov (1711-1765)

Mikhail Vasilevich Lomonosov was not in a strict sense an historian; yet his name can hardly be dissociated from Russian historiography. Though primarily a man of science, his learning embraced a wide range of knowledge. He conducted astronomical observations and proved proficient in physical science, particularly physics and chemistry. Preceding Lavoisier by several decades, he used the chemical balance for the first time and did pioneering work in modern quantitative analysis. He made a mosaic portrait of Peter I and wrote odes dedicated to his favorite sovereign and to the Empress Elizabeth, in which he extolled their virtues. He improved the rhythm of Russian verse and modernized the literary language as distinct from the Old Church Slavonic, thereby helping it to become a vehicle of

[23] *Russky biografichesky slovar,* XXIII, 343-44.

much more eloquent expression. He was the author of a new Russian grammar that remained for many years the standard textbook. Lomonosov held the posts of professor of chemistry and later rector of the University of St. Petersburg and ranked high among the members of the Academy of Sciences.[24]

It was as a member of the Academy that Lomonosov became one of the leading opponents of his German colleagues. Some of the Germans were careerists who through special favors gained membership in the Academy and whose presence caused much resentment. Another source of even more militant opposition was the "Norman" interpretation of history, which Lomonosov came to consider a purely German invention; it led to his indiscriminate battle against any German influence whatsoever. Though chiefly a scientist, he laid aside his laboratory research, plunged headlong into battle with historians, and took up the literary cudgels to defend his own thesis—that the Russian state had developed long before the Normans arrived upon the scene of history. His knowledge of history or of available sources was scant, and yet the influence Lomonosov exerted proved lasting in an historiographic sense.

The "Norman" incident was provoked by a paper delivered at the Academy by Müller in 1749 on the subject of the origin of the Russian state and the derivation of the name *Rus*. A self-made man with a profound sense of national pride, Lomonosov instantly attacked Müller and soon expanded the offensive against Fischer, Bayer, and Schlözer, criticizing their entire

[24] M. V. Lomonosov, *Drevnyaya Rossiiskaya istoriya ot nachala rossiiskogo naroda do konchiny velikogo knyazya Yaroslava Pervogo ili do 1054 goda* [Earliest Russian History from the Beginning of the Russian People Until the End of the Grand Prince Yaroslav the First or to the Year 1054], St. Petersburg, Academy of Sciences, 1766; Pekarsky, *op. cit.,* Vol. II; S. M. Solovyev, *op. cit.,* 1317-88; P. N. Milyukov, *op. cit.,* 31-33; M. N. Tikhomirov (Ed.), *Ocherki istorii istoricheskoy nauki v SSSR* [History of Historical Science in the USSR], Vol. I, Moscow, 1955, 193-204; N. L. Rubinstein, *op. cit.,* 86-96.

philosophy and method of approach; he stressed the fact that they had not learned the Russian language sufficiently and pointed out that they failed to consult native sources and depended usually upon documentary evidence in foreign languages abroad, therefore falsifying the entire course of Russian history.

In defense of his own national philosophy of history Lomonosov argued that the obligation of an historian was not merely to compile factual data, but to synthesize these and show the interdependence of all past events in the long process of history. This, he continued, required lucid vision, consistent thinking, integrity of character, and ability to discern historical unity. When such a narrative of the past is successfully composed, he concluded, it must serve to awaken in the reader a sense of pride, admiration, and respect for his native history. The verdict was thus simple: Müller dismally failed to accomplish his task, for he vilified and falsified history.

Lomonosov's violent attack against Müller led to an official request that he be assigned to write the history he so ardently advocated. This Lomonosov accepted; with the pattern already designed, to show that the past of Russia "equals that of ancient Greece and Rome, except for the absence of historians to prove it," he immediately commenced preparing himself to play the part of a Russian Herodotus. He began to examine the Nestor Chronicle, the earliest Slavic codes of laws, the first part of Tatishchev's manuscript; he read Greek and Byzantine historians, consulted Helmold's *Annales Slavorum* and Martin Cromer's *De origine et rebus gestis Polonorum;* he gathered copious citations that might support his thesis and prove that his opponents were entirely wrong. Lomonosov contemplated an extensive four-volume study which he was not destined to complete nor even to see partially in print: it was a year after his death, in 1766, when his first and only volume came off the press. It was entitled *Earliest Russian History from the Beginning of the Russian People Until the End of the Grand Prince Yaroslav the First or to the Year 1054.*

Lomonosov started to gather his material in 1751, began to write three years later, and sent his manuscript to the press in 1758. According to his annual report to the Academy, the three years were spent compiling citations from a wide range of documentary and secondary sources; he collected data on toponymy and comparative philology as part of the ammunition for his battle with the "Normanists." He quoted Slavic names of settlements of the fourth century and sought proof of earlier civilization preceding the "coming of the Varangians." He contemplated accompanying the published text with lengthy commentaries similar to those of Tatishchev, but his death prevented completion of the plan. From the lengthy lists of original sources which Lomonosov incorporated in the text he argued that Müller unjustifiably complained about the absence or scarcity of documentary evidence. Furthermore, he made an endeavor to prove that whatever source material Müller did use was selective and deliberate and that the latter discarded any evidence that might conflict with his preconceived theories.

The general thesis of Lomonosov can be summarized thus: History represents an endless process of the rise and decline of nations. The fifth century he came to regard as the dividing period between ancient and medieval history. The latter began with the invasions and defeat of the Roman Empire by the Germanic and Slavic tribes and the ensuing internal disorders within the Empire. To prove his thesis Lomonosov cited copiously from many writers, Pliny, Tacitus, Strabo, Procopius, Livy, Nepos, and Ptolemy among them. To Lomonosov history was a universal drama in which the Slavs played a part no less glorious than that of any other people. The coming of the Varangians was only an episode in and not the beginning of Russian history. Nor did the Varangians or "invited Normans" represent a homogeneous people of Baltic origin. On the contrary, contended Lomonosov, they included a most heterogeneous group of tribes and tongues, united by a common cause—plunder. He used philology as evidence, arguing that the origin of the name *Rus* was *Prus*, or "Prussian," a contention which later scholars have most convincingly disproved but which to Lomonosov was good enough for driving a point home.

Lomonosov's *History* cannot be considered as a contribution of enduring value to history; it serves rather as one sign of an awakened national consciousness which clamored for riddance of foreign intrusion in its intellectual life, and was destined to blossom a century later. Furthermore, it demonstrated with increasing evidence that in the absence of a complete publication of sources, as shown by Schlözer, history would provide a wide field for emotional discussion and writing but never a truly integrated, scientifically sound synthesis of Russia's past. This task was largely left the succeeding century to accomplish.

### Shcherbatov (1733-1790)

Historical study and the publication of source material became, in the second half of the eighteenth century, the occupation of many members of the Russian elite. The reign of Peter I and the following years of confusion, the struggle against foreign domination in intellectual life, and the endeavor to create in Russia a culture of her own, all conspired to bring this about. On the one hand, there was an ardent effort to write a pragmatic history of Russia; on the other, a desire to explore all archival material in order to justify by documentary evidence every claim to intellectual independence, if not superiority.

This was not precisely in agreement with the more scholarly concepts of Schlözer, but so far at least as students began to search for sources, it coincided with his ideas. Among these students two were preeminent, Prince Mikhail M. Shcherbatov and Major General Ivan N. Boltin.

A descendant of an illustrious old family, Prince Shcherbatov was one of the most cultured Russians of his time. He had received an excellent education, was thoroughly familiar with world literature, and had built up an enormous private library. As a member of the Legislative Assembly of 1766, Shcherbatov demonstrated an amazing acquaintance with the teachings of Beccaria and Montesquieu. In his observations on the relations between church and state he showed an equal familiarity with the literature of the Encyclopedists and most of all with Voltaire. He was familiar with the theories of the physiocrats, particularly concerning the role of agriculture in national economic life. He agreed with Schlözer on the importance of statistics and even attempted to write a "statistical survey" of Russia. Among his many political and social occupations, Shcherbatov became intensely interested in Russian history.[25] This was fortunate: for not only was his own library of great assistance, but he enjoyed access to some of the Papal archival materials and state archives as well, of which he availed himself largely through the assistance of Catherine II. This enabled him to advance historical writing much further than any of his predecessors.[26] The Emancipation Act of 1762, freeing the nobility from compulsory service to the state, allowed Shcherbatov the leisure to devote himself to the writing of history.

[25] V. Myakotin, *Iz istorii russkogo obshchestva* [Notes on the History of Russian Society], St. Petersburg, 1902, 112 ff.
[26] M. M. Shcherbatov, *Neizdanniye sochineniya* [Unpublished Works], Moscow, 1935, 112-13; *Russky bibliografichesky slovar*, XXIV, 115.

Shcherbatov was familiar with many of the Russian sources of which Schlözer had no knowledge whatever or the existence of which he only suspected. For this reason his history encompasses a far wider scope and is not of the nature of chronicle writing. Yet Shcherbatov still shows the signs of the eighteenth-century dilettante historian rather than the *Geschichtsforscher* of the Schlözer caliber. It is to be regretted that the erudition of Schlözer and the advantages derived from the social position of Shcherbatov could not somehow have been amalgamated; for, in spite of his prodigious industry and excellent opportunities, Shcherbatov sadly lacked training in handling historical sources, with the result that he often committed more errors than a careful scholar would have made without any sources at all. In his work Shcherbatov displayed little originality either in approach or organization of material and often followed the chronicles uncritically.

Economic or social factors were alien to his concepts; it was in politics that he was mainly interested, and the status of the nobility in society was of particular concern to him. An aristocrat to the core, he pursued a single theme: only in cooperation with the nobility could the monarchy remain strong and enduring. He cited at great length the reign of Ivan IV, with its senseless persecution of the nobility, and quoted copiously Prince Kurbsky's correspondence with the first tsar; he interpreted Ivan's military defeats as proof of the dangers of divorcing the interests of the nobility from the state. The numerous peasant uprisings were cited as further evidence for his thesis.

For two decades Prince Shcherbatov toiled over his bulky volumes of *Russian History from the Earliest Times,* which he never managed to complete. The seventh and last volume ends with the year 1610; the author's original intention was to lead up to the reign of Peter the Great. At the end Shcherbatov himself acknowledged that he was not entirely successful in his endeavor to present the historical synthesis he originally intended. He recognized his failure, but justified his labor by the hope that some future historian would utilize his writings and find in them the necessary material for a superior work. Besides his seven-volume history, Scherbatov also published source materials: *A Chronicle of Many Revolts, A History of the War with Sweden,* and various essays. The style of his writing throughout all his works is the typical ponderous one of his time, which makes tedious going for a modern reader. Being a rehash of the chronicles he had read indiscriminately, it therefore represents rather a guide than a study, as the author himself justly sensed at times. The chief merit of Shcherbatov's labor lies in the fact that he was the first to utilize some of the church and diplomatic documents, particularly the correspondence between the Muscovite sovereigns and the Crimean khans. During the following century Karamzin made good use of the materials which Shcherbatov presented and of his bibliographical references in general.[27]

Shcherbatov lived during a period when the demarcation between the old and the new Russia was becoming more and more distinct. As a typical aristocrat of the old Russia, in spite of his flirtation with Voltairian philosophy and his Freemasonry, he could see nothing good in the new ideas and could only lament the moral degradation that had come over his

[27] M. M. Shcherbatov, *Istoriya Rossiiskaya ot drevneyshikh vremyen* [Russian History from the Earliest Times], 7 vols., St. Petersburg, 1770-91; German tr., Danzig, 1779. On Prince Shcherbatov see: N. Chechulin, "Khronologiya i spisok sochineny kn. M. M. Shcherbatova [A Chronology and List of Works of M. M. Shcherbatov]," *Zhurnal Ministerstva Narodnogo Prosveshcheniya,* VIII, 1900, 337-64; Bestuzhev-Ryumin, *op. cit.;* Milyukov, *op. cit.;* A. N. Pypin, "Russkaya nauka i natsionalniyi vopros v XVIII v. [Russian Science and the National Question in the XVIII century]," *Vestnik Evropy,* III, 1884, 212-56; N. L. Rubinstein, *op. cit.,* 116-37; Tikhomirov, *op. cit.,* 286. *Russky bibliografichesky slovar,* Vol. XXIV; M. M. Shcherbatov, *Neizdanniye sochineniya* [Unpublished Works], Moscow, 1935.

fatherland. For him the old Russian customs and institutions held a peculiar virtue which the ruthless onslaught of Western ideas, forced through by Peter I, and the loose morals of Catherine II tended to destroy. He detested the prominence that various court favorites came to assume during the "Times of Catherine" and often expressed his feelings with a rare and mordant frankness. Shcherbatov's last work, *Concerning the Corruption of Morals in Russia,* is an obituary for old Russia and an appeal for the preservation of its forgotten virtues. Acknowledging the progress toward Western civilization which these two sovereigns had assured to Russia, he could not overlook the price which the people had paid for it in the disesteem that had befallen the virtues of the national character.

## Boltin (1735-1792)

Like Prince Shcherbatov, General Ivan Nikitich Boltin was a true son of his age and representative of the "amateur school" of historians. He was a familiar figure in the literary circles of St. Petersburg, knew Lomonosov personally, and was imbued with the spirit of the Age of Enlightenment. At one time he flirted with the ideas of the French *philosophes,* advocated religious tolerance, quoted Voltaire frequently, gently criticized the church and monastic orders for their accumulated wealth, cautiously favored legislation that would curtail the rights of serf owners or at least define them more precisely, and on occasion expressed faint hopes of emancipation.

General Boltin spent a good deal of his spare time, which was none too plentiful, in gathering sources and familiarizing himself with archival materials and private collections. This work was greatly assisted by the well-known collector of Russian antiquities, Count A. I. Musin-Pushkin. The "antiquarian dilettantism" of Boltin proved to have a more serious aspect than the superficial observer might have detected. He was not interested, as was Shcherbatov, in a tedious, minutely detailed paraphrasing of the chronicles. "Trivialities mentioned in chronicles are irrelevant to history," wrote Boltin. It was the philosophy of history that fascinated him. Boltin was absorbed in a comparative study of Russian and western European historical developments: he showed keen interest in national origins and in the history of the institution of serfdom, a subject that was soon to become of major importance. In this respect, it may be added, Boltin was better qualified than his opponents, since few men of his time either saw the essence of history so clearly or traveled so widely and knew conditions in Russia so intimately as he did. He was particularly familiar with the southern part of the country, where he spent many years as administrator in various official capacities. Catherine II sought his advice on many occasions and appreciated his wide knowledge of history, geography, and ethnography. Finally, it should be noted, a great deal of his writing was devoted by Boltin to an analytical study of other historians with whom he crossed swords.

In 1759 a French physician, N. G. Le Clerc, visited Russia at the invitation of the court, and on the basis of this visit wrote nothing less than a six-volume history of that country.[28] He boldly entitled his work *Natural, Moral, and Political History of Early and Recent Russia*. "The brazen-faced slanderer" so deeply hurt Boltin's patriotic pride by numerous misrepresentations that the gallant general took up his literary cudgels in defense of his country. "Judging Russia by comparing her with other European states," he declared, "is like trying to fit a dwarf's suit of clothes to a full-grown man." Since Le Clerc had relied greatly on the first two volumes of Shcherbatov's history,

[28] Nicolas Gabriel Le Clerc, *Histoire physique, morale, et politique de la Russie ancienne et moderne*, 6 vols., Paris, 1783-94.

Boltin unbridled his wrath against both writers. This criticism resulted in an impressive four-volume work, two volumes for each opponent. In these tomes the author displayed not only a considerable knowledge of the subject, as well as a good deal of historical acumen, but also a surprising capacity for original thought.[29] The criticism of Le Clerc's work so impressed Catherine II that she ordered the two volumes to be published at state expense.

Boltin first challenged Le Clerc's "Norman" theory that Russian political life dates to the coming of the Scandinavians. According to the chronicles, argued Boltin, Novgorod had been a self-governing state long before the Scandinavians arrived on the national scene; the level of Slavic civilization, furthermore, was much the same as throughout medieval Europe. Agricultural development, growth of town life, trade in the Baltic area, and commerce were recorded by chroniclers long before the ninth century. Culturally the Scandinavians who descended on Kiev were no further advanced than the Slavic peoples with whom they came in contact. Similarly, Boltin denied the idea expounded by Le Clerc that bondage was a typical Russian institution. He cited the institution of the *veche* (assembly) and similar democratic medieval institutions which allowed voting privileges, thus showing that Le Clerc was wrong. There was feudalism in Russia, said Boltin, but that was

[29] I. N. Boltin, *Primechaniya na istoriyu gospodina Leklerka* [Critical Notes to the History of Russia by M. Le Clerc], 2 vols., St. Petersburg, 1788; *Kriticheskiye primechaniya gen.-mayora Boltina na perviy-vtoroy tom istorii knyazya Shcherbatova* [Critical Notes of Major General Boltin to volumes I and II of the History of Prince Shcherbatov], 2 vols., St. Petersburg, 1793-94; *Otvyet gen.-mayora Boltina na pismo Kn. Shcherbatova* [Reply of Major General Boltin to a Letter of Prince Shcherbatov], St. Petersburg, 1793. On Boltin see: V. O. Klyuchevsky, *Ocherki i rechi* [Sketches and Speeches], Moscow, 1913, 163-98; P. N. Milyukov, *op. cit.*, 50 ff.; A. N. Pypin, "Russkaya Nauka i natsionalnyi vopros [Russian Science and the National Question]," *Vestnik Evropy*, III, 1884, 212-56; V. Ikonnikov, "Boltin," *Russky biografichesky slovar*, Vol. III; M. N. Tikhomirov, *op. cit.*, I, 210-14; N. L. Rubinstein, *op. cit.*, 137-50.

an institution not unfamiliar in western Europe. His theory, an original one, that Russian serfdom was similar to western feudalism was to be developed by other Russian scholars more than a century later.

Boltin regarded Russian annalistic literature as one of the most valuable sources for historical study, far above any foreign accounts of his country. It was reliance upon the latter that caused Prince Shcherbatov to commit some of the grave errors in his writings, stated Boltin. Yet he was entirely aware that one had to be cautious in relying upon the chronicles, and warned historians, therefore, that they must make comparative studies and carefully sift all evidence before their accounts could be accepted with any degree of finality. He correctly declared that the Primary Chronicle of Nestor must have been preceded by other chronicles. Finally, he cautioned, historians must not follow the pattern of events as cited in the chronicles—that was the error of Tatishchev and Shcherbatov—but must present an all-embracing picture of the complex national life and of the people at large. The historian, he advised, must see not only the achievements of individual leaders but the national accomplishments as well, and must explain the effects of historic causes upon the course of events. Such a presentation must incorporate the interdependence of general natural environmental conditions, the form of government, the prevailing judicial system, the peculiar geographic circumstances of the country, and other factors that were liable to contribute to the molding of Russian history.

Boltin was one of the earliest historians in Russia to attempt an analysis of historical processes; he held the view, as did Montesquieu and Bodin, that climate is one of the most important factors in determining social and political institutions. Criticizing Le Clerc's thesis that Russia was a barbaric country governed by whimsical despotism, Boltin endeavored to show that, on the contrary, only through their cultural superiority and monarchical form of government had the Russian people succeeded in surviving and overcoming foreign domination. Like Shcherbatov, he was a typical aristocrat of eighteenth-century Russia, favoring the Muscovite period and skeptical of the reforms of Peter I and Catherine II;[30] unlike Shcherbatov, however, he demanded that the subject of westernization be presented critically. Boltin reminded Shcherbatov in no uncertain terms that if one lacks skill in handling historical sources, it is preferable to leave them alone altogether.[31] He also insisted, as did Schlözer some years later, that history could never be rightly recorded unless all the documents, within the country as well as without, were properly gathered and organized. This was not a task for one person; whoever undertakes by himself both to compile all the sources pertaining to national history and to write that history is bound to fail, as had Tatishchev and Müller. With rare insight Boltin wrote, while criticizing both Shcherbatov and Le Clerc, that the labor which must precede the writing of history is as important and difficult as the writing itself. To create history, particularly good history, is very difficult and is hardly possible for one man, no matter how long his life or how gifted he may be. Before such a history can be written, all the necessary sources must be collected, analyzed, clarified, and comprehended; this requires more time and labor than the writing itself.

The influence of Boltin upon many nineteenth-century Russian writers is much in evidence. He was particularly admired by the later Slavophile school, which held history to be a science of national self-realization. Utilitarian in his view, he tried

---

[30] *Russky biografichesky slovar,* III, 199-200.
[31] *Ibid.,* III, 193-94.

to link his own time with early periods and to derive practical lessons therefrom. Logical and level headed, he maintained that historical interpretation should be based only on authentic sources. Schlözer, who held a very low opinion of Russian historians with the exception of two or three names, singled out Boltin as the only native historian worthy of special mention. Despite his original mind and intellectual foresight, Boltin, being a product of his time and intellectual climate, accepted erroneous theories. Some of his ethnographic theses and ideas concerning the origins of the Slavs, for example, are ludicrous.[32] He was incapable of grasping fully the implied historic importance of issues of his own time. He failed to appreciate the gravest of all such current problems: serfdom. He believed in solving the agonizing issue "step by step and slowly" and lived under mortal fear that precipitate action might be taken; in that case, he prophesied nothing but disaster for the peasants and economic ruin for the country.[33] The more, however, one studies Boltin's general approach to history and his views concerning methodology, purpose, and causation in history, the more one is prone to overlook his false views. Boltin is a symbolic figure in Russian historiography: he stood on the borderline of two distinct eras, with one foot in the quickly-fading eighteenth and the other in the nineteenth century, a century relentlessly advancing with new developments in historical writing.

## Golikov (1735-1801)

Among the men of the eighteenth century who diligently cultivated the fields of historical science must be included the name

[32] V. O. Klyuchevsky, *Ocherki i rechi,* 188.
[33] A. N. Pypin, *Istoriya russkoy etnografii* [A History of Russian Ethnography], I, 147 ff.

of Ivan I. Golikov. He represents the "amateur school" of historian of a different social group: all his life he remained a leaseholder and merchant and in 1766 served as deputy of the Third Estate in the Legislative Assembly summoned by Catherine II. Though leading a busy life, he managed to devote much of his time to the collection of sources on the reign of Peter I. Among these he succeeded in including many primary sources, memoirs of contemporaries, and folk tales about the colorful personality of Peter. The result of this amassed material was a staggering thirty-volume publication: twelve volumes of *Acts of Peter the Great, Wise Reformer of Russia,* and eighteen volumes of addenda, including extensive indices.[34]

This imposing set includes a chronological narrative of the life of Peter and numerous citations of rare documents painstakingly collected by Golikov. The material was obtained at considerable financial cost from many Russian provinces. The title of the voluminous collection in itself is revealing—to prove with almost reverential admiration the "acts of the wise reformer." Historians of a later date came to look with unconcealed disdain upon Golikov's collection; yet many writers relied heavily upon its contents. Golikov himself never pretended to scholarship; he humbly confessed that he was not a man of learning and knew nothing about the rules of critical evaluation of sources, his sole aim being to gather documents that might cast more light upon the time and the illustrious personality of Peter the Great.

As a member of the merchant class he professed special interest in the economic policies of his hero-emperor and in Peter's

---

[34] Ivan I. Golikov, *Deyaniya Petra Velikogo, mudrogo preobrazovatelya Rossii; sobranniye is dostovernykh istochnikov i raspolozhenniye po godam* [Acts of Peter the Great, the Wise Reformer of Russia; Collected From Authentic Sources and Arranged by Years], 12 vols., Moscow, University Press, N. Novikov, 1788-89; *Dopolneniye* [Addendum], 18 vols., Moscow, 1790-97.

aspiring drive to expand trade and commerce, to introduce industry, and to improve means of transportation. He praised Peter's policy of compulsory labor regardless of class origin, thereby expressing the views of the rising middle class. Contrary to the opinions of the aristocratic writers of history such as Shcherbatov, who expressed grave misgivings concerning the "demoralizing effects of westernization" and the decline of the indigenous virtues of the Russian people, Golikov took the opposite view: with the characteristic optimism of his class and the energetic drive for economc expansion, he detected in Peter's reforms only praiseworthy progress for the future. The very appearance of a man like Golikov in Russian historiography heralded some forthcoming changes during the following century.

## A Summary of the Eighteenth Century

With Shcherbatov, Boltin, and Golikov we may bring to a close the story of Russian historical writing during the eighteenth century. In general it can be said that none of the eighteenth-century historians had accomplished any critical study. Schlözer, because of his departure from Russia, was unable to analyze the wealth of new material which Müller had gathered in the east. His only notable accomplishment by the turn of the century was the annotated publication of the Nestor Chronicle.[35] The vast bulk of documentary materials remained virtually unknown to students of history; such was the case

[35] *Nestor. Russische Annalen in ihrer Slavonischen Grundsprache verglichen, übersetzt und erklärt von August Ludwig Schlözer,* 4 vols., Göttingen, 1802-05; Russian tr. by D. Yazykov, 3 parts, St. Petersburg, 1809-19; *La Chronique de Nestor,* tr. en français d'après l'édition imperiale de Petersbourg, manuscrit de Königsberg, 2 vols., Paris, 1834-35; also tr. by Leger, Paris, 1884. See also the edition by R. Trautmann, *Die altrussische Nestorchronik, Povest vremennykh lyet,* Leipzig, 1931. The latest English edition: *The Russian Primary Chronicle. Laurentian Text,* translated and edited by Samuel H. Cross and Olgerd P. Sherbowitz-Wetzor, Cambridge, Mass., The Medieval Academy of America, 1953.

with Müller's collections. Golikov's work represented a purely compilatory accomplishment from which later generations, especially the "Westerners," were to draw needed references during the nineteenth century. Its main purpose was the exaltation of Peter's reforms. The collection of sources remained throughout the eighteenth century largely a matter of the amateur's hobby and rarely a state-supported function. These private collectors nonetheless rendered an inestimable service to the field of history. It suffices to mention such faithful men as Müller, Tatishchev, and Boltin, or such benefactors as Count Rumyantsev and Count Musin-Pushkin.

During the last quarter of the eighteenth century an historian-economist, Mikhail Dmitriyevich Chulkov, succeeded in compiling an impressive seven-volume collection of statistical data on the history of Russian commerce.[36] This represents a rare labor of love and covers a wide range of information. It starts with the trade of pre-Mongolian Russia and the economic relations between the Republic of Novgorod and the Hanseatic League and continues with development of trade in the Baltic, in Asia, in the north by way of Archangel, and in the West. As in the case of other writers, Chulkov's compilatory work proved to be of immense aid only to later students of history. The national archives were still *terra incognita* to almost all historians, partly because of the enormous difficulty of early investigation but chiefly because the government remained reluctant to open them to students of history.

Müller's services to Russian historiography can hardly be

[36] M. D. Chulkov, *Istoricheskoye opisaniye rossiiskoy kommertsii pri vsekh portakh i granitsakh ot drevnikh vremyen do nynye nastoyashchego, i vsekh preimushchestvennykh uzakoneny po onoy Gosudarya Imperatora Petra Velikogo i Gosudaryni Imperatritsy Ekateriny Velikiya* [A History of Russian Commerce at all Ports and Boundaries from Earliest Times to the Present, and all Important Legislation of Peter the Great and of Empress Catherine the Great], 7 vols., St. Petersburg, Academia Scientiarum Imperialis, 1781-88.

overestimated. His preoccupation with the gathering of source materials did not permit him to do the historical writing he had hoped he could; he remained basically a *Geschichtssammler* throughout his lifetime. His ambitious undertaking of the *Sammlung russischer Geschichte* (previously referred to), his *Monthly Publications* published in Russian from 1755 to 1764 (twenty volumes), and later his attempt to write a recent history of Russia—which, incidentally, received the severe rebuke of Lomonosov—all these accomplished little except to supply the future *Geschichtsforscher*.[37] Subsequently, with his appointment as archivist in Moscow, Müller had to abandon even his editorial work and devote his entire attention to the tedious yet vital labor of investigation of hitherto unexplored archives. Again, it was only the generation to follow that reaped the benefits of his toil.

The latter half of the eighteenth century stands out as a schooling period in the field of research and the publication of available historical records. In this connection the year 1767 assumes special significance, for it was then that the first volume of the projected series of chronicle publications made its appearance. The planned series carried the characteristically long eighteenth-century title of *Russian Historical Library Containing Early Chronicles and Various Notations, as an Aid to the Understanding of the History and Geography of Early and Medieval Russia*. Eight volumes appeared between the years 1767 and 1792. During the very year that marks the appearance of the first volume of the chronicles, Tatishchev found the rare historical document, *Russkaya pravda*, the earliest codified laws of eleventh- and twelfth-century Russia. An enlarged edition of this valuable discovery was published twenty years later.

[37] A. N. Pypin, *Istoriya russkoy literatury* [History of Russian Literature], Vol. III, 510; *Sbornik II otd. russkogo yazyka i slovesnosti Imperatorskoy Akademii Nauk*, XXX, 1883, 193-95.

It was, however, not until 1940 that the complete document was gathered from all later-found chronicles, edited, and annotated by the distinguished scholar of this period, B. D. Grekov. Another equally important discovery was the *Sudebnik,* the code of laws of 1551 during the reign of Ivan IV. This document was published in 1768 and accompanied by the commentary notes of Tatishchev. Various other source materials were gathered and published during the second half of the eighteenth century, including the decrees promulgated since 1551 and Golikov's voluminous collection covering the reign of Peter I. In summary, it can safely be said that the second half of the eighteenth century had laid the foundation for the enormous projects which unfolded during the following century.

Closely linked with such initial publications is the name which no historiographer can neglect, that of Nikolay I. Novikov (1744-1810). Novikov was not only one of the greatest publishers of his time but also one of the most eminent bibliophiles, whose special interest was history. In 1779 he rented the University of Moscow Press, and the ensuing ten years saw what one eminent historian called the "Novikov decade." Novikov successfully combed the country to try to locate church and state charters, which he published at a cost that at times nearly ruined him. In 1773 he initiated a plan to publish materials located in private, state, and church collections. The result was his *Early Russian Library* (*Drevnyaya rossiiskaya vivliofika*), which included a mass of historical though indiscriminately accumulated material. It is to be regretted that the career of this pioneer publisher ended abruptly and sorrowfully: in 1792 Catherine II, while passing her last panicky years, detected "subversive Masonic" tendencies in Novikov and ordered his imprisonment. Though released later by Paul I, Novikov never recovered from the experience: he retired broken in heart and in spirit and ruined financially for the remaining years of his life.

The chief link between the eighteenth and nineteenth centuries was the common awareness of the need to gather all historical records and their publication. Both generations ardently sought means to enable the future *Geschichtsmaler* to recreate the past and the *Geschichtsschreiber* to compose an historical synthesis of the entire course of history. At the same time the historian began to free himself from patriotic fervor and to follow, perhaps unconsciously, the wise counsel of Schlözer—freedom to pursue historical truth without patriotic, national, religious, or political bias. The sole allegiance of the historian is to the truth.

By slow degrees Russian historical writing began to dissociate itself from Biblical chronology, annalistic methods and patterns, and folk legends; it commenced to cast off the crude utilitarianism of some writers and the panegyrical pomposity of others. Already eighteenth-century writers began to insist upon more scholarly methods in recording the past. Tatishchev refused to incorporate miracles and Biblical legends in his writings, Boltin denounced Le Clerc and Shcherbatov for failure to substantiate their interpretations with authentic documentary evidence, Müller insisted upon the objective handling of source material, and Schlözer spoke in terms of universal history. Together they left an impressive legacy that helped to crystallize nineteenth-century thought. Ironically, both Müller and Schlözer came to be associated with the Norman school, whose views on the origins of Russia caused bitter feuds and endless controversy among historians. Nonetheless, the intellectual heritage which the eighteenth century passed on to Russian historiography is an impressive one and cannot be lightly overlooked in the analysis of subsequent progress in historical writing.

# The Nineteenth Century
# and After

*THE ROUGH* hit-or-miss historical work during the eighteenth century was not wasted. To students of the subsequent century it proved of considerable aid either in planning the publication of available sources or in the search of still uncovered materials. During the nineteenth century Russian historiography entered a new stage of development when the swelling volume of studies was submitted to analytical study and editorial preparation. The enormous assistance which the newly published historical evidence rendered scholarship can hardly be overestimated. However, the publication of these sources presented a number of inextricable problems. The first and seemingly insurmountable difficulty was that of co-ordinating dispersed efforts in the gathering of materials; another was the evaluation and classification of gathered materials and the order in which these should be published to preclude a haphazard dumping into single volumes. Besides these fundamental questions there were also numerous problems concerning methods of publication, introductory remarks, annotations to textual contents, elucidation of stylistic peculiarities, and agreement on the meaning of obscure or obsolete terms; there was the question, too, of whether to reproduce the texts faithfully or change them to more recent spellings and modernized syntax. These were all pertinent issues that required serious study and specific answers.

One of the most bewildering riddles concerned critical appraisal of recently discovered records. During the preceding century, students of history sadly lacked the knowledge which such editorial work inevitably involved. The new sciences vital in this field, paleography and archeography, flowered much later, which fact explains many of the errors committed during the initial stages. For the same reason most of the eighteenth-century published materials called for a thorough editorial revision as well as more up-to-date textual annotations. The appearance in Göttingen of the Nestor Chronicle, edited by Schlözer in 1802, indicated the path scholarship must follow. This work produced such a favorable impression that two years after the first volume made its appearance, Alexander I ordered the formation of a society for the advancement of historical knowledge at one of the universities in the Empire. The honor of sponsoring the society was bestowed upon the University of Moscow, and so in 1804 there was founded the first Russian historical organization, the Moscow Society of History and Russian Antiquities.[1] The Society existed for 125 years, ending in 1929. Among its members were the most illustrious figures in the field of history: Count Musin-Pushkin, Karamzin, Kalaydovich, Bantysh-Kamensky, Schlözer, and others.

The fact that it was a government-sponsored organization carried with it a degree of restraint. By its charter the membership was limited and the presiding officer had to be approved by the Minister of Education. The activity of the Society was limited to a critical analysis of Russian chronicles, for the political climate that prevailed during the second half of the reign

---

[1] V. S. Ikonnikov, *Opyt russkoy istoriografii* [A Study of Russian Historiography], Kiev, 1891, Vol. I, Book I, 297-99.

of Alexander I and throughout the reign of Nicholas I hardly favored the flourish of free thought. When in 1848 the government was displeased with the choice of Giles Fletcher's *The Russe Commonwealth* for publication in Russian, it banned the Society's annual *Studies* altogether. A year later this publication reappeared under a new name, and its contents, the administration was assured, were to be confined strictly to documentary materials. It was not until 1858 that the publication resumed its original nature and became a quarterly.

Despite the adversities which the Moscow Society had to face, it managed to accomplish a surprising amount in the field of historical studies: aside from the stimulating effect it had on Russian historical scholarship, it kept pressing as well for a wider publication of national sources. Though fettered by official restrictions, the Society nonetheless managed from time to time to publish materials, some of which proved later to be of considerable value to Karamzin and other historians in their writings. The Moscow Society managed to collect and edit not only chronicles but also charters, official and private records of historical interest, and accounts of travels by natives and foreigners; it searched out all available sources and published them in its quarterly or kept them for later study and eventual publication. The amassed materials led to the development of such other allied sciences as numismatics, paleography, diplomatics, and sphragistics. Under the influence of the Moscow Society various local archival institutions began to announce their inventories, carefully listing some of their most treasured accumulations. Furthermore, the Moscow Society eventually inspired other universities to organize similar groups, which were eventually destined to play an important part in the development of historical research. Within no more than a year after the founding of the Society at Moscow, the University of

Kazan initiated a similar organization; the University of Kharkov followed suit in 1817, as did in 1839 the University of Odessa and gradually many other institutions. Each society became actively engaged in research and published its discoveries of materials pertinent to history in its own periodical *Studies*.

In the capital a different situation had developed. Here the Academy of Sciences took the initiative instead of the University of St. Petersburg. It was also the Academy's good fortune to discover in the capital the presence of a veritable Maecenas, the distinguished diplomat, statesman, and benefactor, Count Nikolay Petrovich Rumyantsev (1754-1826). By a fortunate confluence of circumstances it came about that the collective efforts of the Moscow Society and the feverish activity of a dilettante drove a deep furrow in the field of historical research in Russia.

Russian historical science owes a profound debt to Count Rumyantsev for his enthusiasm and devotion to its cause. By his relentless drive in promoting research and the writing of history he erected himself a monument which not even the Revolution was able to delete from the records of the past. Entirely to his efforts was due the founding, in 1831, of the Rumyantsev Museum, to which he donated his immense private library. This included valuable manuscripts, coins, medals, maps, and a vast book collection that included many bibliographic rarities. The museum was later transferred to Moscow and considerably expanded into what is now the Lenin Library.

When in 1809 Count Rumyantsev became State Chancellor and Minister of Foreign Affairs, the Moscow archives came under his jurisdiction. Rumyantsev was thus in a position to avail himself of every publishing opportunity, and he missed none. Since the Moscow Society had been entrusted with the publication of the chronicles, Rumyantsev determined to publish, at his own expense, the diplomatic sources that were kept in the Moscow archives. He spared neither money nor effort to make the edition a luxurious one. In 1813 he presented the Academy with a sum of 25,000 rubles for the purpose of examining and eventually publishing the documentary sources to be found in the Moscow archives of the Foreign Office. The motivation, according to Rumyantsev, was that no adequate history could be written unless the historian were able to make use of all the available source material in the country.[2] For the publication of the forthcoming State Charters and Treaties the historian owes most to Count Rumyantsev.[3]

*The Collection of State Charters and Treaties of the Ministry of Foreign Affairs* included documents covering the period between 1229 and 1696. The editing involved many difficulties and conflicting opinions concerning annotations, spelling, preservation of the old orthography, punctuation, and correction of obvious errors. In this respect Rumyantsev had been fortunate in enjoying the advice and assistance of several of the most able experts in the field of archeography and archival art, such as P. M. Stroyev, K. F. Kalaydovich, A. Kh. Vostokov, N. S. Artsybashev, and P. I. Koeppen. As the work advanced both Rumyantsev and his assistants came to the conclusion that unless the complete collection of chronicles was added to the other sources at their disposal in the archives of Moscow, the entire undertaking would fail. Referring to the chronicles that were

[2] Ikonnikov, *op. cit.,* I, 135 ff. A graphic account of Rumyantsev's role in collecting national sources may be found in *Sobraniye gosudarstvennykh gramot i dogovorov* [Collection of State Charters and Treaties], V, ii-xiii. For a more detailed study see A. A. Kochubinsky, *Admiral Shishkov i Kantsler gr. Rumyantsev. Nachalniye gody slavyanovedeniya* [Admiral Shishkov and Chancellor Rumyantsev. Initial Years of Slavic Studies], Odessa, 1887-88; *Vestnik Evropy,* X, 1888, 703 ff.; Tikhomirov, *op. cit.,* I, 215 ff.; Rubinstein, *op. cit.,* 212-22.

[3] *Sobraniye gosudarstvennykh gramot i dogovorov* [Collection of State Charters and Treaties], 4 vols., Moscow, 1813-28; a fifth volume appeared in 1894.

Сышеръбла · илиниже · ибоѧрина
имати потому росчетъ · ѿполеты
пошлина Адосудапгсадопола ·
аѹполанестоѧцъпомирать · ибо
ѧринахидіаисѹ · потомуросчетоу ·
боѧринхеръбла , дпадатына · дди
аисѹсладдемтъ · дѡколничемуи
діаисѹ · имедлщинко , пощдйполеты
нтъ · Аѹполастоѧцпомирасѧ ·
ибоѧринахидіаисѹ · иматипотому
росчетъ · пошлиныспои · Дѡколни
чемучетпертъ , дамедвлщинкѹхиасче
годадатына · Апобіютсѧнапо
ли · изаемнодвлъ · ипибою · ибоѧ
ринхедіаисомьизанаѹбипиомпро
типень · протипхисцпл · Дѡколни
чемуполтина , дідіаисѹчетпертъ · д
недвлщинкѹхпотина , дамедвлщинкѹу
пасчего , д · датыны · Апобіюсѧ
наполипопожгтъ · илипдшегхъестѡъ ·
илипразбой · илиоптатеъ · инонлѹ
битонецеподопрапити ; дѡколничему
илидхчетпертдтынызастою · дмедвлщицоочетпертъ ·

scattered hither-and-yon, Rumyantsev asked: "Is it believable that one of the greatest nations of the enlightened world and the single possessor of a treasure so significant not only for that nation, but also for all engaged in the writing of history—is it believable that this nation, which ought to be proud of its past, should not hasten to announce and display this treasure to the world?" [4] He therefore began to support lavishly the next plan, the publication of a complete collection of all available chronicles, and donated altogether forty thousand rubles for this purpose.[5] He urged that a Commission be sent to explore such monastic repositories as those of Volokolamsk and New Jerusalem, where he hoped many treasures might be found.

In 1817 the first expedition set out to investigate all book and manuscript collections in various monasteries and towns. At the head of this expedition was the able archivist P. M. Stroyev, who spent about two years in visiting some of the oldest monasteries. The results were most gratifying. Among the treasures found were such records as the previously unknown Code of Laws (*Sudebnik*) of Ivan III and several chronicles. These were carefully and fully copied and subsequently incorporated into the projected publications. The success of the first expedition served as additional proof to Stroyev that only a specially organized Archeographic Commission could handle the unfolding problems of further research.[6] He elaborated a detailed project which provided for a group of specially trained men to investigate systematically all libraries and archives throughout the Empire and compile detailed inventories of everything they found.

In 1825 there appeared *A Detailed Account of Slavo-Russian*

[4] Ikonnikov, *op. cit.*, I, Book I, 150.
[5] *Ibid.*, 149-50.
[6] See N. Barsukov, *Zhizn i trudy P. M. Stroyeva* [Life and Work of P. M. Stroyev], St. Petersburg, 1878.

*Manuscripts of the Moscow Library of Count F. A. Tolstoy,* compiled by Stroyev and Kalaydovich. Four years later an additional publication was issued, *A Detailed Account of the Old Slavic and Russian Books of the Library of Count F. A. Tolstoy.* Thus were published the first inventories of private collections for use by scholars; to follow were similar accounts that opened up a wealth of new material.

In May, 1828, the Academy of Sciences voted ten thousand rubles for the project recommended by Stroyev. A year later the famous Archeographic Expedition, headed by Stroyev, set out through Russia in further search of new source materials. The Expedition represented a semi-private, semi-state enterprise and as such operated under many handicaps. Nonetheless, the story of this Expedition is a dramatic tale in itself, with a record of which Stroyev could be justly proud: during its three years of travel, covering twelve guberniyas, more than two hundred libraries and various archives were searched and about three thousand documents copied.[7] These laid the foundation for the voluminous publications that were to make their appearance throughout the nineteenth century. The quantity of valuable material unearthed compelled the government to pursue the work further, and in December, 1834, the Ministry of Education was instructed to form an Archeographic Commission to be placed in charge of the publication of materials gathered by Stroyev. This task was successfully carried out in 1836, and a year later the Commission was made a permanent one with a regular annual budget.[8] The Archeographic Com-

[7] S. F. Platonov, *Lektsii po russkoy istorii* [Lectures on Russian History], St. Petersburg, 1913, 34-35.

[8] During the long stretch of years the Archeographic Commission amassed and published a large number of volumes containing sources of various nature. To mention only some of them published by the Commission: *Akty, sobranniye v bibliotekakh i arkhivakh Rossiiskoy Imperii Arkheograficheskoyu Ekspeditsieyu* [Documents Gathered in Libraries and Archives by the Archeographical Expedition of the Rus-

mission led virtually an independent life until 1922, when by government decree it became a division of the Academy of Sciences of the Union of Soviet Socialist Republics.

Each set of documents published by the Archeographic Commission is supplemented by a detailed place and subject index. The bulk of the historical material covers the thirteenth through the seventeenth centuries. It includes numerous charters, various legislation and judicial acts, ecclesiastical commentaries, and regulations regarding trade and industry, growth of towns, fiscal laws and budgetary problems, and military and foreign affairs. Simultaneously, the Archeographic Commission undertook the enormous task of publishing the entire collection of Russian chronicles. Armed with experience and aided by a legion of experts in various allied fields, the Commission could now handle these valuable sources more scientifically. The publication which began in 1841 continued throughout the century. During this period revisions and new editions were issued; to date, the latest edition includes twenty-five volumes of the *Complete Collection of Russian Chronicles* (*Polnoye sobraniye russkikh lyetopisey*), published by the Institute of History of the Academy of Sciences.

The Archeographic Commission also sent out a number of scholars to gather all material to be found in foreign archives. The result of this expedition was the publication of archival

---

sian Empire], 4 vols., St. Petersburg, 1836; *Akty, yuridicheskiye ili sobraniye form starinnogo deloproizvodstva* [Juridical Documents or Collection of Old Forms of Procedure], St. Petersburg, 1838; *Akty otnosyashchiesya do yuridicheskogo byta drevney Rossii* [Documents Pertaining to Juridical Conditions of Early Russia], 3 vols., St. Petersburg, 1857-84; *Akty istoricheskiye* [Historical Documents], 5 vols., St. Petersburg, 1841-42; *Dopolneniya k Aktam istoricheskim* [Supplements to the Historical Documents], 12 vols., St. Petersburg, 1846-72; *Akty, otnosyashchiesya k istorii zapadnoy Rossii* [Documents Pertaining to the History of Western Russia], 5 vols., St. Petersburg, 1846-53; *Akty, otnosyashchiesya k istorii yuzhnoy i zapadnoy Rossii* [Documents Pertaining to the History of Southern and Western Russia], 15 vols., St. Petersburg, 1863-92.

material found abroad.[9] One set includes much of the source material found in the Vatican Library, covering the period between 1075 and 1719. Another ten-volume set covers the subjects of Russian relations with the western European countries.

Like many of his contemporaries, Rumyantsev was interested in the origins of the Russian people; unlike others, however, he looked deep into the past, which included the history of both the Near East and the Byzantine Empire and Arabian medieval trade routes. He hoped to trace the ultimate key to early Russian history not only in his own country but abroad as well, and for this reason he sought the assistance of many foreign authorities in Byzantine and Oriental history. For the same reason he dispatched a number of men to Germany, Italy, England, and Poland to investigate the archives of these countries and copy from them all the important documents relating to Russia.[10]

Thus, Rumyantsev saw to it that every document bearing any relation to Russia's past would find its place in the collections to be published.[11] "The fuller and better this collection appears," he wrote to one of his assistants, "the more it will bring honor to you and pleasure in executing this enterprise to me. And whatever sums the expenses of its publication may require, I am ready to make sacrifices to supply them. . . ."[12] Rumyantsev remained loyal to his promise, contributing his time

[9] *Akty istoricheskiye, otnosyashchiesya k Rossii, izvlechenniye iz inostrannykh arkhivov i bibliotek* [Historical Documents Pertaining to Russia Drawn from Foreign Archives and Libraries], ed. by A. I. Turgenev, 2 vols., St. Petersburg, 1841-42; *Dopolneniya k aktam istoricheskim* . . . [Supplements to the Historical Documents . . . ], St. Petersburg, 1848; *Pamyatniki diplomaticheskikh snoshenii drevney Rossii s derzhavami inostrannymi* [Documents Concerning the Relations of Early Russia with Foreign Countries], 10 vols., St. Petersburg, 1851-71.

[10] Ikonnikov, *op. cit.,* 164.

[11] The nature of these sources is discussed by A. Starchevsky in *Zhurnal Ministerstva Narodnogo Prosveshcheniya,* XLIX, 1846, 14-40.

[12] A. A. Kochubinsky, *op. cit.,* 70-75; also *Appendix,* vii ff.

—especially after his retirement from office in 1812—his money, and his energy. As a collector of sources for later historians, and the person financially responsible for their publication, he occupies a prominent place in the dramatic tale of Russian historical research.[13]

From this brief survey it can be safely said that the Archeographic Commission accomplished a monumental work in the field of Russian historiography. Nor must the student of history neglect the publication of *The Complete Code of Laws*. At the head of this project was the eminent statesman, M. M. Speransky, who was assigned the task of collecting all laws from 1649 to the time of the reign of Nicholas I. Beginning with 1830, when the first volume made its appearance, the publication continued throughout the rest of the century until the end of the Empire. *The Complete Code of Laws (Polnoye sobraniye zakonov)* added another principal source of historical information for subsequent scholars.[a]

The ever-increased outpouring of published documentary evidence inspired the founding of provincial societies with similar purposes, notably those at Kiev, Vilna, Tiflis, Voronezh, and Odessa.[14] Accounts of travels in Siberia, local official records, and diaries of native and foreign travelers in the particular provinces found their way to publishing houses. In this connection must be mentioned the important contribution which contemporary periodicals made to history by publishing newly found sources from time to time. A valuable index to the scattered material in periodical literature was compiled by S. R.

[13] A. Starchevsky, "O zaslugakh Rumyantseva, okazannykh otechestvennoy istorii [Concerning the Services Rendered by Rumyantsev to National History]," *Zhurnal Ministerstva Narodnogo Prosveshcheniya*, XLIX, 1846, i ff., 51-56; Kochubinsky, *op. cit.*, Part 2, 37 ff.; Milyukov, *op. cit.*, 204-42.

[a] Marc Raeff, *Michael Speransky*, The Hague, 1957, ch. 11.

[14] A. N. Pypin, *Istoriya russkoy etnografii [History of Russian Ethnography]*, IV, ch. 7.

Mintslov.[15] He was also responsible for the compilation of two bibliographies of writings on Russian history in foreign languages, one entitled *Russica,* the other, *Peter the Great in Foreign Literature.* As the volume of historical writings increased, bibliographical literature increased proportionately. In 1861 the two Lambin brothers began a ten-volume Russian historical bibliography which still stands as one of the most notable contributions in its field.[16]

The work undertaken by the Lambin brothers was continued by another distinguished bibliographer, Vladimir Izmaylovich Mezhov (1831-1894).[17] During the 'eighties he published a six-volume historical bibliography covering the period 1865-1876 and two supplementary volumes of indexes. Having accomplished this much, Mezhov next commenced a more extensive scheme, a bibliography covering the period 1800-1859. Three volumes of this projected work appeared; death precluded the completion of the plan as originally conceived. During his lifetime, however, Mezhov succeeded in compiling a three-volume bibliography on Siberia and two volumes on central Asia.

In 1866 the Imperial Russian Historical Society was founded.

[15] S. R. Mintslov, *Obzor zapisok, dnevnikov, vospominanii, pisem i puteshestvii, otnosyashchikhsya k istorii Rossii i napechatannykh na russkom yazyke* [A Survey of Memoranda, Diaries, Reminiscences, Letters, and Travels, Pertaining to Russian History and Published in Russian], (three issues), Novgorod, 1911-12.

[16] Pyotr i Boris Lambiny, *Russkaya istoricheskaya bibliografiya* [Russian Historical Bibliography], 10 vols., St. Petersburg, 1861-84.

[17] V. I. Mezhov, *Bibliografiya Azii* [Bibliography of Asia], 6 vols., St. Petersburg, 1891-94; *Krestyansky vopros v Rossii. Polnoye sobraniye materialov dlya istorii krestyanskogo voprosa na yazykakh russkom i inostrannykh, napechatannykh v Rossii i za-granitsey, 1764-1864* [The Peasant Problem in Russia. Complete Collection of Sources Concerning the History of the Peasant Problem in Russian and Foreign Languages, published in Russia and Abroad, 1764-1864], St. Petersburg, 1865; *Russkaya istoricheskaya bibliografiya za 1865-76 vklyuchitelno* [Russian Historical Bibliography for the Years 1876 Until 1876 Inclusive], 8 vols., St. Petersburg, 1882-90; *Sibirskaya bibliografiya. Ukazatel knig i statey o Sibiri na russkom yazyke i odnyekh tolko knig na inostrannykh yazykakh* [Siberian Bibliography. A Guide to Books and Articles in Russian and to Books only in Foreign Languages], 8 vols., St. Petersburg, 1891-92.

This organization began to publish documents related to the eighteenth and part of the nineteenth centuries in Russian history. Although much criticism had been heaped upon the Society for its careless editorial work and, what was worse, for its arbitrary textual "amputations" before publication, nonetheless the collected materials represent a valuable aggregate of sources. Altogether the Society published 146 volumes of extractions from foreign and Russian archives. These included the valuable papers of the Great Legislative Commission summoned by Catherine II in 1766; the correspondence between Catherine II and Frederick II as well as Voltaire, d'Alambert, Grimm, and others; documents pertaining to Poland and Russian financial policies during the eighteenth century; sources relating to the war of 1812; diplomatic correspondence with Napoleon; the exchange of letters between Constantine and Nicholas I; and a multitude of others.

The student of history must not neglect the published family archives which began to appear by the end of the nineteenth century. The archives of the Vorontsov, Rayevsky, Mordvinov, and Vyazemsky families shed much light on various aspects of Russian cultural, economic, financial, and political history.[18] Nor must the historical journals, *Russky Arkhiv* [Russian Archive] and *Russkaya Starina* [Russian Antiquity], be overlooked. The former, published by P. Bartenev, and the latter, by M. I. Semevsky, contain invaluable source materials on the preceding two centuries of Russian history.

Needless to say, the extraordinary interest in history during the past century proved helpful in the development of many

---

[18] *Arkhiv knyazya Vorontsova*, ed. by P. Bartenev, 40 vols., Moscow, 1870-97; *Arkhiv grafov Mordvinovykh*, 10 vols., St. Petersburg, 1901-03; *Ostafievsky Arkhiv knyazey Vyazemskikh*, 5 vols., St. Petersburg, 1899-1909; *Arkhiv Rayevskikh*, 5 vols., St. Petersburg, 1908-15; *Arkhiv knyazya F. A. Kurakina*, ed. by M. I. Semevsky, 10 vols., St. Petersburg, 1890-1902.

of the sciences allied to history: paleography, metrology, genealogy, numismatics, sphragistics, heraldry, historical and economic geography, economic history, and statistical science. In addition, interest was awakened in regional history, notably that of Siberia and the Ukraine. A cult of historicism seemed to have enveloped an entire generation. Looking back, one can safely say that by the end of the last century Russian historiography demonstrated a record of accomplishment of which the nation can be rightly proud. The extensive publication of sources enabled a legion of historians to delve into the past with greater enthusiasm and with a firmer faith that their labor was bound to be richly rewarded.

## Karamzin (1766-1826)

The true heir of the eighteenth-century historians was Nikolay Mikhailovich Karamzin. Son of a Simbirsk squire, he was sent to Moscow to receive his education at a private school and then at the university in the same city. In his younger days he associated himself with the distinguished publisher, N. I. Novikov, was on friendly terms with the leading Freemasons, I. P. Turgenev, A. M. Kutuzov, and I. V. Lopukhin, favored Masonic liberal ideas, and for a while even toyed with the ideas of Rousseau. From May, 1789, to September, 1790, Karamzin toured western Europe, including England, and recorded his impressions in his widely read *Letters of a Russian Traveler*.[19] While abroad, he observed closely the life of western Europe, chiefly from the point of view of a philosopher and

---

[19] N. M. Karamzin, *Pisma russkogo puteshestvennika* [Letters of a Russian Traveler], 2nd edition, 2 vols., Moscow, 1846; *Briefe eines reisenden Russen*, 6 vols. in 3, Leipzig, 1801-03; *Travels from Moscow, through Prussia, Germany, Switzerland, France and England*, tr. from the German, 3 vols., London, 1803; *Lettres d'un voyageur russe en France, en Allemagne et en Suisse (1789-1790)*, Paris, 1867. See the latest edition of Karamzin's *Letters* published by Columbia University Press, 1957.

*literatus.* His first impressions inclined him to a great admiration for Western civilization. England failed to arouse the enthusiasm of the "Russian traveler," and except for a warm appreciation of the Anglo-Saxon judicial genius he left the British Isles "as cold as the English themselves"; but Paris made an overwhelming impression upon him and nearly converted him to cosmopolitanism.[20] This city, the pulse of European political and social life, made him believe that nationalism must eventually yield to universalism. One must be a man first and a Slav after. What is good for mankind is good for Russians.[21]

While in Paris, Karamzin already bemoaned the absence of an adequate interpretative history of Russia written in the style of a Tacitus or a Gibbon. He resented any suggestion that Russia had no past. On the contrary, he argued, Russia had a glorious history which she could proudly present before western Europe; all she needed was a Russian Tacitus and Michelangelo to demonstrate her greatness. Russia, wrote Karamzin in one of his letters from Paris, "had her own Charles the Great —Vladimir; her own Louis XI—Tsar Ivan III; her own Cromwell—Godunov," and such an emperor as Peter I western Europe had never seen." [22] In later years Karamzin seems to have reserved the role of Tacitus for himself.

Karamzin's spontaneous outburst of poetic enthusiasm about the West proved of short duration. Even while journeying in

[20] M. Pogodin, *N. M. Karamzin, po ego sochineniyam, pismam i otzyvan sovremennikov* [N. M. Karamzin, as Revealed in His Work and Letters and in the Opinions of His Contemporaries], Moscow, 1866, Vol. I, 139-44.

[21] V. V. Sipovsky, *N. M. Karamzin, avtor "Pisem russkogo puteshestvennika"* [N. M. Karamzin, Author of "Letters of a Russian Traveler"], St. Petersburg, 1900, 416-17; *Russkaya Mysl'*, VII, 1891, 22-23. See also *Starina i Novizna*, I, 60; *Pisma Karamzina k I. I. Dmitriyevu* [Letters of Karamzin to I. I. Dmitriev], St. Petersburg, 1866, 248-49.

[22] Pypin, *Istoriya russkoy literatury* [History of Russian Literature], St. Petersburg, 1913, IV, 222-23; Koyalovich, *op. cit.*, 143; Pogodin, *op. cit.*, II, 1-2.

western Europe, Karamzin cautioned against rash adoption in Russia of outside ideas for fear that it might do violence to entrenched traditions and ancient customs. Such a policy, he warned, must in the end lead to nothing but ruin. Later he began to discard other vestiges of the cosmopolitan idea he cherished in his earlier years, exchanging it for conservative nationalism. The violent nature of the French Revolution, climaxed by Bonapartism and the devastating wars, forced him to recoil. He began to revise his earlier views; by 1811 Karamzin vacillated no longer for he knew precisely where he stood. In his famous *Memorandum on Old and New Russia,* presented during that year to Alexander I, he proved himself *plus royaliste que le roi.* His former enthusiasm for Peter's reforms now came in for a more "rational" re-examination; he came to regard the changes as an unhappily forced breakdown of old institutions, valuable customs, and manners. He blamed his former idol for interfering with the natural course of national history and for undermining the spirituality of the Russian church. He criticized Peter for curbing the privileges of the nobility, without which class the monarchy itself was inconceivable. He warned that the nobility and the institution of serfdom were two pillars on which autocracy rested.

Casting off his former cosmopolitanism, Karamzin based his new views upon historical precedents as he saw them. If Peter I, he said, had made Russians citizens of the world, he also contributed to their neglecting to be citizens of their own country. His relentless drive, continued Karamzin, forced Peter to employ tyrannical methods. He uprooted the traditional old capital of Moscow and exchanged it for the swampy northern city of St. Petersburg. He tampered with the hereditary privileges of the gentry and thereby endangered the social structure; he modified the status of the church and thereby stripped the faith of spirituality. After Peter's death, he said, political pygmies replaced the giant and proved instrumental in further weakening Russian autocracy.

Catherine II saved the monarchy from an oncoming catastrophe: though her reign was not entirely free of blemishes, her brilliant rule restored the prestige of autocracy. Here, incidentally, Karamzin and Shcherbatov were in complete agreement, though reaching it by somewhat devious paths. Their common link was the tender subject of the place of nobility in Russian society, a subject upon which both writers could see eye to eye. Karamzin reprimanded the enlightened Empress for the notorious favoritism at court, which in the end was bound to have a demoralizing effect upon the prestige of the Russian nobility. In the reign of Catherine II he detected "more glitter than validity," and, though appreciating the accomplishments of the period, concluded that there was another side to the picture which Russia must blushingly admit, a deterioration of morals. The ghost of Shcherbatov must have smilingly nodded when Karamzin recorded his views. And after the brief and sorrowful rule of Paul I, came Alexander I, whom Karamzin urged to learn his lessons from history and under no circumstances to consent to any form of limited monarchical government. "Autocracy founded and resurrected Russia; any change of the established political order was bound to lead to complete ruin." [23] Such is briefly the political physiognomy of Karamzin. We must now return to the subject that concerns us most, Karamzin the historian.

On his return from abroad, Karamzin continued to lead an easygoing life, occupying himself chiefly with literary writing —poetry and prose. As he grew older, his interest in history

[23] N. M. Karamzin, *Zapiska o drevney i novoy Rossii* [Memorandum on Old and New Russia], St. Petersburg, 1914.

increased. What made him popular at court were his panegyrics to Catherine II and the famous ode dedicated to Alexander I on the occasion of his accession to the throne, as well as the frequent articles in the *Messenger of Europe,* which Karamzin published and edited. He had already demonstrated his reverence for monarchy and his firm belief that all virtue radiated from the purple robe.[24] In 1803 Karamzin petitioned Alexander I to grant him an allowance so that he would be able to devote himself entirely to the writing of history. By imperial decree on October 31, 1803, the state granted Karamzin the title of "Historiographer" and allowed him an annual pension of two thousand rubles on condition that he write a complete history of Russia. The following year he retired as editor of the *Messenger of Europe* and began to write his *History of the Russian State,* a work which gave him wide publicity and initiated the legend of his being the "first Russian historian." [25] The work appeared in 1816 in eight volumes; it was followed in 1821 by the ninth and in 1824 by the tenth and eleventh volumes. In 1826 he died without completing the twelfth volume, which leads up to the seventeenth century.[26]

The title of Karamzin's history is in itself revealing: it is a history of the Russian state, not of the Russian people. It is not even that: it is a rhetorical, panegyrical narrative which endeavors to prove that autocracy alone has bestowed all the blessings that the Russian Empire ever enjoyed; it is an album of sovereigns accompanied by descriptions of the most florid style. The approach of the author to his subject encompassed, no doubt, a gigantic sweep, but he was badly handicapped by

[24] N. M. Karamzin, *Istoricheskoye pokhvalnoye slovo Ekaterine Vtoroy* [A Historical Word of Praise for Catherine II], Moscow, 1802.

[25] Pogodin, *op. cit.,* I, 396-97.

[26] N. M. Karamzin, *Istoriya gosudarstva rossiyskogo* [History of the Russian State], 12 vols., St. Petersburg, 1816-29; another edition, Moscow, 1903; French tr. by St. Thomas and Jauffret, 11 vols., Paris, 1819-26; German tr., 11 vols., Riga, 1820-33.

his "monarchical blinders." Besides, Karamzin began his history without proper training for such work; critical history was totally alien to him. His contemporaries, Schlözer or Niebuhr, had no influence whatever upon him. Being more a representative of sentimental romanticism in fiction than of scholarly historical writing, he was naturally inclined to consider history to be in large part a beautiful narrative, in which the characters were either heroes to be worshiped or villains to be deplored. The masses did not count, everything emanated from a single source—strong government, and justice "radiated from the purple robe." Such an outlook was not unexpected since already during his journey abroad Karamzin had been inspired with the idea of the seemingly empty past of Russia made into a beautiful dramatic narrative. All one must possess, Karamzin thought, was "mind, taste, and talent"; then he could "select, inspirit, and illuminate, and the reader would be amazed to see how, for instance, a Nestor Chronicle could be transformed into something attractive, powerful, worthy of the attention not only of Russians but also of foreigners."[27] With such aims and a generous pension from the state, Karamzin could give free rein to his artistic pen, his poetic vision, and his political bias.

Naturally, Karamzin could not avoid discussing the question that had already been debated since the times of Lomonosov: the origins of the Russian state. He went back to the early Greek writers, chiefly Herodotus, glided hastily over the confusing morass of ancient references to a legion of tribes in the north and the south, and—for fear of bogging down—conveniently accepted the Scythians as the most logical precursors of Russian history. Karamzin thus brushed aside the Norman theory; the legend of the "invitation" extended to

[27] Pogodin, *op. cit.*, II, 2.

the Varangians "to come to rule and reign" over the Slavs he dismissed as of no importance by giving the general impression of a Varangian admixture in the early Kievan state and nothing more.

According to Karamzin, early Kievan Russia reached a high degree of development because of its strong monarchical government. The downfall of old Russia he explained by the established political custom of dividing the state among the royal heirs and by the bitter rivalry among the princes, which in the end contributed to the triumph of the Mongols. As for the princes, in Basil III, Karamzin saw an extremely colorful figure; without him history would have looked like a "peacock without a tail." But of all the Muscovite grand princes who built the future state of Russia, Ivan III was considered by Karamzin as the greatest of them all; he looked upon this ruler not only as the true founder of the national state but also as the father of Russian autocracy. This was the traditional "Great Russian" interpretation, the theory that the entire historical process was centrifugal rather than centripetal, a theory later to be vigorously opposed by members of the Ukrainian school, notably M. Hrushevsky.

In fairness to Karamzin, it must be stated that his *History of the Russian State* is not without its merits, in spite of its pontifical presentation and obvious bias. Throughout all the volumes there was a novel unity in his narrative that made the course of Russian history seem meaningful. The fact that Karamzin was primarily a literary artist with no pretense to scholarship had one positive effect: his manner of writing. His florid literary style tended to liberate Russian writing from the antiquated church-Slavonic terminology that was greatly admired by members of the old school and to introduce a style more elegant, vigorous, and flowing—even though rhetorical

—a style that appealed to the literary aesthetes of his time.[28] Many people compare Karamzin's writings with those of Sir Walter Scott, while some detect a definite influence of the latter upon him. Undoubtedly, as the volumes began to make their appearance, they awakened an unprecedented interest in national history.[29] To Pushkin, Karamzin was the "Columbus of Russian History."

Finally, and most significantly, Karamzin's *Notes,* or appendices, that accompanied the volumes included an extraordinary number of references to various rare sources formerly unknown or previously not utilized. Here, it can be said most assuredly, the author accomplished a prodigious feat. The value of these *Notes* became even greater when during the Moscow fire of 1812 many of the cited sources, including Karamzin's private library and the state archival depositories, completely and irretrievably perished. The nature of the lost documents is known to us only through Karamzin's voluminous references.[30] Altogether, Karamzin's *History of the Russian State* contains 6,538 references, veritably a history in itself!

Karamzin enjoyed the rare privilege of access to many private and state archives. He utilized the private collection of manuscripts of Musin-Pushkin and the equally valuable library of the Synod. He familiarized himself with numerous chronicles: the Hypatian, the Laurentian, the Troitsky (which, incidentally, perished during the Moscow fire), and others. He consulted the various Codes of Laws of the fourteenth and fifteenth centuries, and the medieval literary writings, such as *The Lay of the Host of Igor*; he read the early accounts of

[28] *Zhurnal Ministerstva Narodnogo Prosveshcheniya,* CXXXIV, 1867, 20 ff.
[29] *Chteniya v Imperatorskom obshchestve istorii i drevnostey rossiyskikh pri Moskovskom universitete,* III, 1862, 23.
[30] *Zhurnal Ministerstva Narodnogo Prosveshcheniya,* CXXXIII, 1867, 17-18.

foreign travelers in eastern Europe. No preceding writer could claim more extensive consultation of sources than Karamzin; to date he crowned all efforts whether in literary style or in historical synthesis.

Despite these merits, his work is now a mere curiosity rather than acceptable study and reading material. It totally lacks historical perspective, since Karamzin could not conceive of an historical process; like the eighteenth-century rationalist, he saw in history only evil or benevolent sovereigns who led the country either to disaster or to glory. It is very doubtful that Karamzin could have examined sufficiently the sources to which he refers in his footnotes, though the archives were at his disposal and he was generously aided by high officials and friends, among them M. Muravyev, the Assistant Minister of Education; Count N. Rumyantsev; A. Malinovsky, Head of the Archives; and his close friend, A. I. Turgenev, who gathered and copied documents for him abroad, particularly at the papal archives. It was a physical impossibility within the comparatively short period of his time, interrupted by frequent illnesses, for him to go over the voluminous amount of material referred to; and though he never mentions them, Karamzin relied in great part upon references cited in secondary authorities, thereby creating an impression of extraordinary erudition.[31]

Of the secondary authorities which greatly aided Karamzin, Schlözer's edition of the Nestor Chronicle must be mentioned for the earlier period of Russian history, and Shcherbatov's for the later. The history of Shcherbatov was not only a ready pattern for the literary embroidery of Karamzin but also the best guide to the sources. Professor Milyukov, by comparing page after page, has shown quite convincingly how closely

---

[31] Compare the different views of M. I. Koyalovich, *Istoriya russkogo samosoznaniya*, 143 ff., and P. N. Milyukov, *Glavniye techeniya russkoy istoricheskoy mysli*, 152 ff.

Karamzin followed the general outline of Shcherbatov.[32] To Shcherbatov's bulky work all Karamzin had to add was stylistic refinement and poetic imagination, precisely the qualities Prince Shcherbatov had lacked, and history was indeed bound to become well "selected, inspirited, and illuminated." A single citation from Karamzin, describing the eve of the historic battle of Kulikovo of September 8, 1380, will prove better than any lengthy discourse the accuracy of this statement:[33]

The noise of arms had not quieted down in the town, and the people looked with emotion at the brave warriors ready to die for the Fatherland and the Faith. It seemed as if the Russian people had awakened after a deep sleep: the long terror of the Tartars had vanished from their hearts as if removed by some supernatural power. They reminded one another of the glorious Vozhsk battle; they enumerated all the evils they had suffered from the barbarians during the hundred and fifty years and wondered at the shameful patience of their forefathers. Princes, boyars, townsmen, peasants, all were fired with equal enthusiasm, for the tyranny of the Khans oppressed all equally, from the throne to the hut. What was more just than the sword at such a noble and unanimous call?

Patriotic? To this skeptical query Karamzin's disarming reply was that where there is no love, there is no soul. He never shrank before such accusations. "I know that I need the impartiality of an historian; forgive me, but I was not always able to conceal my love for the Fatherland." [34] It was this very "soul" that made his history so popular; the first edition of three thousand sets at the prohibitive price of fifty-five rubles a set was sold out within twenty-five days.[35] But the very qual-

[32] Milyukov, *op. cit.*, 161-63; also 187-190.
[33] Karamzin, *Istoriya gosudarstva rossiyskogo*, St. Petersburg, 1819, V, 64.
[34] Pypin, *Istoriya russkoy literatury*, IV, 224.
[35] *Russky istorichesky zhurnal*, I, 1917, 14.

ities which made Karamzin's history popular undermined its value in the eyes of the critical scholar.

Even in Karamzin's lifetime his work drew fire because of its patriotic bias and its obsolete interpretation of the past.[36] As a precursor of Slavophilism, the criticism came naturally from the Westerners, or "skeptics" as they were called in Russian historiography, who were under the influence chiefly of Schlözer and Niebuhr. Polevoy considered Karamzin's *History* an outdated piece of work before it was produced; Pogodin thought even the title of the twelve-volume work a mistake and the author as far from Gibbon as intellectual England was from Russia.[37] In 1818 M. Kachenovsky, editor of the *Messenger of Europe,* wrote a review in which he described it as "a chronicle masterfully recorded by an artist of superb talent, but not a history." The poet Vyazemsky called Karamzin the Field Marshal Kutuzov of History for he saved his country from the "invasion of oblivion"; in the field of history he demonstrated to the world that the Russians had a fatherland much as did Kutuzov on the field of battle in 1812.

Most of the Decembrists condemned Karamzin for his panegyric presentation of autocracy. Nikita Muravyev disapproved of it on the grounds that "history belongs to the people and not to tsars"; M. Fonvizin thought Karamzin concealed the political freedom which the Russian people had enjoyed in their earlier period of history, and instead forced Russian autocracy to the footlights of the national scene. N. Bestuzhev

[36] *Zhurnal Ministerstva Narodnogo Prosveshcheniya,* XVVVIII, 1867, 47.
[37] N. Barsukov, *Zhizn i trudy M. P. Pogodina* [The Life and Works of M. P. Pogodin], St. Petersburg, 1889, II, 333. See also E. Kovalevsky, *Graf Bludov i ego vremya* [Count Bludov and his Time], St. Petersburg, 1866, 232; *Dekabrist N. I. Turgenev. Pis'ma k bratu S. I. Turgenevu* [The Decembrist N. I. Turgenev. Letters to his Brother S. I. Turgenev], Moscow, 1936, 349; Bestuzhev-Ryumin, *op. cit.,* 205-30; Rubinstein, *op. cit.,* 166-188; Tikhomirov, *op. cit.,* 277-88.

lamented that thus far all people wrote about was tsars and heroes, but few mentioned the sufferings and needs of the people. M. Lunin declared that autocracy was immoral and that God alone was entitled to the power claimed by autocracy. N. I. Turgenev recorded in his diary of 1818, after he read Karamzin's history, that the record of the past was the possession of the people and not the tsars and that despotism was concealed from the eye of the reader of this account. A. Pushkin, though considering the history a "creative work of a great writer" and referring to Karamzin as the "Columbus of Russian history," nonetheless discerned the weakness when he dedicated the biting four-line epigram which reads:

> In his history, beauty and simplicity
> Prove without bias
> The necessity of autocracy
> And the charm of the knout.

Among Karamzin's critics may be mentioned the later historian N. G. Ustryalov (1805-1870). He expressed his views in an historical essay in which he credited Karamzin with much that was due him, yet cautiously adding a few subtly formulated notes to his praises. History, he stated, is not a gallery of princes and tsars, but a chain of interlocking events. The purpose of the historian is to show pragmatically the gradual changes that the state has undergone and to explain how the state came to be what it is. Karamzin's *History of the Russian State,* declared Ustryalov, failed completely to come near such an accomplishment; he crowded his pages with accounts of royal members and failed in the end to reveal the genuine moving forces in Russian history.

But these were only isolated voices drowned by the general

hosannas to the author; "Old Russia" extolled Karamzin as the first national historian, and his twelve-volume work remained for a long time the official history of Russia.

## Polevoy (1796-1846)

Among the earlier successors of Karamzin who undertook the reinterpretation of Russian history was Nikolay Alekseyevich Polevoy. Born in Irkutsk as the son of a merchant, he was a typical self-made man and representative of the rising "classless intelligentsia." In his early youth he read Golikov's work on Peter I, which fascinated him to such a degree that he decided to devote himself to history. He read voraciously, though failing to attend the University or receive any regular training. Material circumstances compelled him to assist his father in business; it was not until 1822 that the death of his father freed him from the tedious chores of business, and three years later he settled permanently in Moscow. Here he plunged at once into literary activity and associated with the most prominent writers of the time. His chief interest was journalism, and Polevoy soon assumed the editorship of one of the most progressive magazines of the time, *The Moscow Telegraph*. A man of undoubted literary talent and endowed with an indigenous critical capacity, Polevoy nevertheless lacked the refinement of Karamzin.[38] His disapproval of Karamzin's *History* caused Polevoy considerable difficulties: his friends, among them some of the most influential literary men of the time, left him. It was not too long before his journal was to end entirely. In 1834 the *Telegraph* was closed down for an article which did

[38] A. Borozdin, "Zhurnalist dvadtsatykh godov [A Journalist of the 'Twenties'],"
*Istorichesky Vyestnik,* LXIII, 1896, 946-59. Interesting material may also be found
in M. I. Sukhomlinov's *Issledovaniya i stati* [Studies and Essays], St. Petersburg,
1889, II, 367-431; and Rubinstein, *op. cit.,* 242-54.

not meet with official approbation, an action which caused Polevoy endless financial embarrassment and eventually undermined his moral and physical strength.

From his early days Polevoy had been an enthusiastic admirer of Guizot, Thierry, Schelling, and, particularly, Niebuhr, whose teachings, along with Golikov's inspired him to engage in historical writing. The title of Polevoy's six-volume work, *A History of the Russian People,* indicates the basic idea of the author. Nor does it require much speculation as to Polevoy's real motive for beginning to write history. In 1829 he contributed a critical review of Karamzin's *History of the Russian State* to the *Moscow Telegraph.* The essence of the article was that, though only of recent completion, this work could be regarded as entirely obsolete. Behind the whole story of Karamzin's historical narrative, said Polevoy, there is no philosophy, no indication of any relationship between world history and developments in Russia. Unless, insisted Polevoy, a national history revolved within the orbit of universal history, it must fail dismally in its purpose. Furthermore, the historian cannot deliver verdicts of approval or condemnation; his task is to present facts objectively arrived at.

Though he never favored any other form of cosmopolitanism, Polevoy saw things differently when it came to the field of history: here he detected certain "historical processes" which are universal in character, and Russian as well as any other national history is incapable of escaping participation in them. In postulating his views Polevoy based his arguments exclusively on the philosophy of Schelling, whom he admired most. Only in the spirit of Schelling was he willing to see Russian history as an organic part of universal developments, thereby inviting oblivion for himself in the face of the advancing Hegelianism that came to dominate his generation.

Polevoy dedicated his *History* to Barthold Georg Niebuhr.[39] The aim of the author was to follow the school of Western historians, to narrate without bias the past of his people, and to show the part the Russian nation had played in the general historical drama of the Western world; he did not aim to paint a mere gallery of sovereigns.[40] Moreover, Polevoy was not content with the humble role of a chronicler; to him history was a "practical revaluation of philosophical conceptions concerning the universe and mankind, an analysis of a philosophical synthesis." He therefore hoped to write national history, not from a purely local point of view, but in the light of universal developments.[41] In this respect Polevoy went beyond not only contemporary historians but even his immediate successors in the field of history. The formulation of purpose was far ahead of his time.

However, the task which Polevoy assigned himself proved much beyond his capacities. His six-volume work represented a valorous intellectual effort, yet it served as only one more proof of the futility inevitable when a noble ambition fails to be accompanied by adequate intellectual equipment. Polevoy's extensive reading in the field of philosophy and history, and his eclectic search for some acceptable formula, in the end only confused him in his earnest attempt to construct a basis for a philosophy of national history. At best Polevoy's endeavor represented a healthy reaction to the prevailing errors in current historical writings, errors which he correctly sensed but was

---

[39] N. A. Polevoy, *Istoriya russkogo naroda* [A History of the Russian People], 6 vols., Moscow, 1830-33; *Istoriya Petra Velikogo* [A History of Peter the Great], 2nd edition, Moscow, 1899; *Obozreniye russkoy istorii do yedinoderzhaviya Petra Velikogo* [A Survey of Russian History to the Absolute Reign of Peter the Great], St. Petersburg, 1846.

[40] Pypin, *Istoriya russkoy literatury*, IV, 471-72.

[41] *Istorichesky Vyestnik*, LXIII, 1896, 958; *Russky biografichesky slovar*, XIV, 299-300.

not strong enough to rectify. The sad part is that Polevoy never understood how woefully backward he was when Hegelianism triumphantly reigned over his generation. Loyally adhering all his years to Schelling, he thereby invoked upon himself the fate of being cast by the wayside of history during his own lifetime.

## Pogodin (1800-1875)

The name of Mikhail Petrovich Pogodin is closely linked with the so-called "official school," since these historians staunchly supported the nationalist policy of the administration of Nicholas I.[42] At the outbreak of the Crimean War Pogodin cried out for nothing less than Constantinople. Threats of revolution, he wrote, cannot intimidate Russia, for Russia is not the West. When, however, the prospects of victory were dimmed at Sebastopol, he sang a different tune: now motivated by fear of a complete collapse of the political order, Pogodin began, in his famous *Historico-Political Letters,* to urge reforms. "We do not fear a Mirabeau," he declared; "what we fear is a Yemelka Pugachev."[43] During his lifetime he advocated ideas which sometimes coincided with Slavophile and Panslav philosophies; on other occasions he seemed to have taken the side of the opposite camp, the "skeptics" or those noted for their Western proclivities.

[42] M. P. Pogodin, *Istoriko-politicheskiye pisma* [Historico-Political Letters], Book I, Moscow, 1846; Book II, Moscow, 1867; *Issledovaniya, zamechaniya i lektsii o russkoy istorii* [Investigations, Annotations, and Lectures on Russian History], 7 vols., Moscow, 1846-50; *Drevnyaya russkaya istoriya do mongolskogo iga* [Early Russian History to the Time of the Mongolian Period], 3 vols., Moscow, 1871; *N. M. Karamzin, po ego sochineniyam, pisman i otzyvam sovremennikov* [N. M. Karamzin, as Revealed in His Works and Letters and in the Opinions of His Contemporaries], 2 vols., Moscow, 1866. *Nestor: eine historischkritische Untersuchung über den Anfang der russischen Chroniken,* tr. by F. Löwe, St. Petersburg, 1844.

[43] Pogodin, *Istoriko-politicheskiye pisma,* Book II, 187, 202, 261-62.

Like Polevoy, Pogodin was descended from a humble family; his father was a serf, belonging to Count Saltykov. But, living in Moscow, the boy somehow came into contact with university life; and after being graduated, he joined the faculty. Both Karamzin and Schlözer were great heroes of his, though strictly speaking he was a follower of neither. He worked out his own method of writing, but the reactionary era through which he lived deeply stamped its imprint upon his work. Thus in 1830, as a result of the revolt in Poland, Pogodin wrote an essay, "Reflections on Russo-Polish Relations," which pleased the Third Division (Intelligence Department) so much that it paid the author an honorarium. Yet, when he applied for permission to go abroad, the government refused him the privilege, announcing that "present circumstances make it useless to send this master to foreign lands to complete his studies, for it is more convenient to give him in the university that kind of education which the government would consider profitable." [44] It was not until 1835 that Pogodin made his first journey abroad.

Like many of his contemporaries, Pogodin was interested in early Russian history, and especially in the Varangian or Norman problem. His master's thesis of 1824, *Concerning the Origins of Russia,* was highly praised by Karamzin and opened to the author the doors of his alma mater.[45] Ten years later he published his analysis of the Nestor Chronicle, a study which is still considered an important contribution in the field. On his second sojourn in western Europe Pogodin visited Paris in 1839, met some of the eminent scholars of his day, including the Slavicist, P. J. Šafařik, and the French historian, F. P. G. Guizot. and acquainted himself with Western thought. Upon his return

[44] *Entsiklopedichesky slovar* (Brokhaus-Efron), XXIV (1), 32. See also, Rubinstein, *op. cit.,* 254-70; and Tikhomirov, *op. cit.,* 319-21.

[45] Bestuzhev-Ryumin, *op. cit.,* 235-36, 239-40.

from abroad there followed the decade of his most fruitful period of writing and of collecting valuable sources.

His association with the University of Moscow dates to 1835, when he was appointed as Professor of Russian history, taking the place of his former teacher, M. T. Kachenovsky. The appointment was well fitted to the general policy of the current administration, for Pogodin had no sympathy with the beliefs of the "skeptics" concerning a "universal philosophical synthesis"; anything even remotely related to "universality" was considered at that time a perilous threat to the three pillars of autocracy, orthodoxy, and nationalism, upon which the entire social structure rested.

In 1884 Pogodin resigned his professorship at the University of Moscow in order to devote himself entirely to the editing of the journal *Moskvityanin* and to his government position with the Ministry of Education. The vacated chair was shortly afterwards given to his opponent, S. M. Solovyev, about whom more will be said later. Though Pogodin entirely severed his relations with academic life, he never ceased writing in the field of history. In his seven-volume *Early History of Russia* Pogodin reveals an amazing knowledge of the early historical sources available during his time. It is an enormously detailed study, though it sadly lacks an historical synthesis or consistent architectonic pattern. For this reason the seven volumes can be more aptly described as a voluminous gathering of source information than as a history.

According to Pogodin two forces assisted in the formation of the Russian state: Greek or Byzantine Christianity from the south and Slavic learning from the southwest. Since Russia was strong in the possession of these two mighty forces, Pogodin did not fear, as did others, to acknowledge the existence of Norman influence in early Russian history. The foundation laid by the Normans was unstable, as the ease with which the Mongols overthrew it demonstrates. It was only with the rise of Moscow that a true national state appeared and was given final expression by Peter the Great. Much of this hypothesis Pogodin borrowed from Schlözer, but he added a strong national tinge and a touch of providential destiny to the general picture which he drew of the past.

It was in his doctoral dissertation, his analysis of the Nestor Chronicle, that Pogodin excelled in his writings. The thesis constitutes a superb supplement to Schlözer's study. Here Pogodin analyzed quite ably the chronicle as an historical document and discussed at great length the style of the author as well as biographical and chronological data; he made a skillful comparison between the Nestor and other preceding chronicles of foreign origin, showing the influence of the latter upon the contents of the Russian document. Schlözer was interested in presenting the original text, freeing it from all foreign sources which were incorporated by the author. Pogodin was more interested in the sources that influenced Nestor and in this respect considerably advanced the method of study of annalistic literature. But even here Pogodin did not fail to add a touch of national sentiment characteristic of all his work. His reverence for Nestor stands out quite conspicuously. Pogodin urged the Russian people to "proclaim his eternal memory and to worship him so that he may grant us the spirit of Russian history, for the spirit alone, my friends, uplifts, while the letter alone kills. . . ." Such lines could have been written only by a native "soul-searching" historian of the era of Nicholas I and not by a "Euclidian-minded German academician of the Era of Enlightenment." [46]

Though Pogodin was fond of citing similarities between

[46] *Russky bibliografichesky slovar*, XIV, 159-60.

Russian and western European history, he was equally emphatic in stressing the vital differences. Some of these parallels are of the nature of sweeping generalities and therefore are extremely problematic. He interpreted the conquests of the Normans in early Russia and in western Europe as of identical character; in both cases the conquests led to the foundation of states. The appanage system in Russia was similar to the Western feudal system. The crusades and the Mongolian invasion resulted in both cases in the undermining of feudalism and were instrumental in establishing or consolidating absolutism. The Reformation and the reforms of Peter I, according to Pogodin, accomplished similar changes—secularization of the state. Having acknowledged such similarities, Pogodin then continued, as if by lapse of memory, to draw vital differences which are equally sweeping and even more problematic. In western European history he saw only wars, conquests, division, class struggle, social hatred, and revolution, while in Russia none of these could be found. The reason for this was, as Pogodin explained it, that Russian statehood was based on a peaceful agreement between the people and the government best illustrated by the "invitation of the Normans to come and govern." To soften the injury which this might cause to sensitive national pride, Pogodin hastened to add that, naturally, even if the Normans had never been invited, the course of history would still have been the same. Be that as it may, the Norman theory thus was dismissed with no offense to national feelings. If the first contention, stressing the similarities between Russian and Western history, delighted the Westerners, the second one, minimizing the historical significance of the Normans, pleased the Slavophiles. Pogodin could truly pride himself as the proverbial merchant, being ready to serve all alike!

On occasion Pogodin found himself tied up by contradictory theories of his own creation. A single illustration will suffice. Pogodin asserted that a mass revolt for people's sovereignty was inconceivable because of the "uniqueness" of Russian history. Revolutions in Russia, if they occur, are initiated from above and not below, as in the case of the reforms of Peter I. Russian authority rested upon a totally different principle than authority in the West. In Russia the people "invited" the government, made a contract between themselves and the ruler, and consented to be ruled by the chosen prince. The deduction one could naturally draw was that if the same people happened to be displeased with the sovereign, they had the right to nullify the contract and choose a more suitable ruler. But this was a dangerous doctrine, too strongly flavored with the spirit of the American Declaration of Independence. Therefore Pogodin hastened to add, almost in the same breath, that once the power to rule was granted it was irretrievable and the people had nothing more to say about it. The Slavophiles seized upon the "uniqueness" of political development in Russia; the Westerners deduced the theory of government by consent of the people as a traditional institution.

Though Pogodin received a far broader education than Polevoy, he set sail on shallower waters. With Pogodin it was almost axiomatic that Russia was destined to defend and maintain peace and social order on the continent and that, as an historian, he must clarify that mission for the public. He predicted that the destiny of Europe and mankind might be determined by his country. Though no admirer of the philosophy of the Westerners, he had some praise for Peter I as he saw his place in history. Pogodin considered that rebel tsar as presenting the most unique illustration of a nation where profound revolutionary changes emanate from a lawful source rather than from mob action. To Pogodin this was one of the vital differences between Russia and western Europe.

Pogodin's reverence for Russian antiquities in the strictest orthodox sense suited the prevailing philosophy during the reign of Nicholas I. As lecturer in the University of Moscow and later as employee of the Ministry of Education, or as editor of the *Moscow Messenger* (1827-1830) and subsequently of the *Moskvityatin* (1841-1856), he consistently followed an extremely nationalistic line. How one could embrace both the broad principles of Schlözer and a homespun patriotism was a mystery even to his contemporaries, but that was the mystery, also, of his time.[47] Did not even Polevoy, crushed by many reverses, become, according to A. Herzen, "within five days a loyal subject?" The duality of Pogodin allowed both Westerners and Slavophiles to cite his writings in order to prove their contentions.

Pogodin's contribution to historiography has been recognized mainly for the following. He carried on further studies of the chronicles which proved of great aid to subsequent scholarship in the field of earlier Russian history, particularly his publication of several volumes of hitherto unknown chronicles. Pogodin collected many valuable manuscripts which subsequently became the property of the Leningrad Public Library and are known as the Pogodin Collection. He revived the publication of the long forgotten two-volume work of I. T. Pososhkov, *On Wealth and Poverty,* written during the reign of Peter I. The purpose of Pososhkov was to present an extensive project for economic reform in Russia based on the mercantilist philosophy of the time. Though not an advocate of the emancipation of the serfs, Pososhkov urged the restraint of the nobility in their rights over the peasants and recommended the sum-

[47] See Barsukov, *op. cit.,* IV, 252-53.

moning of a legislative assembly and the adoption of appropriate legislation to carry out the projects elaborated. Instead of
becoming a national hero the author ended in 1725 as a prisoner
in the Peter and Paul fortress, where he died a few months
later. The new edition of Pososhkov's writings by Pogodin was
to pay honor to an overlooked work and a martyr historian-
economist.

In one of his essays on the origins of serfdom in Russia entitled "Is Boris Godunov to be Considered as the Founder of
Serfdom?" Pogodin argued that the state was in no way responsible for the introduction of that institution; the government cared only for the welfare of the peasants and was
indirectly involved in the approval of serfdom.[48] Serfdom, Pogodin concluded, came, not through some single legislative
action, but through gradual development, the initiative resting
exclusively with the landlord class. Such was the new interpretation as presented by Pogodin in 1858 on the eve of the collapse
of the entire medieval order of society that prevailed in Russia. By then it did not much matter what theory of the origin
of serfdom one might suggest; the most essential issue at that
time was how to end serfdom. For nearly two decades Pogodin
was destined to witness the crumbling of the social order which
he so vainly defended. One is inclined to wonder if the two
different phases of history through which Pogodin lived may
explain at least in part the two contradictory points of view
that are frequently found in his writings.

## THE TURBULENT MID-CENTURY DECADES

"Westernism" and "Slavophilism" constitute a complex phenomenon, which can be referred to here only as far as the im-

[48] Pogodin, *Istoriko-kriticheskiye otryvki* [Critical Essays], Book II, pp. 197-257.

mediate subject is concerned. Nicholas I's policy of isolating Russia from the revolutionary contagion plaguing western Europe stimulated thinking concerning Russia's destiny; and subsequent discussions involved the use and often abuse of history. They also accelerated the process of sharper demarcation between two schools of thought, Western and Slavophile. The two diverged markedly in their interpretation of Russian history and accordingly a literary battle ranged over a wide field of subjects involving historical interpretation. Various ideologies had been fermenting quietly until 1836, when the famous *Philosophical Letter* of Chaadayev brought the brewing process to a violent end.[49] The tenseness of the arguments led to extreme theories, often totally devoid of reality. Involved in the conflict were three views which should be briefly discussed to show how each employed history as its weapon.

## Chaadayev (1796-1856)

The Slavophiles believed that Russia had a great history but lost it with the ascendancy of Peter I; the Westerners held that Russia's past was hardly worthy of her until the Petrine era; Chaadayev argued that Russia had no history at all of which to be proud, either in the past or the present. With this sweeping assumption Chaadayev plunged into the flood of controversy and was all but drowned. The dikes, meanwhile, had gone down before a wave of arguments that continued throughout an entire generation between the other two schools of thought.

Peter Yakovlevich Chaadayev represented the theocratic aspects of Russian Westernism; in the historical past he traced three stages: "at first savage barbarism, then primitive supersti-

---

[49] P. Y. Chaadayev, *Sochineniya i pisma* [Works and Letters], 2 vols., Moscow, 1913-1914.

tion, followed by brutal, humiliating foreign oppression, characteristics inherited afterward by the national government." [50]
He showed an ill-concealed sense of contempt for Slavophile
jingoism and was equally skeptical about the philosophy of its
opponents. Chaadayev was oppressed by the sorrowful state of
*spiritual isolation* of his country. He turned to history because,
as he said, only the past can explain a people.

The first tragic development in Russian history, according to
Chaadayev, was the fact that while in search of a new religious
faith Russia, as if impelled by a fatal destiny, turned not to
Rome, the genuine source of Christian teaching, but to Byzantium. And this had happened at a time when the Byzantine
church, led by an egotist, Patriarch Photius, broke away from
"universal brotherhood." Thus, a religion distorted by human
passion made its initial appearance in Russia. By embracing
the faith that emanated from the south, the people of Russia
dissociated themselves from the Western brotherhood of Chris-
tendom. The Russians became Christianized and civilized,
added Chaadayev wryly, but so did the Abyssinians and the
Japanese. In effect the country remained, as before, in a spiritual
and cultural vacuum.

Russia's geographic position offered unusual opportunities,
Chaadayev argued. "Resting with one elbow on China and
with the other on Germany," he wrote, "we ought to unite
in ourselves the two great fundamentals of knowledge—imagination and reason—and correlate in our civil education the
history of the whole world." Nothing of the kind happened;
Russia remained immune to both and let opportunities pass
by. At one time Peter I had every noble intention and "threw
the mantle of civilization" to his people. What happened in
fact was that the Russians "picked up the mantle and left the

[50] *Ibid.*, I, 6-7.

civilization untouched." Alexander I later led Russia in triumph across the continent of Europe, but when his armies returned, they brought back only ideas and aspirations; the end was a tragic fiasco, the Decembrist Revolt, which set the clock of history back half a century.

The deduction Chaadayev arrived at was one easy to guess: take the road to Rome. In the Roman church Chaadayev saw the foundation of Christian civilization and the genuine cohesive force of Western society. He considered the Reformation the most deplorable event in modern history: it resulted in the tragic demolition of Christian unity and a division that had prevailed ever since.

### *Westerners*

Those who advocated a Western national orientation did not share the dim view of Chaadayev nor did they let themselves be swayed by the Catholic romanticism of the time. Though not seeing eye to eye with Chaadayev on many issues, they did agree with him in their negative opinion of Russia's past. They envisioned national salvation, not in mystical religious revival, however, but in political and economic emancipation of the masses, as it had been attained in western Europe. In parliamentary government based on a Western model they saw a higher stage of development which Russia could not neglect if she expected to move forward.

The Westerners could also agree with Chaadayev on the question of the historical significance of Peter I: both regarded his reforms as the initial step toward change. Chaadayev was disheartened by what had happened, but the Westerners refused to be swayed by his melancholy reflections; they considered the reign of Peter I as the true era of enlightenment in Russian history. They rejected other arguments such as that Petrine reforms constituted a violation of the natural evolution of national progress. This idea the Westerners branded as crude homespun patriotism, which served no other purpose than to perpetuate Asiatic despotism.

In the summer of 1847 the famed literary critic and leading figure among the Westerners, Vissarion G. Belinsky, was provoked by the publication of Gogol's *Choice Passages from Correspondence with Friends*. He wrote a review of this book in the form of a *Letter* to the author. Though the occasion bore no direct relation to the ideological battle presently to be discussed, the *Letter* can be justly regarded as the first salvo fired by the Westerners. The document contained all the accumulated wrath and revulsion against Slavophile views in whatever form these might appear. Gogol's morose piety only antagonized the militant ranks of the Westerners; behind the smooth seamless front of Christian morality was hidden a defeatist spirit.

Russia's salvation, declared "Raging Vissarion," was not in mysticism and prayers, "but in awakening among her common folk a sense of human dignity (for so many ages have been lost amid the mire of manure) and rights and laws. . . ." What the country needed most was abolition of serfdom, introduction of justice, and restraint of the unbridled tyranny of the administration. In essence, glorification of Orthodoxy signified blind praise of Cimmerian darkness and Mongolian morals.

Centuries of cultural isolation, asserted the Westerners, served to perpetuate the harmful legacies of Byzantium and Tartar domination. Many of the worse characteristics were engrafted upon the national character: mental sloth, a sense of inferiority, widespread illiteracy and superstition, cunningness, and evasiveness. These were not inherent traits, only influences absorbed during forced association with the Mongols while they dominated the country.

Peter smashed all barriers that stood between the West and his country; for the first time, through the crashed "window," came a gust of fresh Western air. Catherine II assured further benefits from contacts with western Europe forced by Peter I. A close relationship did not mean that the Russians would turn into slavish reflectors of Western culture; rather, it would make them European Russians. From Western experience Russians could gain much: they could dissociate genuine cultural values from false appearances; they might avoid all the faults of capitalism and ensure a pattern of social and economic development more advanced than that of the West. Furthermore, it should be borne in mind that institutions which collapsed in the West were destined to meet the same fate in the East. Contrary to Slavophile allegations that western Europe represented a decaying civilization, the Westerners urged that Russia take cognizance of the enormous progress which the continent had attained and Russia must overtake. They advised their opponents to lay aside their Oriental yardsticks and admit that the West remained a great reservoir of vitality which nourished much of the world.

The frequent rebuttals carried one feature particularly worthy of notice: both sides used history as their chief weapon. Seldom had the past been studied more intensively in order to illustrate the points each ideological camp wished to drive home. Whatever ends each side pursued, history meanwhile made gains, being widely studied, written, rewritten, and reinterpreted by an agitated generation.

## Slavophiles

Chaadayev's savage criticism, which stripped his country of its history, and the philosophy of the Westerners, which shared to a degree the views of Chaadayev, aroused the ardent nationalists. In self-defense they elaborated a curious thesis of their own: a mixture of sentimental patriotism and a romantic interpretation of history, known generally as Slavophilism. Slavophile opponents of the West asserted with adolescent zeal that the Russian people were in possession of a civilization of their own and needed no imitation of others. Russia, they said, was a world in her own right, to which Western yardsticks were totally inapplicable; her stability was due to the social and political institutions the country had enjoyed.

The course of Russian history, continued the Slavophiles, is reflected in the two capitals of the land, Moscow and St. Petersburg. These cities are uniquely symbolic, one representing the epoch of traditional relationship between the people and their government, a time when a genuine bond of common interests prevailed between the two; the other representing a later period when the authorities, motivated by a foreign spirit, established a government apart from the people and alien to their true national aspirations. "You [Peter I] have detested Russia and all her past," wrote one of the Slavophile champions, Constantine Aksakov. "For this reason a seal of malediction is imprinted on all your senseless work. You heartlessly repudiated Moscow and went out to build, apart from your people, a solitary city, the reason being that you and the people could no longer dwell together." The reforms of Peter I, so highly glorified by the Westerners, were anathema to the Slavophiles; all the violent changes of Peter I were considered as some sort of blundering Teutonic intrusion of national life, for they superimposed upon the nation a philo-European form of government and legislation historically, traditionally, and spiritually alien to the people. Though the Slavophiles admitted that the country was at a critical turning point, their remedies could hardly be considered a solution to the problem since they sought an answer, not in the future, but in a past which they idealized as totally "unique" and apart from the Western world.

Slavophilism thus can be regarded as a conservative, romantic nationalism that sensed the urgent need for reforms. However, these reforms could be enforced peacefully by a national assembly which would curb, if not abolish, the institution of serfdom and partition the land, though preserving the revered institution of the village commune. Thus far there was nothing that would radically differ from any program of a bourgeois western European party. Yet there was a difference in the Slavophiles' approach to history, most marked by their blind faith in the past. They believed that Russia occupied a position in history distinct from that of the West and that her future as well was to be gloriously unique. To uphold their views the Slavophiles searched through history and discovered three bases upon which to build their philosophy: Orthodoxy, autocracy, and the commune.

The first, Greek Orthodoxy, represented to the Slavophiles more than a Western form of religious organization; it was a truly spiritual bond that held men together by a common loyalty to God and to each other. No other religious organization allowed the individual member a greater degree of freedom than Orthodoxy; no other had managed to preserve the qualities of the original founders of the church as had Greek Orthodoxy. Roman Catholicism is based on the authoritarian despotism of one man, Protestantism on an unprincipled revolt and a book; but Greek Orthodoxy is based on free unity, on a genuine spirit of freedom and Christian love.

The second and peculiarly Russian institution, autocracy, was as unique as the first. Autocracy in early Russia represented patriarchal authority and had nothing in common with other autocratic governments, which were usually based on physical compulsion and therefore violently opposed by their subjects. In western Europe the state is based on sheer force and thus rests, according to the Slavophiles, on artificial unity and internal contradiction. The Western state, then, is bound to witness constant revolts of those coerced to accept imposed authority. But upon Russia, a nation of a different political complexion from the dawn of history, autocracy never imposed itself; it had been "invited" by voluntary consent of the people. Here authority was based on persuasion, unity, communal interests, and genuine spirituality, according to P. V. Kireyevsky. For this reason Russia had no need of the Western type of democratic institutions, which resulted only in political and social strife, sharp economic rivalry, and class antagonisms.

Finally, there was the commune, the symbol of a truly "moral union of men," a "fraternal triumph of humanitarian spirit." This institution the Slavophiles interpreted as an answer to the Western utopian ideals cherished by socialists. According to the Slavophiles the commune practiced socialism long before the socialists in the West conceived their economic doctrines; in Russia socialism operated without the political convulsions manifested elsewhere in Europe. Moreover, whereas in the West socialism had been enforced from above, in Russia the organically Christian commune had applied social and economic justice voluntarily through its local members. This fact explained the absence of class struggle and of a proletariat, the class that constituted a constant revolutionary peril and contributed to the decline of European society.

While challenging this idyllic interpretation of the past, the Westerners, as well as later critics of Slavophilism, had erred on one point: they identified Slavophilism with the absolutism of the period of Nicholas I. This was either a deliberate distortion or an unconscious misconception of their views. There was one cardinal difference between autocracy as the Slavophiles envisioned it historically and as it existed in Russia. In the past, the Slavophiles pointed out, the people played a different part in relation to the state: the latter was the creation of the people, the instrument chosen and accepted by themselves. Sovereignty of the people was the *raison d'être* of the state in early Russian history, that state being a party to a contractual agreement that served the interests of the masses. On this score the Slavophiles and official authorities disagreed, for, in the opinion of the latter, admission of such a precept might have led to perilous political deduction. It carried with it some delicate questions, such as the need to summon a national assembly or the problem of inviolable rights of the people which the state was bound to honor under any circumstances. The Slavophiles cannot be regarded as in opposition to absolutism in a Western sense; merely representing a political concept, they endeavored to delineate more clearly the interests and rights of the state and those of the people. How the two could be kept apart, without fundamental political changes, the Slavophile exponents never succeeded in explaining. Because of this lack of clarity on such a vital point the government looked upon Slavophilism with misgivings, while the Westerners came to interpret it as another disguised device to perpetuate "Byzantine autocracy" in Russia.

While envisioning reforms, the Slavophiles could not accept

the measures advocated by their opponents; and it is here that they revealed their ideological vulnerability. The Slavophiles were essentially retrogressive in their aspirations, insisting upon a restoration of the status quo of bygone days when true Christian freedom prevailed, and harmony between the people and sovereign served as the basis of "unique" Russian government. This presentation of history irked even such a poised historian as S. M. Solovyev, who caustically dismissed it as the Buddhist concept in Russian historical thought. The Slavophiles asserted that the old harmony between faith and politics, between church and state, was destroyed by the devastating policies of Peter I. This destruction was bound to lead, they thought, to the creation of a Westernized minority and an unaffected majority, thereby alienating the leaders from the masses, the majestic imperial state from the Russian people. Peter's reforms introduced an air of artificiality, of aping alien culture while casting overboard traditional institutions and the national way of life. Slavophile interpretation of Russian history represented a curious mixture of idyllic loyalties to institutions and traditions that had never existed and a negation of the obvious realities of political life.

*Summary*

The intellectual conflict that raged in Russia during the middle of the nineteenth century was part and parcel a reflection of the German romantic movement and of the outburst of Slav nationalism in central and southeastern Europe during the same period. The idealization of traditionalism, of early national institutions, and the worship of the "national and cultural spirit" characterized the generation of the mid-nineteenth century. The idealization of the past can be regarded as an escape from the sordid present. Perhaps, to use the apt observation of Sir John Maynard, all of them had a tendency to mix their wish with its fulfilment. And yet, as one contemplates retrospectively this turbulent period and endeavors to summarize the intellectual tempest, certain facts stand out significantly. The verbal encounters between the opposing camps of Slavophilism and Westernism were not without some salutary effects. On the ideological battlefields were tempered a number of eminent national figures: liberals like Herzen, literary critics like Belinsky, famed pedagogues like Granovsky, and writers and publicists like Yury Samarin, A. S. Khomyakov, the Kireyevsky brothers, or C. S. Aksakov. The conflict stimulated an unprecedented interest in ethnography, Russian folklore, and particularly in Russian history, since each camp cherished a majestic sense of destiny and sought in the past a revelation of universal reason upon which to build its philosophy.[51] Seizing upon the ideas of Hegel and Schelling concerning the successive ascent of nations with historic missions for mankind, they tried to find justification for their hopes that the next message to the world would be delivered by Russia.

Those who took sides in this dispute—and it was difficult to remain neutral—turned not only to national history but to western European history as well. Young men absorbed themselves in the writings of the French Encyclopedists and were fascinated with the philosophies of Kant, Fichte, Schelling, and

---

[51] The Literature on the subject is vast. The following may be suggested: A. S. Khomyakov, *Polnoye sobraniye sochineny* [Complete Works], Moscow, 1900; Vols. I and III are of special interest. I. V. Kireyevsky's and C. Aksakov's essays dealing with the basic tenets of Slavophilism may be found in the *Moskovsky sbornik*, see especially Vols. I and III, 1852, and in the *Moskvityanin*, 1845 and 1847.

See also Aksakov, C., *Sochineniya istoricheskiye* [Historical Works], Moscow, 1889; G. A. Maksimovich, *Ucheniye pervykh slavyanofilov* [The philosophy of the First Slavophiles], Kiev, 1907; M. Gershenzon, *Istoricheskiye zapiski* [Historical Notes], Moscow, 1908; Michael B. Petrovich, *The Emergence of Russian Panslavism 1856-1870*, New York, 1956; see Chapters 1-2.

Hegel. Whereas the Slavophiles remained basically loyal to Schelling, the Westerners came to idolize Hegel, read his writings voraciously, and make appropriate deductions to support their own philosophy. The intellectual fever of the middle of the nineteenth century brought forth a series of brilliant scholars, whose names, with only a few exceptions unfortunately, mean little to Western readers. Suffice it to mention A. N. Popov, I. Ye. Zabelin, or I. D. Belyayev, the last-named known for his studies of earlier periods of Moscow life, chiefly concerning the peasant problem, communal landownership, and conditions of the Slavic tribes before the coming of the Varangians; or K. D. Kavelin and I. I. Dmitriyev, later to be followed by that prolific scholar, A. N. Pypin, noted for his works on recent Russian political and social history, Russian Freemasonry, Slavic literature, and Russian ethnography;[52]

---

[52] A. N. Popov, *Materialy dlya istorii vozmushcheniya Stenki Razina* [Sources Concerning the History of the Revolt of Stenka Razin], Moscow, 1857; *Poslednyaya sudba papskoy politiki v Rossii, 1845-1867 gg.* [Papal Policy in Russia, 1845-1867], St. Petersburg, 1868; *Russkoye posolstvo v Polshe v 1873-77 godakh* [The Russian Legation in Poland in 1673-77], St. Petersburg, 1854; I. Ye. Zabelin, *Domashny byt russkikh tsarey v XVI i XVII st.* [Domestic Life of Russian Tsars During the XVI-XVII Centuries], Moscow, 1872; *Istoriya goroda Moskvy* [A History of Moscow], 2nd. ed., Moscow, 1905; *Opyt izucheniya russkikh drevnostey i istorii* [A Study of Russian Antiquities and History], 2 vols., Moscow, 1872-73.

I. D. Belyayev, *Zemskiye sobory na Rusi* [A History of the National Assemblies in Russia], Moscow, 1867; *Krestyane na Rusi* [The Peasantry in Russia], Moscow, 1891; *Otnosheniye pridneprovskikh gorodov k vyaryazhskim knyazyam do vzyatiya Kieva v 1171* [Relations Between the Dnieper Towns and the Varangian Princes Prior to the Capture of Kiev in 1171], Moscow, 1848; *O russkom voyske v tsarstvovaniye Mikhayla Feodorovicha i posle ego, do preobrazovany sdelannykh Petrom Velikim* [Russian Armed Forces During the Reign of Michael Feodorovich and After Until the Reforms of Peter the Great], Moscow, 1846.

A. N. Pypin, *Istoriya russkoy etnografiii* [A History of Russian Ethnography], 4 vols., St. Petersburg, 1890-92; *Istoriya russkoy literatury* [A History of Russian Literature], 4 vols., St. Petersburg, 1902-03; *Histoire des littératures slaves*, Paris, 1881; *Geschichte der Slavischen Literature*, Leipzig, 1880-84; *Russkoye masonstvo XVIII i pervaya chetvert XIX v.* [Russian Freemasonry of the XVIII and First Quarter of the XIX Centuries], Petrograd, 1916; *Obshchestvennoye dvizheniye v Rossii pri Aleksandre I* [Social Movements in Russia During the Reign of Alexander I], St. Petersburg, 1900.

or V. I. Sergeyevich, the distinguished student of legal history, whose *Antiquities of Russian Law* remains to this day a monument to scholarship; or B. N. Chicherin, Hegelian, eminent jurist, and philosopher, whose chief contribution was in the field of Russian local government of the eighteenth century. The list could be greatly augmented, but the limited scope of this study does not permit a detailed account of this period of "storm and stress" in Russian history. Since this survey can include only the pillars of modern historiography, produced by the intellectual fermentation of the time, the most imposing of them must be considered next, namely S. M. Solovyev.

# The Second Half of the
# Nineteenth Century

## Solovyev (1820-1879)

*SERGEY MIKHAYLOVICH SOLOVYEV* appeared at a time when Russian historiography was in need of a writer who could amalgamate all the divergent theories accumulated through preceding decades into a single work. This was a task too great for any one man, but Solovyev assumed it and carried it an almost unbelievable distance.

Solovyev was born in Moscow and, until he was fourteen years old, received his education at home. His father was a priest and teacher, and the young man inherited a profound religious faith, which subsequently colored strongly his philosophy of history. In 1838 Solovyev entered the University of Moscow, where he was a pupil of both M. P. Pogodin and T. N. Granovsky. The former aroused little admiration in the future scholar, but to Granovsky, Solovyev felt deeply indebted for the rest of his life. The historical synthesis presented by Granovsky at once arrested the young student, Solovyev.[a] In 1845 he completed his master's thesis, *The Relations Between Novgorod and the Grand Princes,* and two years later successfully defended his doctoral dissertation, *A History of the Relations Among the Russian Princes of the Rurik Dynasty.* In

[a] Ivashin, "Rukopis' publichnykh lektsii T. N. Granovskogo," *Istorichesky zhurnal* (Moscow), Nos. 1-2, 1945.

98

the latter he stressed the internal rather than external factors that contributed to the consolidation of the Russian state. Later the idea was developed further when Solovyev brushed aside the "Norman" as well as the "Mongolian" theories. He came to regard both as inconsequential compared to the facts of internal political development.

Like many young people of his day, Solovyev had to sail toward intellectual maturity between the Scylla and Charybdis of Westernism and Slavophilism. For a time he leaned toward Slavophilism, until, by careful reading of Russian history, he was "cured." But the "cure" was evidently not thorough: Solovyev retained his faith in the religious and political Messianism of Russia; his continuing firm belief in the monarchical form of government was softened only by an amendment that rule should be by consent of the "better portions of the nation." Among the historians who determined the career of Solovyev was J. P. G. Ewers,[1] whose studies of early Russian history marked an epoch in Solovyev's intellectual life. Later recalling his training, Solovyev wrote: "From Karamzin I gathered only facts; Karamzin stimulated my feelings, but Ewers stimulated my thinking and compelled me to contemplate Russian history."

During the years 1842-1844 Solovyev traveled abroad as tutor in the family of Count Stroganov and made wise use of every available hour. In Paris he audited the lectures of the French historians Jules Michelet, Edgar Quinet, Charles Lenormant, successor of Guizot, and Victor Chasles; here he also made the acquaintance of the greatest of all poets of Poland, Adam Mickiewicz. In Prague he met the leading philologist and

---

[1] Johann Philipp Gustav Ewers (1781-1830) was a student of Schlözer at Göttingen. In 1803 Ewers came to Russia and established there his permanent residence. His most important contributions are *Vom Ursprunge des russischen Staats* (1808) and *Das älteste Reich der Russen in seiner geschichtlichen Entwickelung* (1826).

Slavophile, Pavel Josef Šafařik; in Berlin he audited the lectures of Leopold von Ranke, Karl Ritter, and the eminent church historian, Johann August Wilhelm Neander. During his short sojourn in western Europe he also familiarized himself with Western historical literature and was fascinated with the writings of Henry T. Buckle. He returned to Russia with warm reverence for Giovanni Vico as the great thinker of the eighteenth century and for François Guizot as the eminent historian of his own time.[2] The breadth of Solovyev's interest is characteristic. Unlike many historians, especially of the later generation, he demonstrated an amazing knowledge of universal history. He was also excellently versed in European history and culture, in the broadest sense, and was a keen student of ancient civilization.

Upon his return from western Europe in 1844, Solovyev was appointed to the faculty of the University of Moscow to teach Russian history, a chair formerly held by his recently retired teacher, Pogodin. As lecturer and writer, Solovyev stood forth as the champion of the theory of national development as an "organic whole"; he was a determined opponent of the old periodizations in Russian history, whether Norman, Mongolian, appanage, or any other. All "epochs," "periods," and "eras," he maintained, were misleading and obscured the organic unity of historic events. The first obligation of historical science, he taught, was to cast overboard all notions of epochs; instead of dividing history one should stress continuity throughout the centuries of national development. "People live, develop according to certain laws, and pass certain ages as individuals, just as all living organisms [do]." In recording the past, Solov-

[2] V. O. Klyuchevsky, *Ocherki i ryechi* [Studies and Addresses], Moscow, n.d., 2-3; M. N. Pokrovsky, *Borba klassov i russkaya istoricheskaya literatura* [Class Struggle and Russian Historical Literature], Petrograd, 1923, 59-60.

yev insisted, one must show how the separate components of the past came together to form the organic present. History is never aware of beginnings and ends; every event is rooted in the past and projects into the future. There was no "Norman period" because the Normans were soon absorbed by the Slavs; there was neither a "Mongolian" nor an "appanage period" because the process of organic growth never ceased.

This new view was bound to leave indelible marks on the development of Russian historiography. The historian was warned never to overlook the dramatic unity in the course of past events. With such a design, Solovyev set out to rewrite history, and in 1851 the first volume of his famous *History of Russia from Earliest Times* appeared. In the next twenty-eight years there followed volume after volume, twenty-nine altogether, ending with the date 1774. His original project was to lead up to the nineteenth century, which would have required at least six more volumes; death, interrupting the author in the middle of a sentence, prevented the completion of the plan.[3]

As the immense tapestry of Russian history unrolled, Solovyev did not limit his work to a mere recording of events but endeavored to explain them by tracing their origins, linking

[3] S. M. Solovyev, *Ob otnosheniyakh Novgoroda k velikim knyazyam* [Relations Between Novgorod and the Grand Princes], Moscow, 1845; *Istoriya otnosheny mezhdu russkimi knyazyami Ryurikova doma* [A History of the Relations Among the Russian Princes of the Rurik Dynasty], Moscow, 1847; *Sobraniye sochineny* [Collected Works] (This bulky volume includes Solovyev's monographic studies such as the essays on Russian Historiography, the History of the Fall of Poland, The Near Eastern Question, and others.), St. Petersburg, n.d.; *Geschichte des Falles von Polen*, tr. by Spörer, Gotha, 1865; *Imperator Aleksandr I. Politika-Diplomatiya* [Politics and Diplomacy in the Reign of Alexander I], St. Petersburg, 1877; *Istoriya Rossii s drevneyshikh vremyen* [History of Russia from Earliest Times], 29 vols., St. Petersburg, 1897; *Histoire de Russie* (tr. of the abridged, one-volume edition), Paris, 1879.

On Solovyev see: V. O. Klyuchevsky, "S. M. Solovyev," *Ocherki i ryechi*, Moscow, 1913, 1-35; Bestuzhev-Ryumin, *op. cit.*, 255-72; M. N. Pokrovsky, *Istoricheskaya nauka i borba klassov* [Historical Science and Class Struggle], Moscow, 1933, 7-100; Rubinstein, *op. cit.*, 312-42.

their correlations, and deriving plausible conclusions. According to Solovyev three conditions mold the history of a people: the character of the natural environment in which the people settle; the character of the people, or "national physiognomy"; and the external pressures to which the people are subjected. He made an analysis of the social, economic, and political forces and of the geographic environment which contributed to the changes in society, beginning with the time when ancient Slavic tribes lived, as he thought, along the Danube; then he proceeded with the development by which the Slavs were forced eastward by some other people to a totally bare and inhospitable territory, later to become known as Russia, and left behind them the fertile and strategically more convenient lands. Scattered along the Dniester, Dnieper, and Oka rivers, they required a long time for readjustment, while constant invasions of Asian hordes from the east and bitter rivalry with Poland and Lithuania along the western frontiers made progress difficult and slow. Whereas in western Europe nature served as the mother of the people, in eastern Europe nature was destined to be their wicked stepmother. Herein lay the main reason for Russia's backwardness and desperate need for centralized authority to control the "fluid condition." The more favorable geographic position of the Muscovite principality aided its political growth. Being farther away from immediate danger and exploiting every occasion for consolidating its powers at the expense of its weaker neighbors, this principality gradually laid the foundation for the future Moscow state, from which, later, the Russian Empire was to arise.[4] Moscow's destiny was shaped not only by exceptionally able leaders but also by strategic advantages and favorable material resources. Personali-

[4] *Russky biografichesky slovar*, XIX, 85, 86.

ties interested Solovyev to a small extent only, for he could never admit that history stemmed solely from the operation of personal force; nor did he believe that the dynamics of national history involved either blind force or destiny, for only human will added shape and meaning to the course of national life. The so-called "Era of Peter I" therefore becomes only an accelerated course of events derived from preceding developments. The new course is determined by pressure forces of internal and external nature. Nothing is accidental, since no historic event begins suddenly or ends abruptly; the new begins at a time when the old is still continuing. Circumstances forced Peter I to leadership in a struggle for a cause already determined before his ascendancy. Ivan IV was instrumental in delivering a fatal blow to the old boyar class that had already been receding from the scene of national history.

Solovyev developed his thesis concerning the rise of the Russian state somewhat as follows. State and nation, he explained, are inseparable, the one deriving from the other; the history of Russia is a history of its government. National leaders do not rise by accident; they are products of their times and social environment: their caliber is measured by the nation they stem from and the latter by the part it plays in history. The influence of Hegel and Ranke is obvious; Solovyev read Hegel's *Philosophy of History* avidly, absorbing every thought, and later incorporated it as part of his entire outlook upon history. In the presence of the broad conception and logical deductions Solovyev had made, the works of the earlier writers were bound to be superseded by the new pattern of interpretation. Solovyev boldly attacked Karamzin at a time when his nine-volume work was still considered officially as the last word in Russian historiography. Nor did he ingratiate himself with the Slavophiles when

he warned against their idealization of the past, defined it as
"Buddhism in the science of history," and described it as philosophical stagnation.

It was the first time that a history of Russia had been conceived on such a scale, with the narrative based always on the
authentic source and held fast to the principle of pure, objective
truth. In this comprehensive conception both of history and of
the nation in all aspects of its life, Solovyev emphasized three
main factors—political, religious, and cultural—and found their
expression in "loyalty to the State, devotion to the Church, and
struggle for enlightenment." Peter I, that "rebel on the throne,"
fascinated Solovyev on account of the reforms he himself had
witnessed during his own lifetime. As he observed the oncoming
reaction to the reforms of the 'sixties and compared Alexander
II with Peter I and other historical personalities, Solovyev com-
mented: "Fate did not send Alexander II a Richelieu or a Bismarck, but it is doubtful that he would have been capable of
using a Richelieu or a Bismarck. Alexander had pretenses; he
was a weak man who feared to appear weak or dependent.
Compelled by fear, he would, one beautiful morning, have expelled both Richelieu and Bismarck."

Solovyev's emphasis upon cultural development was in accordance with the prevailing tendency of historical writing in
western Europe. His main thesis of depicting Russia's history
against a background that ranged beyond mere national limita-
tions also brought him closer to the philosophy of the Westerners. At the same time his broad knowledge of his subject and
his strictly critical approach to every problem of his work won
respect even among those who could not agree with his contention. Yet even Solovyev himself did not consider as final the
work to which he had devoted his whole life: he regarded it as
only a tool to be used in clearing the way for a closer, fuller, and

perhaps more penetrating, study of Russian historical development.[5]

Particularly Solovyev's last volumes are based on sources obtained in St. Petersburg and Moscow archives that were either unknown or not utilized before. In many respects the voluminous work represents an encyclopedia of the nation's growth rather than a mere history. In this fact lies its merit as well as its weakness. One of its shortcomings is that, notwithstanding the author's insistence upon "organic unity," his twenty-nine volumes constitute a mass of historical material laced with Hegelian design but lacking any proper integration. Solovyev himself had described his work as only a tool for later scholars; and it still offers sufficient raw material to be well worth consulting. The numerous documents cited by Solovyev and formerly unpublished are of considerable value to this day. Solovyev did not possess a speculative mind: whatever was obscure he omitted, and he never indulged in hypothetical interpretations. This is the main reason, says Klyuchevsky, why Solovyev's history contains so little "learned trash" and may explain also why the author has been labeled a "dry historian." [6]

Solovyev lacked the literary gift and the architectonic skill of Klyuchevsky, nor did he have the time to be concerned either with style or design; he was occupied with "pick and shovel" work, composing largely for the student of history rather than for the average reader. Solovyev is truly an historian's historian; how else could he have produced a twenty-nine volume history, not to mention many articles and a number of important monographs? He never dwelt in an ivory tower but always responded to current issues, lectured, and contributed numerous articles

---

[5] E. Shmurlo, "S. M. Solovyev," *Entsiklopedichesky slovar* (Brokhaus-Efron), XXX (2), 798-803.

[6] V. O. Klyuchevsky, *Ocherki i ryechi*, 39.

during the agitated period of reforms. "Life," he said on one occasion, "has its full right to present questions to science; science has an obligation to answer questions of life." After his death Solovyev left a mass of raw material with numerous threads hanging at loose ends. It became the task of his pupil and successor, the *Geschichtsmaler* Klyuchevsky, to weave these threads together into a beautiful design, embodying in his historical writing of supreme excellence a summary of all the efforts of Russian historians, beginning with Tatishchev in the eighteenth century. It fell to the later generation of writers to utilize the broad outlines of Solovyev's philosophy for further studies in comparing Russian and western European institutions, as serfdom and feudalism. The greatest contribution Solovyev made to historical science was to map the road for those who detected in history a universal design. The path of development, as Solovyev saw it, was not regular to be sure; at times it followed zigzags, sometimes retracing itself, sometimes advancing, but in the end it was a relentless surge forward. The pilgrimage of Solovyev through the maze of materials set the way for Klyuchevsky, Pavlov-Silvansky, and others who—with greater success—sought the pattern of events rather than accept history as simply a "tissue of disconnected accidents."

### *Chicherin* (1828-1904)

Hagelian philosophy and the German school of Ranke, Niebuhr, Eichhorn, and Savigny influenced many other writers in Russia besides Solovyev. The writings of Boris Nikolayevich Chicherin, a contemporary of Solovyev, may be cited as the best illustration of this influence. The stress upon the role of the state in the development of a nation could already be noted in the writings of Solovyev. It gave rise to a trend in historical writing

known in Russian historiography as the "juridical school."
The basic idea of this school was that behind the entire historical development of the nation had always been the state. The
state, accordingly, represents "the highest form of social life"
and national development; the obscure concept of nationality
assumes concrete form in the embodiment of the state. The most
prominent member of this school was Chicherin, author of
numerous works, all of which contain the same thesis.[7]

The central theme was that the beginning of the Russian
state begins history; that the formation of the state came while
the people represented nothing but a "lonely, wandering face"
and played only a passing or opposing part in the process. From
the day of the Muscovy Principality and throughout subsequent
events the initiative always emanated from the center, from
sovereign authority that acted as the moving spirit of national
will and unity. The role of the middle class, according to Chicherin, was to serve as ballast to keep the ship of state on an
even keel. It was this class that acted as an instrument of social
leveling, a factor evenly distributing wealth within the nation
and thereby precluding extremes of either wealth or poverty.
The strength of the state was determined by the role the masses
played; the less they interfered in public affairs, the more chance
there was for the state to fulfill its mission.

Developments within a society were determined not by its
economic production and class rivalry, but by the actual needs
of the state. Chicherin even traced the origin of the institution
of serfdom directly and exclusively to the interests of the state,
while the privileges of the landed aristocracy came as a by-

[7] B. N. Chicherin, *Opyty po istorii russkogo prava* [Studies in History of Russian
Law], Moscow, 1858; *O narodnom predstavitelstvye* [National Representation], Moscow, 1866; *Russky dilettantizm i obshchinnoye zemlevladeniye* [Russian Dilettantism
and Communal Landownership], Moscow, 1878; *Philosophische Forschungen,* Heidel-
berg, 1899.

product and were entirely accidental. The dominant fact was service of all, in whatever form it might be, to the state. The conclusion was that the parent of all institutions within a society is the state; it was within the power of the state to retain, alter, or abolish any institution it chose.

At times his philosophy led Chicherin to rather curious generalizations which tested the patience of the rising liberal elements in the country. He explained the "invitation" of the Normans or Varangians, for example, by the fact that the Slavs were always noted not only for their inability to get along among themselves but also for their readiness to sacrifice themselves for the fatherland and sovereign. Needless to say, the view was not a palatable one to the younger generation of his later life. On the other hand, as a mild liberal—though of a proud, aristocratic family—he came to be regarded by the authorities as an "unreliable." In 1868 he resigned as professor of History of Law at the University of Moscow in protest against the policy of the administration and returned to his native estate in Tambov, where he devoted most of his time to local administration. In 1881 he was elected mayor of the city of Moscow, a post which proved of short duration: by an order of Alexander III he was dismissed two years after he assumed office. The reason for this drastic action was a speech which Chicherin delivered at a gathering of city mayors in which he urged the "united action of all local governments to assure the welfare of Russia." The career of Chicherin manifests the plight of even the mildly liberal elements, the anguish of inner conflicts which the Russian intelligentsia had suffered during the last decades of the past century: men were torn between lingering and deep-seated loyalties to the past and budding enthusiasm for the future.

## Kavelin (1818-1885)

Another representative of the "juridical school" was Konstantin Dmitriyevich Kavelin. In his earliest work, *A Survey of the Juridical Conditions of Early Russia,* published in 1846, Kavelin leaned more toward the views of Solovyev. He endeavored to show that national development represents an organic process based on immutable laws which neither the individual genius nor historical incidents can offset.[8] Not the genius of the leader but the genius of the people ultimately shapes the destiny of a nation; and, very much as the *Iliad* and the *Odyssey* represent products of the collective genius of the Greek people, so is social life the product of the collective rather than of the individual effort, no matter how pre-eminent the individual may be.

Kavelin stressed but little the economic or cultural aspects of social life and dwelt more upon those "immutable laws" which control the historical procession of changes that a society is bound to undergo.[9] The fundamental law of history, he believed, is the organic growth and transformation of the community from a loosely-knit tribe into a modern state. The reign of Ivan IV, according to Kavelin, heralded the rise of the Russian state, while Peter I expressed its final form. To use Kavelin's formula, Ivan served the state as the poet, Peter as the practical statesman. In its development toward the highest form of social organization, society has to go through three stages: the tribal, the patrimonial, and, finally, the institutional form. To Kavelin the first symbolized the primitive step, lead-

[8] K. D. Kavelin, *Sobraniye sochineny* [Collected Works], 4 vols., St. Petersburg, 1900.
[9] *Russky biografichesky slovar,* VIII, 364-65.

ing to the family, while the last marked the formation of the modern nation.

In brief, the history of a society is entirely a part of the history of the state; only in the latter can one find the key to an understanding of the hidden forces that mold a nation. The process naturally has its ramifications, but historical law relentlessly drives society toward its goals; resistance to this law explains the social unrest that occurs from time to time in history. It was in accord with this law that Kavelin conceived the rise of the Muscovite state. So far his views coincided with those of Solovyev; thereafter, however, Kavelin departed to join the "juridical school." Whereas Solovyev believed that the centralized Russian state had evolved largely because of a number of favorable historical coincidences, Kavelin insisted that a state had to emerge as an historical inevitability, since society cannot escape the prescribed course "from the tribal stage with its form of communal ownership to the family with its patrimonial estate or separate ownership, to the individual within the modern state." [10]

One more detail is perhaps worth noting. The rise of the state in Russia, as Kavelin saw it, differed from the ascendancy of the state in western Europe: whereas in the West the process emanated "from below," in Russia it had emerged "from above." Though in both western and eastern Europe the state arrived at the same goal, their historical paths differed. Here Kavelin's view coincides with that of Chicherin. Kavelin accepted the contention that Russia was a "peasant state," yet his faith in the peasant masses had always been thin, gnawed away by skepticism. To Kavelin the peasantry was nothing but an "ethnographic protoplasm" that held out no more than a promise of national life. For this reason Kavelin favored a

[10] Pypin, *Istoriya russkoy etnografiii*, II, 19 ff.

strong, centralized, monarchical authority as the only form of government capable of preserving national life.

Kavelin's interpretation seemed too dogmatic to many students of history. The Slavophiles frowned upon a philosophy that professed little faith in a communal form of social organization. Later, V. I. Sergeyevich carried the theory further by maintaining that the state came into being, not because of historical laws, but by virtue of a civil contract between the Prince and the Assembly, or *veche*.[11] He defined two stages in the development of the state: the first when individual will was supreme, the second when sovereignty of the state superseded individual free will. Sergeyevich was followed later by Klyuchevsky and Kostomarov, the former approaching the problem with an eye mainly upon its social-economic aspects, the latter two concentrating upon its ethnography; thus, little was left of Kavelin's laboriously erected theory. Whatever the validity of each of the philosophical contentions, cumulatively they stimulated historical research, tempered the will to scholarly pursuits, aroused keen curiosity about the past, and compelled many to publish what they considered to be newly discovered historical truth. This development barred any static faith in "eternal verities" and agitated a cultural alertness in the country as never before.

The "Era of Great Reforms" stimulated further the study of law and institutions in Russia. This was a period which subsequently produced a legion of scholars, among whom were such eminent students of history as A. D. Gradovsky, N. M. Korkunov, M. A. Dyakonov, A. V. Romanovich-Slavatinsky, and B. E. Nolde, who investigated Russian institutions; others, like M. F. Vladimirsky-Budanov and S. B. Veselovsky, who

---

[11] V. I. Sergeyevich, *Drevnosti russkogo prava* [Early Russian Law], St. Petersburg, 1911.

made a comparative study of Russian public law and financial legislation; and a third group, typified by A. S. Lappo-Danilevsky, who distinguished himself in the field of diplomatics, and M. K. Lyubavsky, who contributed to the field of historical geography, particularly with regard to the formation of the Muscovite state and its relations to the medieval Grand Duchy of Lithuania.

The towering figure among these writers was Alexander Dmitriyevich Gradovsky (1841-1889), who through his interest in Western political institutions came to advocate the principles of legality and political liberty.[12] To Gradovsky history was mainly a matter of legal development; he viewed Russia's past largely through the development of local institutions, as their functions co-ordinated or conflicted with those of the national agencies. As professor at the University of St. Petersburg, Gradovsky left a considerable following among his former students; of these some were destined to become world-renowned jurists, like N. Tagantsev in the field of criminal law and F. Martens in international law.[13]

### Klyuchevsky (1841-1911)

Vasily Osipovich Klyuchevsky was born in the Province of Penza to the family of a village priest. His early years brought him close to peasant life, an experience that later enabled him to see the vital agrarian problem and the origins of serfdom not only with rare sympathy but also with remarkable insight and intuition—qualities quite alien to court panegyrists and the city-bred intelligentsia. In 1856 Klyuchevsky entered an ecclesi-

---

[12] A. D. Gradovsky, *Sobraniye sochineny* [Collected Works], 9 vols., St. Petersburg, 1899-1904.

[13] A critical appraisal of the "juridical school" is ably presented by N. P. Milyukov in an article: "Yuridicheskaya shkola v russkoy istoriografii: Solovyev, Kavelin, Chicherin, Sergeyevich," *Russkaya Mysl'*, VI, 1886, 80-92.

astical seminary. He made an excellent record there, but after four years he determined to follow a different path. The seminary board was reluctant to grant him a leave, insisting that since he was receiving a government stipend, he was therefore under moral obligation to pursue the career he had chosen; but the bishop looked at the matter differently, and Klyuchevsky was permitted to leave. The following year he enrolled at the University of Moscow. It was the year of great reforms, and many young men were fired with the hope of brighter days for their country. Klyuchevsky plunged into the midst of this feverish period—a turning point in modern Russia—with the utmost interest in everything that concerned the national life.

At the University, Klyuchevsky was fortunate in finding a few remaining members of the "old guard," among them G. Ivanov, the stimulating lecturer on ancient civilization; B. Chicherin, the leading figure of the "juridical school"; and S. Solovyev, the eminent historian. Solovyev was then in the prime of his popularity, and he deeply impressed the young man. It is through Solovyev, his greatly admired teacher, that Klyuchevsky arrived at his broad vision of history, learned the necessity of mastering sources, and gained a sense of purpose in the historical process that did not permit of an aimless flow of events. An early study, based on the accounts of the Muscovite state by foreign travelers, won immediate attention, and at Solovyev's suggestion he undertook a number of other studies. Chief among them was a master's thesis on the lives of early Russian saints as a source of history. Another study dealt with the Solovetsky monastery as a factor in the economic development of the north and further confirmed the expectations of the teacher.[14] But Klyuchevsky's ambition was not attracted to

[14] V. O. Klyuchevsky, *Opyty i issledovaniya* [Essays and Studies], Moscow, 1915, 1 ff.

local developments, however important they might be; he wanted to paint a broad design on a national scale. Endowed with the vision and the temperament of an artist, he was able only by self-discipline and determination to complete a study based on boring accounts of an old monastery. Yet the tedious work was not wasted; it developed in Klyuchevsky qualities indispensable to the historian: patience and a keen analytical ability to scrutinize numerous sources, sifting much sand for a few grains of gold, as well as the capacity to take full advantage of his access to source material never before examined. It also enabled him to familiarize himself with a field rarely dwelt upon in a scholarly manner: the relations between church and state, and the part played by the church in the economic development of the Russian people.

The lectures which Klyuchevsky delivered at the Alexandrian military school and at the University of Moscow for Women demonstrated during the early period of his teaching career not only his exceptional ability as a lecturer but also his rare literary gift and his remarkable vision and talent for imparting a glowing, vivid reality to dusty archival records. Within a few years he had become widely known, and when Solovyev became gravely ill in 1879, Klyuchevsky was given the chair of his teacher. Many students at the University of Moscow looked askance at the young appointee, the teacher from a military school and a women's university! Speedily, however, as one of his pupils recalls, his lectures became so popular that it was futile to offer anything else at the hours when Klyuchevsky lectured: he would empty all other auditoriums.[15]

Klyuchevsky is especially noteworthy for his remarkable

---

[15] *V. O. Klyuchevsky. Kharakteristiki i vospominaniya* [V. O. Klyuchevsky. Essays and Recollections], Moscow, 1912, 13-14.

grasp of the scope of historical processes and for the richness of his cultural knowledge. He was an active member of the Moscow Archeological Society. In 1900 he consented, after continuous and persistent pressure, to lecture at the School of Fine Arts, and there he remained to his closing days. His addresses on Fonvizin, Pushkin, and Lermontov, later published in the form of essays, bear witness to his profound familiarity with literature.[16] The essay on Lermontov, entitled "Melancholy" (*Grust'*), appeared in one of the leading periodicals, *Russkaya mysl'*, and did not bear the name of the modest author; Klyuchevsky's style was so unique that the author was quickly detected by the readers.

His *Course in Russian History,* delivered at the University of Moscow, reveals a genius for presenting a marvelously synthesized history and stands today as a monument to the art of both historical writing and Russian letters. He toiled over every single lecture with rare perseverance. On one occasion a group of students asked Klyuchevsky to deliver an address on the poet Nekrasov. He accepted the invitation, yet when he discovered that the address was to be delivered within a month he withdrew his consent, explaining that one could not prepare himself within such a brief period. "It takes little time to deliver a lecture," explained Klyuchevsky. "It does not take much time to write it either; it takes a long time before the theme begins to 'nibble.'" He would not even think of less than six months preparation.[17]

For a long time Klyuchevsky's lectures were known only through the notes of students. All attempts to persuade him to publish them in book form met with his disapproval because he

---

[16] Published in *Ocherki i ryechi* [Studies and Addresses], 57-89; 117-39; 279-311.
[17] V. A. Maklakov, *Iz vospominany* [Reminiscences], 191.

felt that they were far from being the last word on Russian history.[18] He finally yielded, however, and in 1904 there appeared the first volume of his popular *Course*, which was soon followed by three more; in 1921 there appeared a fifth volume, compiled from the notes of a former student, Y. Barskov.[19]

Klyuchevsky came at a time when Slavophilism, Westernism, and Hegelianism were beginning to fade; the old feudal order was definitely passing away, and everywhere there were signs of the emergence of a new Russia. Thus Klyuchevsky was in the advantageous position of one who could look back at times and at schools which had flourished and gone; and he made the best of his opportunity. In his work he considered the social strata of the past ten centuries of Russia horizontally: at the bottom, the "dark" peasant masses; at the top, the gentry nurtured physically by the masses and intellectually by French culture; between these, the other classes, dependent on both. These social layers were now antagonistic, now allied, as circumstances dictated. In his description of the process of social

[18] *Klyuchevsky. Kharakteristiki i vospominaniya*, 20-22.

[19] The following are the most important works of Klyuchevsky: *Drevnerusskiye zhitiya svyatykh, kas istorichesky istochnik* [Lives of Early Russian Saints as a Source of History], Moscow, 1871; *Pisma V. O. Klyuchevskogo k P. P. Gvozdevu (1861-1870)* [Letters of V. O. Klyuchevsky to P. P. Gvozdev], Moscow, 1870; *Kurs russkoy istorii* [A Course in Russian History], 5 vols., Moscow, 1904-21; tr. by J. Hogarth, 5 vols., London, 1911-31; *Istoriya soslovy v Rossii* [A History of Classes in Russia], Moscow, 1913; *Boyarskaya duma drevney Rusi* [The Boyar Council in Early Russia], Moscow, 1883; *Ocherki i ryechi* [Studies and Addresses], Moscow, n.d.; *Opyty i issledovaniya* [Essays and Studies], Moscow, 1915; *Otzyvy i otvety* [Reviews and Replies], Moscow, 1914; *Skazaniya inostrantsev o Moskovskom gosudarstve* [Accounts of Foreigners Concerning the Muscovite State], Petrograd, 1918.

Essays concerning Klyuchevsky: S. I. Tkhorzhevsky, "V. O. Klyuchevsky, kak sotsiolog i politichesky myslitel [V. O. Klyuchevsky as Sociologist and Political Thinker]," *Dyela i dni* (Petrograd), II, 1921, 152-79; A. E. Presnyakov, "V. O. Klyuchevsky (1911-21)," *Russky istorichesky zhurnal* (Petrograd), VIII, 1922, 203-24; M. N. Pokrovsky, *Istoricheskaya nauka i borba klassov* [Historical Science and the Class Struggle], Moscow, 1933, 167-205; S. A. Golubtsov, "Teoreticheskiye vzglyady V. O. Klyuchevskogo [Theoretical Views of V. O. Klyuchevsky]," *Russky istorichesky zhurnal* (Petrograd), VIII, 178-202; N. L. Rubinstein, *Russkaya istoriografiya* [Russian Historiography], Moscow, 1941, 441-69.

formation certain concrete factors stand out: struggle for national unity, the demands of national defense, the longing for
cultural development, and the desire for economic security.[20]
These factors make his narrative systematic, unique, and pur-
poseful. The only criticism one can make is that the author gave
little space to Russian foreign policy, emphasizing mainly the
internal development of the Empire: the Foreign Office occupies
no place of prominence in Klyuchevsky's history. Even the
Mongolian invasion is presented as an incidental experience
in Russian history, a brief nightmare rather than a period of the
nation's past. Nor did Klyuchevsky show any interest in problems of national minorities incorporated within the Empire,
not even the Ukrainian people; Klyuchevsky was truly a "Great
Russian" historian.

The approach of Klyuchevsky to any past event was never
that of the cold logician-scientist with lancet poised to probe,
but rather that of the keen, sympathetically intuitive psycholo-
gist; yet never did his rich and fertile imagination betray the
scientific accuracy of his observations or his judgment. Therefore his generalizations are usually sound, his characters emerge
from the distant past clothed in flesh and blood, and the whole
process of historical development becomes a vivid, integrated
panorama. His striking accomplishment is his harmonization
within himself of the qualities of an erudite historian, a sociologist, an artist, and a teacher. As the reader turns the pages of
Klyuchevsky's *Course,* he can not but marvel at the vivid revival
of the past before him. How can one not admire the artist-his-
torian who presents such living portraits as those of Ivan III
and Ivan the Terrible, of Boris Godunov, of Patriarch Nikon, or
of Peter the Great and Catherine II? The masterful metaphors
and characterization of personalities once read cannot easily be

[20] *Russky istorichesky zhurnal,* VIII, 1922, 184-85.

forgotten. Many of his vivid portrayals give one the impression not so much of an individual as of an alloy that served to temper the national character. Klyuchevsky compared Patriarch Nikon to a sail—magnificent in stormy weather, but in the calm air an ordinary piece of cloth hanging pitifully. He presented Peter as the epitome of an elemental fury that combined the dynamism of his people with personal pettiness. In Catherine he detected a fusion of French culture, boundless feminine vanity, and voluptuousness.

Not only students of history learned from Klyuchevsky but accomplished artists like Chaliapin as well. Before he undertook the difficult part of Boris Godunov, Chaliapin had a long session with Klyuchevsky. Later the great opera singer recalled "with grateful pleasure the marvellous pictures he painted of Boris, his times and environment." Recalling his visit, Chaliapin writes: "An artist in words, and gifted with a most powerful historical imagination, Klyuchevsky was, in addition to being an historian, a most remarkable actor." [21] If one may use Schlözer's classification, it can be safely said that Klyuchevsky was the rare combination of both the *Geschichtsmaler* and the *Geschichtsschreiber*.

No previous general course in Russian history had given so much space to the peasant problem. The peasant of Kievan Russia in all his multiple appearances—the frontiersman, tradesman, and tiller of the soil, whether free or enslaved in field or factory, whether groaning under the burden of crushing taxes, submissive and downtrodden at the feet of his master, or great and terrifying in the reawakened spirit of his frontier ancestors of the wide plains of Russia—this peasant occupies a prominent place in Klyuchevsky's history. For the historian realized that it is only by the systematic analysis of the peasant himself as

[21] F. I. Chaliapin, *Pages from My Life*, N. Y., 1927, 194-95.

well as the agrarian problem in general that Russian history may be fully appreciated. Yet, for some strange reason, though deeply sympathetic with the peasant masses and profoundly aware of the hidden reservoir of social explosives, he devoted hardly any space to such mass rebellions as those led by Stenka Razin or Pugachev.

Though Klyuchevsky greatly revered his teachers, Solovyev and Chicherin, he left them far behind.[22] Solovyev, like Buckle, later emphasized the influence of "spiritual forces" upon history; his pupil turned more to the political, social, and economic spheres. Of real importance were more the material than the moral forces, those which manifested themselves in social phenomena. And if to Chicherin institutions meant everything, to Klyuchevsky they were simply mechanical things shaped by the sociological process of a nation. Among the works that display this conception are the analytical study of the Council of Boyars, which remains to this day a classic piece of historical literature; the study of the value of the ruble from the sixteenth to the eighteenth century; and, finally, the essay on the origins of serfdom, a reply to J. Engelmann's book, *Die Leibeigenschaft in Russland* (The Institution of Serfdom in Russia), in which Klyuchevsky endeavors to prove that peasant indebtedness was the main condition that led to the establishment of serfdom.[23] This essay presented a highly original view, though it is questioned by present-day scholars, who are inclined to attach more importance to direct state legislation than to any abstract process.

Klyuchevsky destroyed many of the happier notions of the past, notably those held by the Slavophiles. For instance, the

---

[22] *Russky istorichesky zhurnal,* VIII, 1922, 204 ff. See also two excellent essays on this subject in *V. O. Klyuchevsky. Kharakteristiki i vospominaniya,* 45-58; 59-93.

[23] Klyuchevsky, *Opyty i issledovaniya,* 212-310.

Slavophiles were fond of pointing out that in the early days Russia was governed by a limited monarch, the agency to limit his powers being the *Zemsky Sobor,* or National Assembly. Klyuchevsky exploded that theory by proving that so far as the Assembly of the sixteenth century was concerned, it never constituted any limitation upon the monarch's powers, for the simple reason that that chamber of loquacity never constituted an elective body but was appointed by no other than the sovereign himself.[24] The origin of the autocratic state and the rise of the military landowning gentry Klyuchevsky masterfully explained mainly by two factors: continuous territorial expansion and the urgent necessity of defending the frontiers of the wide-flung state. Precisely the same motives dictated the reforms of Peter I.[25] To the delight of the Slavophiles, Klyuchevsky paints these in the most unsparing colors. But he also has pages which would equally delight the Westerners: descriptions of ruthless, shallow, dynastic struggles and of the oppression and exploitation of the peasant in a truly Asiatic manner, with little concern for individual rights. The reason for the mutual satisfaction in both camps is that Klyuchevsky never wrote "patriotic" history, though he was a Russian from tip to toe. He hated national glorification no less than national debasement. He felt with an equal sting of conscience the heart-rending ruthlessness of Ivan the Terrible and Peter the Great, the stupidity of boyar pettiness, the snobbery and class-selfishness of the later gentry, and the brutality and blind hatred of the peasants toward every form of social discipline.

But Klyuchevsky also understood the Russian character. He saw the causes lying behind the bloodstained pages of the past

[24] See *Sbornik statey, posvyashchennykh S. F. Platonovu,* St. Petersburg, 1912, 299. Note also Klyuchevsky, *Opyty i issledovaniya,* 417 ff.

[25] Klyuchevsky, *A Course in Russian History,* IV, Chapters III-VI and X. See also his interpretation of Catherine's reign in *Ocherki i ryechi,* 312-385.

and therefore was able to draw from the story, not embittered
and distorted ideas, but wholesome lessons. It would seem as
if he always bore in mind the words of Dostoyevsky: "Judge the
Russian people, not by the degrading sins which it often com-
mits, but by the great and holy things to which, in the midst
of degradation, it constantly aspires. . . . Judge the people not
by what it is, but by what it would like to become." [26]

### Bestuzhev-Ryumin  (1829-1897)

The list of nineteenth-century historians would be incomplete without the names of Bestuzhev-Ryumin and one of his
pupils, S. F. Platonov. Konstantin Nikolayevich Bestuzhev-
Ryumin, pupil of Pogodin, Granovsky, and Solovyev, and great
admirer of Karamzin, was among the first to steer an independent course through the stormy sea created by the Slavophiles and Westerners of the 'forties and 'fifties.[27] He was more
of a critic than an historian, more of an eclectic idealist than an
original thinker, an observer rather than a warrior—and therefore a less colorful figure than his teachers. Conservative, non-
committal, scholastically sterile, adhering to no particular
school, he naturally had no historical Pleiad of his own and his
disciples were not many; among them, the most distinguished
was the late S. F. Platonov.

[26] See the most recent appraisals of Klyuchevsky by G. Fedotov in *Sovremenniye
zapiski* (Paris), L, 1932, 340-62, and M. Karpovich, "Klyuchevsky and Recent
Trends in Russian Historiography," *The Slavonic and East European Review*, XXI,
1943, 31-39.

[27] K. N. Bestuzhev-Ryumin, *Biografii i kharakteristiki* [Biographical Essays], St.
Petersburg, 1882; *Russkaya istoriya* [Russian History], 2 vols., St. Petersburg, 1872-75;
*Geschichte Russlands,* tr. by T. Schiemann, Mitau, 1877; *O tom, kak roslo Moskov-
skoye knyazhestvo i sdelalos russkim tsarstvom* [How the Muscovy Principality Grew
and Became the Russian State], St. Petersburg, 1866.

See E. Shmurlo, *Ocherk zhizni i nauchnoy deyatelnosti Konstantina Nikolayevicha
Bestuzheva-Ryumina* [A Study of the Life and Scholarly Activities of K. N. Bestuzhev-
Ryumin], Yuriev, 1899; S. F. Platonov, *Stati po russkoy istorii* [Articles on Russian
History], 2nd ed., St. Petersburg, 1912; see article on Bestuzhev-Ryumin.

Of noble birth and refined education, Bestuzhev-Ryumin entered academic life with impressive intellectual baggage, though, as he himself humbly stated, it was rather "chaotic," or, in the words of Pushkin, he had learned "something and somehow." His knowledge was not limited to history alone, but embraced also the fine arts, literature, theology, and philosophy; and he possessed no meager knowledge of the Russian chronicles. Bestuzhev-Ryumin matured amidst the restless decades of the era of Nicholas I, when Westernism and Slavophilism were in full armor against each other. He absorbed much from both camps, though for the rest of his life he sentimentally leaned more toward Slavophile nationalism.

As professor of the University of St. Petersburg and member of the Academy of Sciences, Bestuzhev-Ryumin always maintained that the historian must be impartial, giving nothing but the facts.[28] The duty of an historian, he taught, must be to gather carefully verified factual material and put it together without the embellishments of "social processes." The basis of national history, he taught, is the "complex phenomenon called society." To present it accurately one must be objective about the social components of society and the factors that hold the community together: social authority, government, judicial institutions, social classes, religion, cultural standards, trade, industry, and the institution of the family. Platonov recalls that Bestuzhev-Ryumin particularly endeavored to impress this principle upon his pupils. The insistence upon complete objectivity at times involved Bestuzhev-Ryumin in incidents not much to his credit and indicates how precarious such an attitude may become when applied without imaginative daring or if void of a sense of humor.

Bestuzhev-Ryumin was a true product of the early Germanic

[28] *Russky istorichesky zhurnal,* VIII, 1922, 225-28.

school of Schlözer, in which authenticity and unbiased narration of the past were the highest arts of historical writing. It can truly be said that before Bestuzhev-Ryumin "every bird lay unfeathered." Is it any wonder that he was overshadowed by such a giant as Solovyev and such an artist as Klyuchevsky? Today Bestuzhev-Ryumin is a half-forgotten man, an object of curiosity to the student of Russian historiography. To him, however, the student must pay due tribute for his able analysis of the chronicles and biographical sketches of Karamzin and Pogodin, which, though written in a panegyric vein, characterize the political milieu of the author.

In his *Russian History* Bestuzhev-Ryumin endeavored to follow the pattern he taught his students, emphasized methodology and authenticity of utilized sources, and refrained from delivery of "messages" of philosophical summations. Klyuchevsky's amazing skill at painting on an immense national canvas was alien to the nature of Bestuzhev-Ryumin. Yet his cold-hearted factual objectivity occasionally gave way before sentimental loyalty to admired personalities, manifested in his *Biographical Essays*. His two-volume *History of Russia,* leading up to the death of Ivan IV, is an incomplete work which he planned to extend through the nineteenth century. He also translated Henry T. Buckle's master work, *The History of Civilization in England.*

## Platonov (1860-1933)

Among the "old guardsmen" and pupils of Bestuzhev-Ryumin, Sergey Feodorovich Platonov is pre-eminent.[29] He suc-

---

[29] S. F. Platonov, *Ocherki po istorii smuty v Moskovskom gosudarstve XVI-XVII v. v.* [A Study of the History of the Time of Trouble in the Muscovite State in the XVI-XVII centuries], St. Petersburg, 1899; *Lektsii po russkoy istorii* [Lectures on Russian History], St. Petersburg, 1915; *Boris Godunov,* Petrograd, 1921; *Ivan Grozniy* [Ivan the Terrible], Berlin, 1924; *Histoire de la Russie des origines à 1918,* Paris, 1929; *La Russie moscovite,* Paris, 1932.

ceeded his teacher to the chair of Russian history at the University of St. Petersburg. By his own admission two men primarily influenced his views, Bestuzhev-Ryumin and Klyuchevsky. Grandson of a serf and tutor of the royal heirs, a man of persistent energy and possessing a religious reverence for his country's past, Platonov eventually gained recognition as a man of high scholarship. His main work, *The History of the Time of Troubles,* is a study unique among its kind. Steering cautiously through the feculent pool of politics and masterfully handling all the sources to be found, the author deduced convincing conclusions. With genuine talent and Olympian patience, Platonov examined the amassed sources pertaining to this most complicated period in Russian history (1598-1613), brushing aside biased versions and basing his thesis on more acceptable chronicles and accounts of contemporary writers. Nothing escaped Platonov's vigilant eye, and the concatenated forces lying behind the whole social and political upheaval, with all their consequences, are masterfully elucidated. Particular attention has been given to the tense class struggle between the old boyar class and the rising nobility created by Ivan IV, on the one side, and the urban and rural classes with their interlocking interests now coinciding, now in sharp conflict, on the other.

Platonov's approach to the concurrence of causes that led to the fifteen-year strife preceding the ascendancy of the Romanov dynasty, or the "Time of Troubles," was somewhat new. Platonov kept the problem of foreign intervention and the wars with Sweden and Poland in the background; the main issue, as he saw it, was the internal condition, the conflict of class interests, which by the end of the period assumed proportions of a national social revolution. This enormous conflict was interpreted in terms of a class war, not in the Marxian sense of a mass uprising from below, but rather as a revolution steered from above, gradually forcing the masses from below into the whirpool of violence. Only in the last stages of these national developments did the masses rise, as if against their will, under the leadership of Bolotnikov to assert their rights or to vindicate some deep-seated social grievances. The entire struggle was regarded by Platonov as a predominantly political struggle, while social and economic aspects of the conflict he kept in the wings of the national stage. The theme thus centered around the struggle for political power, and for this reason the question of dynastic aspirations or the problem of restoration of the social order assumed prominence throughout the entire discussion. Yet Platonov could not avoid dwelling at considerable length upon such critical issues as the entrenchment of the institution of serfdom, with all the interests and opposition it implied at this turning point in history. Nor could the author fail to bring in the role of the boyar class, the collapse of parts of the system violently introduced by Ivan IV, such as the *oprichnina,* and the appearance of the new tenant nobility. The work received the highest praise of such eminent scholars as Ikonnikov, Sergeye-vich, and Klyuchevsky, and was recommended for the Uvarov prize.

Platonov lived long enough to get into serious trouble with the authorities after 1917. Conservative, reserved, and alien to materialistic interpretations of history, he could hardly escape a clash with Marxist historians. It was not surprising that his difficulties increased as years went by. Yet he refused to leave his native land and loyally performed his duties as director of the library at the Academy of Sciences until he was forced to resign, shortly before his death, on the charge of concealing some historical records. He was exiled to Samara (Kuybyshev), where he died in 1933 in loneliness and great want.

## Lappo-Danilevsky (1863-1919)

Another member of the "old guard" was Alexander Sergeye-vich Lappo-Danilevsky, who occupies a special place in Russian historiography because he was never an historian in the strict sense of the word.[30] He concentrated his ardent labor, not upon Russian history as such, but upon archeology, sphragistics, pale-ography, and methodology of history. His first work dealt with Scythian culture, and in 1887 he published *Scythian Antiquities,* followed by a study of seals of the later period of the Galich and Vladimir principalities. Subsequently his interest was di-verted to economic history, growth of towns in the seventeenth century, and the status of the serf peasantry. A work on the development of Russian society during the eighteenth century remains in manuscript form in the files of the Academy of Sciences to this day.

Whether Lappo-Danilevsky's project happened to be of the broadest dimensions or only of microscopic nature, it was in-variably subordinated to his main field of interest, the method-ology of history. Yet here is something to be noted: in his voluminous work (which lists 172 titles) the treatment of each

[30] For a complete list of Lappo-Danilevsky's works see *Russky istorichesky zhurnal,* VI, 1920, 29-41. His most important works are the following: *Organizatsiya pryamogo oblozheniya v Moskovskom gosudarstve so vremyen smuty do epokhi preobrazovany* [The Administration of Direct Taxation in the Muscovite State from the Time of Troubles to the Period of Reforms], St. Petersburg, 1890 (See a criticism of this work by P. N. Milyukov, *Sporniye voprosy finansovoy istorii Moskovskogo gosudarstva* [Debatable Questions Concerning the Financial History of the Muscovite State], St. Petersburg, 1892.); *Skifskiye drevnosti* [Scythian Antiquities], St. Petersburg, 1887; *Russkiye promyshlenniye i torgoviye kompanii v pervoy polovine XVIII stoletiya* [Russian Industrial and Trading Companies in the First Half of the 18th Century], St. Petersburg, 1899; *Ocherk istorii obrazovaniya glavneyshikh razryadov krestyan-skogo naseleniya v Rossii* [A Study of the Formation of the Main Categories Within the Peasant Population of Russia], St. Petersburg, 1905; *Metodologiya istorii* [The Methodology of History], St. Petersburg, 1913; *Ocherk russkoy diplomatiki chastnykh aktov* [A Study of Russian Paleography], Prague, 1920; "The Development of Science and Learning in Russia," *Russian Realities and Problems,* ed. by J. D. Duff, Cam-bridge, 1917.

individual topic, despite the fact that it is part of a larger scheme, constitutes a complete piece of work in itself, and each is, moreover, a masterpiece. Such, for instance, is his monograph on the *Russian Industrial and Trading Companies in the First Half of the 18th Century* or his thesis on *The Administration of Direct Taxation in the Muscovite State from the Time of Troubles to the Period of Reforms,* which P. N. Milyukov considered as "the most wonderful phenomenon in Russian historical literature." It is to be regretted that Lappo-Danilevsky's writings lack the stylistic grace of a Klyuchevsky and the daring historical synthesis of a Milyukov. This can be explained partly by the fact that the author was a solitary person and very little in touch with the younger generation. He remained, instead, under the influence of the "juridicial" school of Gradovsky and Chicherin long after it had been shelved by the advancing decades. Out of voluminous, hitherto unearthed sources he constructed a grandiose tower of antiquated architecture.

Lappo-Danilevsky focused his attention mainly upon the seventeenth and eighteenth centuries, to him an absorbing epoch during which the crystallization of social and political Russia might be seen vividly.[31] The emergence of a society with a new cultural physiognomy, new forms of economic life and judicial institutions, and a new sort of social consciousness, fascinated him. Distinguished contributions from his pen include monographs on the attachment of the peasants to the soil, the formation of peasant categories, and patrimonial estates (*votchiny*) of the sixteenth and seventeenth centuries, which constituted the basis of the later structure of Russian society. His course of lectures on the eighteenth century at the University of St. Petersburg is interesting particularly in its organization. He divided the century into four transitional periods: (1)

[31] *Russky istorichesky zhurnal,* VI, 1920, 97 ff.

consolidation of the state under Peter I; (2) consolidation of the nobility, with its asserted privileges, at the expense of the state; (3) the amalgamation of government and aristocratic interests, emancipation of the nobility, and early rise of public opinion; and (4) severance of the bonds between government and society and a period of reaction.

Coincident with his enthusiastic research in this period, Lappo-Danilevsky also engaged in a work that would seem drudgery to others—the systematization of historical materials and their publication, including all the sources concerning Russia to be found in foreign archives. He maintained that for an understanding of the relations between the Eastern Orthodox and Western Catholic churches, as well as of Moscow's role in the Near Eastern problem, the Italian archives were indispensable. It was through his influence that the Academy of Sciences later sent its special correspondents to Rome. Simultaneously, he conducted an extensive investigation of all foreign residents in Moscow during the first half of the seventeenth century: their activities, the purpose of their journey thither, any service they might have rendered the government, or cultural influence they might have exerted. He wrote a notable essay on Peter the Great as founder of the Academy of Sciences, another on I. I. Betskoy and his system of education during the reign of Catherine II, and a third essay on German-Russian relations in the eighteenth century. To Lappo-Danilevsky the final synthesis of history was to be the synthesis of world history. But this goal was not to be attained merely by coining *a priori* formulae similar to those of Spencer, Comte, Hegel, or Marx, nor by intuitive, spontaneous thinking; it was to be gained by an orderly, methodic understanding based on an intimate knowledge of the various stages through which humanity has passed during its long course of history.

## Lyubavsky (1860-1937)

The heavy lot of Platonov during his later years fell also to his contemporary, the historian Matvey Kuzmich Lyubavsky.[32] Lyubavsky belonged to the senior group of Klyuchevsky's pupils, though for his studies he chose a field somewhat remote from that of his colleagues; his interest was concentrated chiefly upon the past of Lithuania, a subject he selected for both his master's and doctoral dissertations. These two bulky works immediately assured the writer an eminent place in his field. Written in a somewhat pedantic style and lavishly supported by references from firsthand sources, they represent a laborious task of investigation in the archives of western Russia. The caution with which the author elaborated his thesis and the frequent citation of references rob it, however, of any literary charm. Like Bestuzhev-Ryumin, Lyubavsky left no school, but only a few individual students.

The central theme of Lyubavsky is the geographic factor in the formation of the Russian state. This in turn led the author to a special study of peripheral Western history. The field was an original one, and Lyubavsky was the only historian to explore the subject with painstaking care. His research led him to the theory that Lithuanian Russia, like Moscow, arose as a direct offspring of Kievan Russia. He elaborated this thesis in his lectures on early Russian history to the end of the sixteenth century, which he delivered at the University of Moscow. These lectures served as a sort of supplement to Klyuchevsky's

[32] M. K. Lyubavsky, *Oblastnoye deleniye i mestnoye upravleniye litovsko-russkogo gosudarstva* [Provincial Division and Local Administration of the Lithuanian-Russian State], Moscow, 1892; *Litovsko-russky seym* [The Lithuanian-Russian Diet], Moscow, 1901; *Ocherk istorii Litovsko-russkogo gosudarstva do Lyublinskoy unii vklyuchitelno* [A Study of the Lithuanian-Russian State Down to the Union of Lublin], Moscow, 1910; *Obrazovaniye osnovnoy gosudarstvennoy territorii velikorusskoy narodnosti* [The Territorial Basis of the Great Russian State], Leningrad, 1929.

general course. If Presnyakov in his work, *The Foundation of the Great Russian State,* felt that Lithuania had arisen as a consequence of political concentration, Lyubavsky, on the other hand, approached the same subject from its ethnographic and geographic aspects, which led him to emphasize territorial concentration. While Lyubavsky saw in the union between the two principalities, Vladimir and Moscow, underlying military and financial causes, Presnyakov interpreted the same phenomena as the outcome of a political tradition.

In his writings as in person, Lyubavsky was detached from surrounding realities. He was, in the full sense of the word, an academician, to whom politics and social activity were alien, his whole life being absorbed in his studies of the past, and his careful weaving of bygone events into a factual narrative. The Revolution was to him, therefore, a fatal blow; for a violent period demanded partisanship and a colorful presentation of current history, not a detached, objective narration of seemingly nullified events. His opponents sought Lyubavsky's removal from his post (he had been Rector of the University of Moscow since 1911), and it was not long before they succeeded. Eventually he was banished to Ufa, where he died a heartbroken man, witnessing the familiar old order around him give way to a new one he was never able to comprehend.

## *Presnyakov* (1870-1929)

Along with Lyubavsky, of the University of Moscow, stood the figure of Alexander Evgenyevich Presnyakov, of the University of St. Petersburg. Though a pupil of S. F. Platonov, Presnyakov in his writings shows himself to have been strongly influenced by the "juridical school," particularly V. I. Sergeyevich, whose ideas underlie his master's dissertation on the authority of the Prince in early Russian history. This Presnyakov expanded into a study on a much broader scale than the topic might suggest. An analysis of the princely authority soon developed into an elaborate investigation of the social order of the period. The result was a pioneering work on a subject that much later became a popular theme—feudalism in Russia. It was Pavlov-Silvansky who subsequently carried the subject to its logical conclusion; Presnyakov plodded in that direction and induced others to accept the idea that western European and Russian feudalism had originated under similar social and political conditions. This assertion seriously challenged the former theory cherished by the Slavophiles that Russian serfdom developed in a peculiarly national environment, totally different from that of the West.

Presnyakov's doctoral dissertation, *The Formation of the Great Russian State,* displays an amazing knowledge of all the Russian chronicles and charters of the fifteenth and sixteenth centuries. The whole topic acquired a new significance and was presented in an entirely different light from that shed by all previous writers.[33] Formerly, the rise of Moscow had mainly been interpreted, not as a result of national and state aspirations, but as either the outcome of the greed of the landowning nobility (Chicherin) or—virtually the same idea (Solovyev, Klyuchevsky)—the logical consequence of economic development leading to expansion. Thus the Muscovite prince was a mere tool of either individual landlords or economic circumstances, or both, and the state as such played only a subordinate part in national expansion.

---

[33] A. E. Presnyakov, *Obrazovaniye velikorusskogo gosudarstva. Ocherki po istorii XIII-XV stoletii* [The Formation of the Great Russian State. Studies in the History of the 13th-15th Centuries], Petrograd, 1918; *Knyazhoye pravo v drevney Rusi* [Prince Law in Early Russia], St. Petersburg, 1909; *Aleksandr I,* Petrograd, 1924; *Apogey samoderzhaviya: Nikolay I* [The Apogee of Autocracy: Nicholas I], Leningrad, 1925; *14 Dekabrya 1825 goda* [December 14, 1825], Leningrad, 1926.

Presnyakov, throwing all these theories overboard, presented his own view, namely, that beneath all the strivings for territorial expansion was not mere individual greed, but a conscientious national aspiration and a political realization of the necessity to form a consolidated state. The internal conflicts between Moscow and the other principalities—Tver, Suzdal, Ryazan, and others—were not simply expressions of the inherent belligerent instincts of their respective princes, but rather expressions of conflicting ideas concerning the policy to be followed in the formation of a centralized national state. In other words, the whole internal conflict represented not the rivalry of acquisitive instincts, but a national centripetal force seeking the best methods for its materialization. The soundness of the theory has been questioned by some scholars, but the originality of the thesis has not been denied; in fact it stimulated the revision of many theories formerly held unchallenged.

Presnyakov's other works deal chiefly with recent Russian history. Among them must be mentioned his two short monographs on Alexander I and his admirable study of the Decembrist uprising. Under the influence of the Revolution he inclined more to the writing of recent Russian history, though even here he was careful to maintain the old standard and avoid flagwaving. He died on September 30, 1929. The Society of Marxist Historians, of which he was a member, casually mentioned his death in the official publication, *Istorik-Marksist* (of which, incidentally, he was one of the editors), promising to publish in the following issue a detailed appraisal of his works; there has been no further reference to Presnyakov in subsequent issues.[34] One reason that might explain this neglect may be found in the *Great Soviet Encyclopedia,* which states:[35] "After

---

[34] *Istorik-Marksist,* XIII, 269.
[35] *Bolshaya sovetskaya entsiklopediya,* Vol. XXXIV, 440.

the Great October Socialist Revolution, Presnyakov tried to revise his theoretical position and actively participated in the work of soviet scientific institutions and institutions of higher learning. However, he was unable to emancipate himself from bourgeois-idealistic methodology in his search for historical processes." Obviously the verdict must have had some relation to the absence of further tribute to the departed scholar, since such heresy as "bourgeois-idealistic methodology" could not be tolerated.

## *Milyukov* (1859-1943)

Another "old guardsman," and student of Solovyev and Klyuchevsky, was Pavel Nikolayevich Milyukov, ardent Westerner in the more modern sense, editor, lecturer, statesman, and author of a number of notable studies in the field of Russian history.[36] His first works, which secured him a wide reputation as an historian, were his master's thesis, *State Economy in Russia During the First Quarter of the Eighteenth Century and the Reforms of Peter the Great,* followed later by an equally penetrating essay on the *Debatable Questions Concerning the Financial History of the Muscovite State.* Both studies embraced such a mass of new material extracted from the files of archives

---

[36] P. N. Milyukov, *Gosudarstvennoye khozyaystvo v Rossii v pervoy chetverti XVIII stoletiya i reforma Petra Velikogo* [State Economy in Russia During the First Quarter of the XVIII Century and the Reforms of Peter the Great], St. Petersburg, 1892; 2nd ed., 1905; *Sporniye voprosy finansovoy istorii Moskovskogo gosudarstva* [Debatable Questions Concerning the Financial History of the Muscovite State], St. Petersburg, 1892; *Glavniye techeniya russkoy istoricheskoy mysli* [Main Currents in Russian Historical Thought], Moscow, 1898; *Ocherki po istorii russkoy kultury* [Studies in the History of Russian Culture], 3 vols., St. Petersburg, 1896-1903; revised edition, 3 vols. in 4, Paris, 1930-37; *Russia and Its Crisis,* Chicago, 1905; *Iz istorii russkoy intelligentsii* [Essays on the Russian Intelligentsia], St. Petersburg, 1902; *Le mouvement intellectuel russe,* tr. by J. W. Bienstock, Paris, 1918; *Histoire de Russie* (in collaboration with Ch. Seignobos and L. Eisenmann), 3 vols., Paris, 1932-33; *Zhivoy Pushkin* [The Living Pushkin], Paris, 1937.

that they flooded with light many questions other than the economic measures of Peter I. They opened the way to other scholars, notably M. M. Bogoslovsky, whose dissertation entitled *Local Reforms of Peter the Great* may be considered an outgrowth of Milyukov's pioneering work. His stimulating essays on the history of the Russian intelligentsia, including one on the "Decay of Slavophilism," showed Milyukov's wide range of interest, while his later book on Pushkin demonstrated his impressive knowledge of Russian letters. Another work, *Main Currents in Russian Historical Thought,* is considered one of the most distinguished studies in Russian historiography. It is regrettable that the work was never completed; the first and only volume ends with Chaadayev and the influence of Schelling on Russian historical writing.

Milyukov's greatest work is his *Outlines of Russian Culture.* This is neither a chronological nor a "scientific" work in the orthodox sense; yet it is valuable and refreshing because of its scope, its critical, realistic vision, and its uniqueness. It is an excellent supplement to Klyuchevsky's *Course in Russian History;* the two should be read together, since Milyukov filled in many of the gaps that Klyuchevsky left. First the author deals with the rise of the state, population, economics, and social developments. The state in Russia, according to Milyukov, passed through three stages of development: tribal, feudal, and national; the last was strongly military in character. Feudalism affected only the southwestern part of the country, adjacent to Poland and Lithuania, with which Russia had close contacts. Because of local peculiarities, the Muscovite state hardly knew feudalism; environmental conditions were instrumental in accentuating the military character of the state. Threats from the East and lack of natural lines of defense forced the government to resort to military policies which in the end gave rise to political institutions, financial needs and taxing methods, and the formation of social groupings.

The geographic factors were largely responsible for mobility of population or a "wandering peasantry," while national interests called for a stable society upon which authorities could rely for manpower and revenue. This state of affairs caused the government to "attach" the peasants to the soil and the gentry to the state. The latter managed eventually to free themselves from their obligations, while the status of the peasantry remained unaltered; serfdom, formerly a public institution, then became a legalized private privilege. The entire development, Milyukov stresses, emanated from state authority; whatever institution, class, or community entered national life was dictated or initiated mainly by the needs of the government. By the second half of the last century, however, conditions had so altered that the government was forced to cast off the social and economic legacy and reorganize national life entirely. Serfdom had to be cast overboard, and the former serf owners who depended upon compulsory labor had to learn quickly to manage their estates within the frame of a free economy. According to Milyukov, they failed dismally at this task, and the gentry soon found themselves in a serious economic plight, largely due to their inability to cope with problems derived from a free economy and the rising capitalistic form of production.[37] By the end of the century the state on several occasions had had to rescue them from total bankruptcy. The solution, as the author envisioned it, lay, not in cherishing these "social relics," which Milyukov considered terribly overestimated by false national pride, but in a nationally concentrated effort to build a freer community in harmony with more recent political and social ideals.

[37] *Ocherki po istorii russkoy kultury*, I, 235-38.

After Milyukov expounded the role of the state, he turned to the church, sectarianism, and education, or, as he states, to the "spiritual" rather than the "material" aspects of culture. Once again Milyukov reached firm conclusions. As in the case of the state, here too the course of events developed differently from that in western Europe. Russian culture found its beginnings not "below" in the masses, but imposed from above. Cultural life descended from the church, supported by the state from the very start. Since the people were neither organized nor in any way able to stand behind the ecclesiastical leaders, the church was soon subordinated to the will of the state. This caused immeasurable damage, forming a wide abyss between the people and the church, which resulted in sterility of the faith, emphasis upon ritualism, and desperate efforts such as those of Nikon to correct the situation, which in turn led to the sorrowful schism within the church. Education shared the same fate: it became a function of and for the government.

Even more important to Milyukov was the fact that Russian nationalism became a state-sponsored ideology, initiated and promoted by the government and subservient to it. The general consequence of this development was a division between government and a minority of intellectuals on one hand and the vast majority of the people on the other. Nationalism thus did not depend upon the people; it did not draw its vitality from the masses, but from the superstructure of society which represented a small minority. Face to face, then, were two groups: the alienated minority and the sullen, passive, and inarticulate masses. A precarious situation thus developed whereby a native population was governed by a culturally alien administration. This isolation of national authority was climaxed by Peter I, whose westernization of the state, now accelerated to a dizzy speed, was truly the task of a single man. Milyukov was at heart a strong Westerner and was the last to oppose on general principles the reforms of Peter I. What disturbed him was the manner in which these were carried out and the sorrowful consequences that were bound to ensue. The reforms of Peter came, as Milyukov saw them, like a storm; the nation was caught unaware, totally unprepared for such changes; they were carried out by men who at best hardly comprehended what they were doing, and at worst were often hostile to the orders of their sovereign. For this reason it could be said that the reforms were the work of a single man; in the words of Pososhkov, "Peter alone pulled uphill, while millions were pulling downhill."

Milyukov stressed particularly the fact that, as in the past, so again during the Petrine period the reforms were a by-product of military necessity rather than a result of keen cultural perception. What was needed first and foremost was an up-to-date military force backed by economic resources, with all the other things implied by these two closely linked objectives. The sum total was the continuation of a tradition that began far back in history—a determined sovereign furiously trying to dislodge an obsolete order while the masses, for whose benefit the sovereign toils, resentfully moan over their fate. With extraordinary lucidity and persistency Milyukov traced the formation of the breach between the masses and the handful of intelligentsia, first on religious grounds, later in other spheres. The ever-present necessity of "overtaking" the West only widened the gulf, since the vanguard of this drive left the rear guard of the nation far behind.

A good portion of the blame for this lamentable state of affairs Milyukov seems to ascribe to Orthodoxy, which had failed to become a powerful lever like the Protestant churches in western Europe and, particularly, in England. He neatly summarized the situation by stating that in England religion nourished the citizen and that culture developed there along with religious thought; hence the Englishman was still religious. In France the situation was different: religion took a definitely hostile attitude toward the development of modern scientific and philosophical thinking, and the national mind, advancing in spite of clerical opposition, left religion behind; consequently, the Frenchman turned against religion. In Russia, Orthodoxy did neither one nor the other; it failed to keep pace with cultural development, and it did not establish an inquisition; therefore the Russian intelligentsia became traditionally indifferent toward any religion.[38]

Though a Westerner to the core, Milyukov by his bold interpretation of history unwittingly delivered much ammunition to his opponents. However, a conscientious perusal of his writings leads to one conclusion: the future of Russia depends on the success of her adaptability to the course of Western civilization. The process, begun in the seventeenth century, will proceed in spite of the frequent opposition it is bound to meet, since it will be aided by economic and military aggression from outside and by the growing needs from within. As an émigré, Milyukov later undertook a revision of his Studies in the History of Russian Culture, but he never completed the laborious task: the political activities into which he plunged headlong at the beginning of the present century seriously handicapped his scholarly pursuits. It is a pity that his energy was so much diverted to other channels; scholars of Milyukov's caliber are rare, and his frequent absence from their ranks has been felt on many occasions.

[38] P. N. Milyukov, Ocherki po istorii russkoy kultury, II, 394-96.

## *Semevsky* (1848-1916)

The peasant question in Russian history has always been a vital problem around which have revolved many national issues. A good many Russian scholars have extended their studies of various phases of the peasant class beyond the confines of their own country: M. I. Rostovtsev has enriched historical knowledge with his investigations concerning the Roman Empire; V. G. Vasilevsky and F. I. Uspensky followed by A. A. Vasiliev have done the same for Byzantine history; N. I. Kareyev and I. V. Luchitsky have made sizable contributions to the study of the French peasantry. The history of the Russian peasant was a subject popularly explored by a legion of scholars, among them B. N. Chicherin, I. D. Belyayev, M. A. Dyakonov, I. I. Ignatovich, V. A. Myakotin, A. S. Lappo-Danilevsky, M. M. Bogoslovsky, B. D. Grekov, A. A. Kornilov, A. Ya. Efimenko, P. B. Struve, and a host of others who contributed to the field of Russian agrarian history.

However, almost all these studies have dealt with the earlier period of Russian history; few of the writers have gone beyond the eighteenth century, nor have they made any effort to embrace the vast field in its entirety. A task of this magnitude was undertaken and successfully carried out by Vasily Ivanovich Semevsky. This profound student and eminent authority on the history of the peasant was branded by his faculty colleagues as a "radical" and partisan unworthy to enter a teaching career; after his death his memory was bespattered by epigonous Marxian writers who labeled him as a "petty bourgeois lacking a knowledge of Marxian dialectic," and a "populist-historian" who could possibly write on labor but was incapable of comprehending the principle of class struggle in history.[39]

[39] See, e.g., P. Paradizov, *Ocherki po istoriografii dekabristov* [A Study of the Historiography of the Decembrists], Moscow, 1929, 161 ff.

Whatever partisan opinion concerning Semevsky may be, calmer judgment will consider his work among the most distinguished contributions to the agrarian history of Russia, from which both friends and foes will draw material for years to come. It is unfortunate indeed that his works are not available in other languages: historical literature might have been spared many mediocre and repetitious accounts of a subject that he so thoroughly explored long ago. His life illustrates the bitter cup that is put to the lips of man who dares to defy the conventional or dogmatic concepts of his compatriots.

Semevsky was born in the Province of Pskov, into the family of a poor squire; he was one of fourteen children and from an early age experienced want and struggle.[40] In 1866 Semevsky entered the St. Petersburg Medical Academy, where he spent two years and had the opportunity to study with the distinguished physiologist, I. M. Syechenov, and the world-famed I. I. Mechnikov. The two years contributed much to his character and immunized his mind against the various forms of intellectual sluggishness which years later afflicted the Russian intelligentsia. In 1868 Semevsky entered the University of St. Petersburg and devoted himself to studying peasant history as well as doing social work among the peasants, whose economic problems became of absorbing interest to him for the rest of his life.[41] "It is high time," he wrote some years later, "for our agrarian country, which has been maintained for a thousand years almost exclusively at the expense of the peasant, to pay due tribute to the class to which we owe everything." [42]

Semevsky spent ten years on his master's thesis, which he

[40] Autobiographical sketches of V. I. Semevsky may be found in *Golos minuvshego* [Voice of the Past], IX-X, 1917.

[41] E. N. Vodovozova, *Na zare zhizni* [At the Dawn of Life], Moscow, 1934, Vol. II, 339 ff.

[42] See Semevsky's "Address" delivered before the examination board, defending his master's thesis, in *Russkaya starina, XXXIV,* 1882, 577-78.

presented in 1881. Later he enlarged this work into two volumes, which were published in 1903 under the title *Peasants in the Reign of Catherine II*.[43] For the first time there was revealed to the public a subject which until 1861 had been completely banned, and which after the lifting of the ban was reluctantly handled because of its extraordinarily complex nature. The warmest sympathy with the peasant did not hinder Semevsky from producing a work of singular merit, in which he demonstrated not only a phenomenal knowledge of archival material but also his special talent for absorbing and properly synthesizing the amassed resources.

After that Semevsky began his thorny career as an historian. When the thesis was presented to the faculty, the candidate was immediately given to taste the bitter fruit of reactionary criticism from the university authorities. Bestuzhev-Ryumin, to whom previous reference has been made, led the opposition against acceptance of the thesis on the ground that the author besmirched Russian history. He considered the conclusions tendentious and alleged that the thesis presented unfair criticism of official policy and generally discriminated in favor of the peasantry. By an unfortunate coincidence it so happened that Semevsky opened his battle for the acceptance of his dissertation during the year of the assassination of Alexander II, which was followed by a strong reaction throughout the country and caused a tremor among the panic-stricken intellectuals.

---

[43] V. I. Semevsky, *Krestyane v tsarstvovaniye Imperatritsy Ekateriny II* [Peasants in the Reign of Catherine II], 2 vols., St. Petersburg, 1903; *Krestyansky vopros v Rossii v XVIII i pervoy polovine XIX vyeka* [The Peasant Question in Russia in the 18th and the First Half of the 19th Century], 2 vols., St. Petersburg, 1888; *Rabochiye na sibirskikh zolotykh promyslakh* [Laborers in the Siberian Goldmining Industry], 2 vols., St. Petersburg, 1898; *Politicheskiye i obshchestvenniye idei dekabristov* [Political and Social Ideas of the Decembrists], St. Petersburg, 1909; *M. Butashevich-Petrashevsky i Petrashevtsy* [M. V. Butashevich-Petrashevsky and his Circle], Moscow, 1922.

All the arguments against the guardians of "pure history" to the effect that the work presented a scholarly achievement based on primary and previously unexplored sources proved futile: the thesis was rejected and Bestuzhev-Ryumin scored his triumph.

Semevsky thereupon shifted the battlefield to Moscow, where, to his surprise, his thesis was finally accepted. Among those who approved it was V. O. Klyuchevsky.[44] With his degree now in hand, Semevsky returned to St. Petersburg to apply for a chair in Russian history, evidently with the intention of facing his opponents on an equal footing. Strangely enough, the chair he sought was granted, but his victory proved of short duration. Three years later, through the pressure of the same Bestuzhev-Ryumin,[45] Semevsky was forced out, despite the fact that he had become the most popular lecturer among the liberal students—and who was not a liberal student in those days? One of the main accusations leveled against Semevsky was that he presented Russian history in colors too black and dared to refer, though subtly, to such a delicate subject as the assassination of Paul.[46] Expulsion from the university was a hard blow to him, and Semevsky, having always dreamed of teaching, was unable for a long time to reconcile himself to abandoning his chosen academic career. "Yes," he wrote in a private letter, "difficult and ungrateful is the work of the economist-historian."

It would seem that there is no evil without compensating good. Deprived of his privilege of teaching, Semevsky was forced to concentrate his attention upon research into fields of special interest. His acquaintance with the work of Georg

[44] *Russkaya starina*, XXXIV, 1882, 578-84.
[45] *Golos minuvshego*, IX-X, 1917, 38.
[46] S. Svatikov, "Opalnaya professura 80-kh godov [Dishonored Professors of the Eighties]," *Golos minuvshego*, II, 1917.

Ludwig von Maurer and his "Mark theory" was an incentive
to Semevsky to make a similar study for his own country.[47] In
1888 his second work appeared, *The Peasant Question in Russia
in the Eighteenth and First Half of the Nineteenth Century,*
a continuation of his previous study. The author was highly
praised, voted the Uvarov prize, and was granted a gold medal
by the Free Economic Society. In a short review an appraisal
of this extensive work is impossible: it is a classic study, not
likely to be enlarged upon by future investigations. Every aspect of the problem—legal, political, social, and economic—is
minutely analyzed. The author's conclusion is that emancipation of the peasants was made inevitable not by the decision of
the upper hierarchy in the capital, but by pressure of the masses
in co-operation with the liberal intelligentsia; if in 1861 the
reforms proved inadequate, as he later tried to show they did,
it was because of unwillingness on the part of the government
to carry the program to its logical end. It may be of interest
to note that in this as well as in all his later works Semevsky
adhered to the belief that communal land ownership must be
preserved, that its abolition would spell nothing less than economic disaster for the peasants.

For a long time Semevsky's attention was focused on Siberia,
where he went in 1891 at the invitation of an eminent industri-
alist, A. I. Sibiryakov.[48] His wide travels and personal acquaintance with peasant conditions, reinforced by use of local archives,
enabled him to publish in 1898 a two-volume work entitled
*Laborers in the Siberian Goldmining Industry,* a study equaling
in thoroughness his previous works. During the following years
he turned his attention to another subject, the liberal movement

---

[47] See G. L. von Maurer, *Einleitung zur Geschichte der Mark-, Hof-, Dorf-, und
Stadverfassung,* 1854. Also his *Geschichte der Fronhöfe, der Banernhöfe under der
Hofverfassung in Deutschland,* 4 vols., N.p., 1863.
[48] Semevsky, *Rabochiye na sibirskikh zolotykh promyslakh,* I, iii-iv ff.

in Russia. As a result the last book published in his lifetime appeared in 1909: *The Political and Social Ideas of the Decembrists*. For the first time the Decembrist movement was subjected to detailed scholarly investigation. The casual treatment of the subject by court historians like N. K. Schilder and M. I. Bogdanovich, by the Westerner A. N. Pypin, and even by the more conscientious writer M. V. Dovnar-Zapolsky, came to be overshadowed by this latest contribution in the field. Semevsky traced the rise of Decembrist ideas from their earliest possible sources, in the eighteenth century, to the increasing demand for liberal reforms which culminated, in the first quarter of the nineteenth century, in the Decembrist movement. He did not, however, deal with the organization of secret societies nor with the uprising itself, but restricted his subject to the social and political origins of the movement. The study of the Decembrist movement led his interest further toward the liberal ideas of the 'thirties and 'forties, resulting in two essays, one on the Petrashevsky circle, the other on the Cyril-Methodius society. Both occupy a recognized place in the historical literature on nineteenth-century Russian liberalism.

Aside from these works, Semevsky contributed numerous articles to various magazines, most of which deserve wider publicity and point to the urgent advisability of collecting his entire works for publication at the earliest possible time. In 1913 he became editor of a well-know magazine, *Golos minuvshego* (Voice of the Past), an ambition he had dreamed of for many years; death prevented his plans to develop his editorial capacities as he had hoped. In an obituary notice one writer summarized Semevsky's accomplishment thus: barred from university lecture halls, this scholar could do nothing but transform his learning into ponderous volumes. These writings have proven a far more enduring monument to Semevsky than the lectures which he hoped to deliver. His voluminous works will be read and consulted for many years to come and by many more students than any university auditorium could have ever accommodated.

# The Federal Idea in Russian Historiography

## Shchapov (1830-1876)

*RUSSIAN* historical writing was predominantly Great Russian and therefore bore a distinct "Moscow mark." Only a few men, very few indeed, endeavored to show that not all roads lead to Moscow. Those who rebelled against Great Russian particularism might be called the "federal school." One of the earliest students to stress the federal principle in Russian historical writing was undoubtedly Afanasy Prokofyevich Shchapov, and if he failed to develop this thesis in his short lifetime, it was largely because he was gagged by the authorities.[1]

Shchapov was born in a Siberian village, Anga, about a hundred and fifty miles from Irkutsk. His father was a Russian parish priest, his mother of Buryat origin. His parental background and place of birth make Shchapov a true product of the national and local milieu of his time. While attending the Divinity School of Irkutsk, he distinguished himself as a student and was sent to complete his higher education at the

---

[1] A. P. Shchapov, *Sochineniya* [Works], 3 vols., St. Petersburg, 1906-08; *Zemstvo i raskol* [Zemstvo and the Schism], St. Peterburg, 1862; *Neizdanniye sochineniya* [Unpublished Works], Kazan, 1926; *Sobraniye sochineny. Dopolnitelniy tom k izdaniyu 1906-08 g.g.* [Collected Works. Supplementary Volume to the Edition of 1906-08], prepared by A. N. Turunov, Irkutsk, 1937.

Kazan Divinity Academy. Upon graduation he was retained as lecturer in Russian history. Taking advantage of the archives recently transferred from the Solovetsky monastery to Kazan, Shchapov began to examine these sources and became interested in church history and the schism.

Subsequently Shchapov was invited to the University of Kazan, where his real academic career began. Russian history was his chosen field, yet it was Henry T. Buckle whom he esteemed highly and read avidly; Russian historians disappointed him. The reason for this he explained in one of his addresses:[2]

When I studied Ustryalov and Karamzin, it always seemed strange to me why in their histories one does not see rural Russia, a history of the masses, the so-called simple, dark people. Must the majority remain inaudible, passive, and outside of history? Has not this overwhelming majority the right to enlightenment, to historical development, to life and importance, as have the nobility and clergy? . . . Yet read the chronicles or the historical records up to the eighteenth century: who built, founded, and populated the land, cleared the Russian soil of forests, and drained it of marshes? Who if not the peasants?

In Shchapov's appeal can be discerned the earliest and the genuine *vox populi* in Russian historiography, an historical materialism, or, better still, a peasant materialism. With his characteristic wit, G. V. Plekhanov, in describing a debate between Shchapov and Chernyshevsky, referred to it as a verbal duel between a democrat and a social-democrat.[3] Like his much earlier predecessor, Ivan Pososhkov,[4] Shchapov was of the flesh and blood of the peasant and was the ideologist of his class.

[2] *Istorik-Marksist,* III, 1927, 9-10.
[3] G. V. Plekhanov, *Sochineniya* [Works], Moscow, 1923, Vol. III, 19.
[4] *Zhurnal ministerstva narodnogo prosveshcheniya,* IX-X, 1875, 72.

He approached the study of the past with the peasant's purely democratic interest, and history was to him a weapon for the defense of the people, as well as a science.

For his master's dissertation, presented in 1858, Shchapov selected a subject which for political reasons students had previously preferred to leave alone—the schism within the Russian church. The new view taken in his thesis was contrary to all former interpretations; the author concluded that the whole matter of the schism was a phenomenon not merely religious in nature, but political and social as well. The essence of the schism was not a mere question of ritualism, as is still commonly thought; in the schism Shchapov saw a much deeper meaning—a conflict between the people and ecclesiastic authorities. It implied popular protest against the church as an agency which collaborated with the state in the enforcement of serfdom and a crushing tax system; it condoned administrative abuses and army recruiting. Subtly Shchapov hinted at the close tie between the schism and the subsequent peasant uprising led by Stenka Razin in 1670-1671. The thesis cast a totally new light upon the origins of the schism. To quote the author himself: "[The schism] proved to be a revolt not only against the church, but against the state, and not only against the reforms of Nikon, but against civic changes and reforms." The schismatics were more than religious rebels; they represented the general rebellious spirit of the masses against the entire state of affairs in the nation. The merits of his study were acknowledged even by such conservative historians as Bestuzhev-Ryumin, who was usually very reserved about committing himself.

Shchapov's concept of the Russian state was equally original and was noted for its interpretative originality. The leitmotiv in Russian history, Shchapov maintained in his lectures at the

University of Kazan, was regionalism, local self-government, and not centralization. He continued to stress this theme in his later writing and throughout his life. In a series of essays on regionalism during the Time of Troubles, on the village community and the village meeting, and on the town meeting in Russia he recurrently referred to the same subject: that democratic rule in Russia must rest on one principle only—regional autonomy within the sprawling Empire of Russia. Shchapov differentiated western European federalism from Russian regionalism: whereas the former was based on ethnographic peculiarities, the latter must be based on historic, economic, and peculiarly local forms of life. Only such a policy can assure successful completion of the continued process of colonization in the nation. Public initiative, and its instinctive reflexes toward national unity without compulsion from above, was an article of faith with Shchapov. This he saw in the village commune, in the locally preserved institution of the town meetings, and in the vanished General Assembly (*Zemsky Sobor*), in which, contrary to Klyuchevsky's view, Shchapov saw true native democracy. Because of his unswerving faith in the people rather than in a centralized state, Shchapov attacked the "juridical school" with particular vehemence, referring to it as "superstate fanaticism," while the Slavophile interpretation of the past he called the "cobweb weaving of history."

In another series of essays on geography and history, on the causes of cultural backwardness, and on the role of the state and the people, Shchapov concluded that the state represents a progressive force only as long as it is an instrument of enlightenment and thereby assists the people to participate actively in its life. Shchapov said the theory, as presented by the "juridical school," of the state as an absolute factor in history was not only false but dangerous, for it would force the masses into a submissive and passive position; such a state invariably would deprive itself of the true forces of national strength and progress. The author logically deduced the necessity for a program of universal education which would enable the people to assume responsibility in the affairs of the state. Only in that case could Russia advance with other nations toward a brighter future. It is not difficult to detect in Shchapov's deduction the current populist philosophy of the 'seventies. Shchapov considered the peasantry as the backbone of national life and the intelligentsia as destined to lead the peasantry toward a free social order and economic progress. For this reason he is considered the pioneer populist-historian of nineteenth-century Russia.

While at the University of Kazan Shchapov became involved in a political affair which ended his academic career. Participating in a session organized by the University students to commemorate the victims of the peasant uprising at Bezdna in 1861, he delivered an address that ended with the cry, "Long live a democratic constitution!" [5] Shortly afterwards he was ordered to appear in St. Petersburg for an investigation, and although the case was hushed up, his relations with the University were severed. While in the capital, Shchapov met some of the leading intellectuals of his generation: Pisarev, Chernyshevsky, Dobrolyubov, and others. They left an indelible impression upon him.

Three years later the authorities ordered him to leave the capital and depart for his native city of Irkutsk, where he devoted himself to the study of Siberia. Removed from political events, friends, and libraries, his scholarly pursuits were gravely handicapped; the indigenous intellectual began to wither away. The untimely death of his wife, along with distressing financial

[5] *Krasniy Arkhiv*, IV, 407-10; *Russky biografichesky slovar*, XXIV, 5.

difficulties and cultural isolation, thwarted Shchapov's talent and undermined his physical health: he died during the most fruitful period of his life, at the age of forty-six. Despite all that, he managed to leave behind him numerous essays, some constituting valuable contributions to the study of Russian religious sects, others giving a refreshing view of the theory of regionalism in Russian history, particularly as demonstrated in the administration of Siberia.

While Shchapov, studying Siberia, came to be a firm believer in the principle of regionalism as an answer to local discontent with centralized authority, a number of writers in other parts of the Empire, notably in the Ukraine, drew identical conclusions. The renaissance among the national minorities within Russia aroused a keen popular interest in the past. Among the intellectual groups arose a considerable contingent of "federalists," or "autonomists," who sought political and cultural autonomy as well as opportunities for national development within corresponding regional delimitations. Of these stand out men like M. P. Dragomanov (1841-1895), V. B. Antonovich (1834-1908), M. A. Maksimovich (1804-1873), N. I. Kostomarov, and a score of others, most of whom were connected with the University of Kiev. Their extensive writings, editing of documents, and research in folklore, ethnography, archeology, and history served to agitate regional sentiments and awaken national consciousness among a people traditionally referred to as "Little Russians."

Dragomanov, who combined historical research with Ukrainian national activities, soon disagreed sharply with both university and official authorities. In 1875 he was dismissed from the faculty of the University of Kiev; a year later he emigrated to Geneva, the haven of many political *émigrés,* where he became editor of a Ukrainian publication, *Hromada.* Between

1878 and 1883 he edited five volumes of essays on Ukrainian folklore, history, and ethnography. Dragomanov was a Pan-Slavist who envisioned a great Slav federation, and a confirmed agrarian socialist as well, so that the publication reflected his strong anti-Marxian and nationalistic ideas and championed the cause of Ukrainian autonomy. Together with Antonovich, Dragomanov also published a two-volume annotated collection of Ukrainian folksongs. Dragomanov's collaborator, V. B. Antonovich, remained in Kiev. Here he became editor-in-chief of the Kievan Archeographic Commission, and under his direction were published nine volumes of collected documents on Ukrainian history, covering the XV-XVIII centuries (*Arkhiv yugozapadnoy Rossii*). Antonovich was also the author of a number of works, notably a study of the last period of the Dnieper Cossack communities and a monograph on Lithuania prior to the middle of the fifteenth century. He conducted several archeological expeditions in southern Russia and was the author of several archeological maps of the Kiev and Volyn' regions. M. A. Maksimovich, though originally a botanist, later shifted his interest to history. His collection of annotated songs of the south won high praise among men like A. S. Pushkin, P. A. Vyazemsky, and other famed national poets.

## Kostomarov (1817-1885)

A more colorful and productive member of the Ukrainian "federal school" was Kostomarov.[6] Nikolay Ivanovich Kos-

[6] N. I. Kostomarov, *Istoricheskiye monografii i issledovaniya* [Historical Monographs and Studies] 21 vols., St. Petersburg, 1903-06; *Russkaya istoriya v zhizneopisaniyakh eya glavneyshikh deyateley* [A History of Russia in Biographies of her Leading Statesmen], 2 vols., St. Petersburg, 1903-07; *Posledniye gody Rechi-Pospolitoy* [The Closing Years of the Polish Commonwealth], St. Petersburg, 1870; *Bunt Stenki Razina* [The Stenka Razin Rebellion], St. Petersburg, 1859.

On Kostomarov: Rubinstein, *op. cit.*, 421-40. G. Karpov, *Kostomarov, kak istorik Malorossii* [Kostomarov as an Historian of the Ukraine], Moscow, 1871. A. N. Pypin, *Istoriya russkoy etnografii* [History of Russian Ethnography], III, 151-87. V. I. Semev-

tomarov was born in the province of Voronezh. His father was a nobleman, who was murdered by his own serfs; his mother was of Ukrainian origin, a former serf girl on his father's estate. It is very likely that Kostomarov received from his mother both an interest in southern Russia and sympathy for the oppressed peasant masses. He tells us that his reading of history left him curious, reminding us of the case of Shchapov. "Why is it," he asks, "that all histories talk about eminent statesmen, sometimes about laws and institutions, but disregard the life of the masses? The poor peasant, the tiller of the soil, seems not to exist in history. Why does not history say something about his general life, about the way he thinks and feels, about his happiness and his sorrows?"

Kostomarov came to believe that history did not consist merely of accounts of political life, of diplomacy, wars, and legislative acts. True history must deal with the lives of peoples, their aspirations, vices and virtues, domestic life, habits, customs, rituals, morals, folk manners. He severely reproached the Slavophiles and criticized historians like Solovyev for giving pre-eminence to the state at the expense of the people. The purpose of history, argued Kostomarov, was not a matter of chronologically stringing events and facts together; that was the function of archeology and ethnography. The historian's mission was the elucidation of the spirit of the people he deals with, embracing all the ramifications and multitudinousness of their daily lives.

In his writings Kostomarov sought the causes for the loss of Ukrainian autonomy and the triumph of Muscovite absolutism despite the freedom-loving spirit that prevailed among the Ukrainian people. He endeavored to retrace old democratic

---

sky, "N. I. Kostomarov," *Russkaya Starina*, I, 1886, 181-212; N. I. Kostomarov, *Avtobiografiya* [Autobiography], ed. by V. Kotelnikov, Moscow, 1922.

institutions among the early Slavs and studied the period of the Novgorod Republic and the causes of its decline. Whatever subject Kostomarov undertook, his object was to see the underlying forces in history rather than merely political events. This led him at times to overgeneralizations and made him the target of much criticism. His characterization of the Russian and Ukrainian people was colorful enough but hardly palatable to many readers except the romantics in favor of Ukrainian separatism.

As a student at the University of Kharkov, Kostomarov studied history, ethnography, and folklore. For his thesis he chose the subject of the Uniate Church in western Russia, but the censor banned it and Kostomarov changed the topic to a study of Russian national poetry in history. In 1846 he joined the faculty of the University of Kiev, though not for long: within less than three years he was arrested as a member of the democratic Pan-Slavist Cyril-Methodius Society, imprisoned in the dreaded Peter and Paul fortress, and—though he belonged to the extreme right wing of the group—banished to Saratov. While in exile, he continued to gather sources on Ukrainian folklore and the peasant revolts under Stenka Razin and Emelyan Pugachev. Here he also developed an interest in archeology, participated in several expeditions, and remained an active member of the archeographic society for the rest of his life.

With the ascendancy of Alexander II, Kostomarov was granted greater freedom and in 1859 he returned to the capital, where he joined the faculty of the University of St. Petersburg to lecture in Russian history. Here he interpreted the past of Russia as a centripetal process, emphasizing the part of the national minorities in the history of the Empire. From the very dawn of history, Kostomarov maintained, Russian rule was based on the principle of broad federalism.[7] Furthermore, he insisted that the role of the state had been placed too much in the foreground of events while the part the masses had contributed to history was woefully neglected. This thesis provoked displeasure among many of his university colleagues, frowns among others, and suspicion on the part of official authorities.

In addition to his lectures at the University of St. Petersburg, Kostomarov also consented to take part in the recently formed "Free University." As a middle-of-the-road liberal Kostomarov came in conflict with the students, who regarded him as too conservative. By 1862 he was compelled to abandon his university post altogether, after which he devoted himself entirely to writing and active participation in the archeological, archeographic, and geographic societies. A prolific writer, he left behind no less than twenty-one volumes of "Historical Monographs," not to mention numerous articles scattered throughout the periodical literature of the country. As a member of the Archeographic Commission he was responsible for the editing of the nine-volume collection of historical documents on southern and western Russia (*Akty, otnosyashchiyesya k istorii yuzhnoy i zapadnoy Rossii*). Simultaneously he served as editor of a three-volume ethnography published by the Geographical Society. The advancement in the fields of archeology, ethnography, and archeography is due to a considerable extent to Kostomarov. These developed sciences proved instrumental in stimulating and inspiring an interest in history among other scholars.

Kostomarov's chief works are concerned with the Ukrainian people and their struggle for independence against aristocratic feudal Poland and absolutist Russia. He published a biography

---

[7] See Kostomarov's *Mysli o federativnom nachalye drevney Rusi* [Thoughts on the Origin of Federalism in Early Russia], St. Petersburg, 1872.

of Ivan Svirhovsky, Ukrainian Ataman of the sixteenth century, and a monograph on the Ukrainian struggle against Poland during the first quarter of the seventeenth century; later appeared his work on the war led by Bohdan Khmelnitsky and the annexation of southern Ukraine to Russia. Following that he shifted his interest to the history of peasant uprisings in Russia, notably the rebellion of Stenka Razin and the mass revolts during the Time of Troubles. Whatever the main subject of study happened to be, the emphasis was always upon its ethnographic rather than political or economic aspects. The haste with which he wrote explains in part the many errors one is able to find in his works; the varied activities in which he enthusiastically participated did not help matters either, a fact that rendered him vulnerable to sharp criticism and provided grounds for considering his writings superficial. A greater fault of Kostomarov was his hero worship and his frequent liberal interpretations which as frequently led him to "liberal" handling of factual material. Characters for whom he felt a personal fondness he painted as legendary knights and relished their part in history with romantic enthusiasm. It is this more than anything else that explains the uncritical fecundity of Kostomarov. His vulnerability as a scholar has been readily admitted even by his admirers; yet his voluminous writings stirred deep interest in a field of history which had been formerly de-emphasized if not entirely neglected by Great Russian writers, who generally included the Ukraine as a mere annex of Moscow.

There were serious weaknesses and self-contradictions in the historical processes which Kostomarov so laboriously tried to set up against the "juridical school." The exalted role assigned to the masses by Kostomarov still leaves one with some misgivings as to either their wisdom or constructive force in history. Like the Biblical prophet, Balaam, Kostomarov begins by cursing the state and ends blessing it. Unwittingly his narrative leads to the deduction that, not the people, but the state did play the primary part in adding meaning and form to national life. Despite their exaltation, the peasant masses remain an abstraction whereas the state looms as an imposing reality. Peasants rising in protest prove in the end to have been void of plan or purpose, and thereby defeat themselves and gradually surrender to the very authority against which they rebelled. But that was the thesis of the "juridical school," which Kostomarov set out to disprove!

In his effort to prove his own thesis Kostomarov insisted that contemporary opinion and beliefs were as important as factual documents. What he meant was that the past could be reconstructed without necessarily utilizing available documentary records. The answer of his critics was that the result of such a method must be historical fiction rather than history, a romanticized narrative of the past which must disclaim any pretense to scientific research. And this is exactly what most of Kostomarov's works are; he is the Carlyle of Russian historiography. To be sure, Kostomarov's knowledge of Russian and Ukrainian folklore was impressive, but its application to historical interpretation was bound to expose him to grave criticism. Aside from a few more enduring contributions to history, most of his writings cite colorful episodes that do not stand up against critical analysis. Hearsay and legendary tales dominate factual evidence; sentimentality and passion overrule rational judgment. The general reader finds the stories about dashing Cossacks, valorous hetmans, and daring rebel leaders entertaining; to the historian, however, it is fiction, upon which he frowns, to be put aside except for his bedtime reading.

Though Kostomarov laments the vanished free life of the

"Cossack days," he could not but sense that the era had passed into history beyond any hope of restoration. He seems to have gravely feared that any effort in that direction would resolve itself into a naked nihilism that spelled violence, bloodshed, and waste of lives. A strange circle thus formed itself: fears of possible senseless violence in the present destroyed the idols he built from the past.[8] Yet some of his writings retain value and lasting interest, such as his work on Polish intervention during the Time of Troubles.

The flowing literary style and colorful characterization of historical figures made Klyuchevsky's studies monumental contributions to both history and the Russian language. These qualities were not altered by lack of either accuracy or objective handling of documentary evidence. Kostomarov is noted, too, for his flawless and racy style, yet the conscientious reader seems to sense a degree of theatricality. Actors appear before a certain artificial stage-setting, cite their lines, and depart; they provoke applause as the curtain is lowered, the lights go out, and the drama comes to an end. "It may not be true, but it is absorbingly exciting," concludes the layman. "It may be absorbingly exciting, but it hardly agrees with the historical evidence," chimes in the historian.

## Hrushevsky (1866-1934)

The leading historian among the Ukrainian "federalists" is unquestionably the patriarch scholar Mikhail Sergeyevich Hrushevsky. He was born in Kholm, formerly Russian Poland, studied at the University of Kiev under Professor V. S. Antonovich, and later taught at the same institution for a brief period. Because of the cultural persecution, the ban on the Ukrainian

---

[8] Kostomarov, *Istoricheskiye monografii i issledovaniya* [Historical Monographs and Studies], St. Petersburg, 1903, Book I, 412.

language, and his personal political views, Hrushevsky's difficulties with the administration became unavoidable. In 1894, on the recommendation of his admired teacher, Antonovich, he accepted a chair at the University of Lviw (Lemberg), then in Austria, where he anticipated a greater degree of cultural freedom and a milder political climate. Within a short time he won the respect of his academic colleagues and the reverence of his students. His field was southeastern European and Ukrainian history, and shortly after his arrival Hrushevsky assumed leadership in the intellectual movement. As president of the Shevchenko Scientific Society he took charge of its publications.

Hrushevsky was recognized not only as a scholar but also as a statesman; history to him was a tool for implementing his beliefs, yet he never vulgarized it and managed to remain loyal to true scholarship. Unlike others, he never employed his historical knowledge for popular writing, propaganda pamphlets, of romantic narration. His whole life was given to a single cause: to erect for his people, in the form of a scholarly history, a monument which could be neither overlooked nor overthrown by his northern opponents. His *History of the Ukraine* is beyond doubt the standard work in its field and a contribution to which Great Russian historians cannot remain indifferent. The author toiled half his lifetime over it, as can be judged by the span of time during which the ten volumes appeared, 1898-1937, the last volume being published posthumously. An abridged one-volume history of the Ukrainian people appeared in 1904 in Russian. A few years later his *Illustrated History of the Ukraine* appeared in the Ukrainian language and has since been translated into English and published in the United States. Distracted by the turbulent years following 1917, Hrushevsky never completed his great study but ended with the seventeenth century. The Ukraine has been the homeland of war for many centuries; again and again that country served as the battleground of conflicts between the East and the West. Yet Hrushevsky's ten-volume history represents more than a record of wars: the volumes incorporate valuable accounts of social, economic, and cultural history as well.[9]

Russian historiography has suffered from one serious defect, which might be called "Muscovite egocentricity." Many outstanding writers persistently neglected peripheral influence upon the general course of Russian national development. Thus, for instance, the Kievan period was most scantily treated, and some still treat it as a casual chapter, a mere episode that only served as a prologue to the rise of the Muscovite state. In most histories the Kievan era seems to vanish after the middle of the thirteenth century as mysteriously as it reappears in the middle of the seventeenth century. The period that elapses between leaves one with an impression of a vacuum in the history of eastern Europe. The period that precedes 1240 is often presented as a political dress rehearsal for the national state destined to rise in the north.

With the rise of nationalism in the peripheral regions, such neglect or misinterpretation of historical facts provoked understandable resentment. Ukrainian students of history regarded the de-emphasis of the role of the southwestern portion of the nation as nothing less than typical Great Russian distortion. While grumblings against "northern distortion of history"

[9] M. S. Hrushevsky, *Istoriya Ukrainy-Rusi* [History of Ukrainian Russia], 10 vols., Lviw-Kiev, 1898-37; *Istoriya ukrainskoy literatury* [A History of Ukrainian Literature], 3 vols., Lviw-Kiev, 1923; *Zherela do istorii Ukrainy-Rusi* [Sources Pertaining to the History of Ukrainian Russia], Kiev-Lviw, Vols. I-VIII and XII, 1895-1913; XXII, 1913; XXVI, 1924; *Istoriya Kievskoy zemli* [History of Kievan Russia], Kiev, 1891; *A History of the Ukraine,* ed. by O. J. Fredriksen, New Haven, 1941; *Ocherk istorii ukrainskogo naroda* [A Study of the History of the Ukrainian People], St. Petersburg, 1904; *Abrégé de l'Histoire de Ukraine,* Paris, 1920; *Geschichte des ukrainischen (ruthenischen) Volkes,* Leipzig, 1906.

became increasingly audible, it was Hrushevsky who openly revolted and successfully challenged the Great Russian writers. And though Hrushevsky undertook to correct the situation out of vengeance, he nevertheless rendered Russian history a service. Furthermore, he inadvertently demonstrated the need to bring the peripheral units together into an historical synthesis rather than treat them as totally separate and even counteracting entities.

Hrushevsky's "revengeful" spirit expressed itself in the form of political separatism. His separatist tendencies compelled him to consider the Kievan period as exclusively Ukrainian history and not as Great Russian or Muscovite. More than any others, his thesis proves the need of treating each nationality—White Russian, Lithuanian, Great Russian, or Ukrainian—in a manner just to its part in national history. Such an approach must inevitably result in an all-embracing account of the past and eliminate the former Muscovite particularism. A realization of the continuous, successive development through the earlier periods that led up to the rise of Moscow will enrich the store of knowledge concerning both Great Russian and Ukrainian historiography. This development must take into account Kievan Russia, Lithuania, and Poland, as well as Moscow, and not abruptly shift the story from the "Decline of Kiev" to the "Rise of Moscow" without properly accounting for the economic and political causes that preceded this shift.

Hrushevsky was not a narrow specialist historian; he felt that a knowledge of political events alone could never be sufficient for an understanding of the past—hence his concentration on various aspects of the cultural life of the Ukrainian people. He was keenly interested in literature, philology, economics, sociology, and the natural sciences, and frequently contributed articles in each of these fields. His *History of*

*Ukrainian Literature* vividly attests to the broad cultural knowledge of the author.

With the advent of the Revolution in March 1917, Hrushevsky immediately returned to Kiev, where he was elected president of the recently formed Ukrainian National Council (*Rada*). From this initial stage began a tense struggle between Kiev and Petrograd for recognition and clarification of the degree of autonomous rights. Later, when the Bolsheviks seized power, the vicissitudes of Ukrainian independence began in earnest: German occupation, followed by the civil war and Allied intervention, ending with the defeat of the independent Ukrainian state and the triumph of Moscow. Hrushevsky left for Vienna, where he turned to writing once again.

In 1924, at the invitation of the Ukrainian Academy of Science, Hrushevsky was induced to return to Kiev with the intention of completing his lifework. Here he was named president of that august institution. However, his hopes for unmolested scholarship were soon to be shattered: after a few years of relative comfort he came to realize that the national freedom and cultural autonomy pledged to his people were in reality a myth: constant suspicion of a revival of "Ukrainian chauvinism," which might lead to clamor for national independence, led in turn to repression and interference with scholarly activities.

In 1930 Hrushevsky was arrested and banished to the north, near Moscow. His ceaseless political and literary activities, with all their adversities, hopes, and disillusionments, finally shattered him. In 1934 he was sent south to restore his health, but it was too late: he died shortly afterwards in the Caucasus, a total physical wreck. Hrushevsky left a contribution to historical literature which, regardless of political feuds, will always have to be taken into account if Russian history is to be seen in its entirety rather than as a series of episodic stages loosely revolving around the Muscovite state.

## SIBERIAN HISTORIOGRAPHY

Closely related to the borderland provinces is the long-overlooked domain of Siberia.[10] Interest in the province was aroused in the eighteenth century when the "father of Siberian history," Gerhard Friedrich Müller, returned from the "Great Northern" expedition after a study of the archives in the east. The fruit of Müller's ten years of exploits in Siberia appeared in 1750 in a work entitled *A Description of the Siberian Kingdom,* followed in 1761 by additional chapters in his *Compilation of Russian History (Sammlung russischer Geschichte).*[11] The *Description* represents a dull narrative, poorly synthesized, yet it incorporated a mass of newly discovered materials which served many later historians. Soon after the appearance of Müller's work, Johann Fischer published a plagiarized version of Siberian history which did not improve the work either stylistically or architectonically.[12]

For years thereafter, the subject of Siberian history was handled mostly by amateurs like G. I. Spassky, who was by profession a mining engineer. His services, like those of earlier amateur historians, were mainly editorial. He was editor of two periodicals in which was published a large amount of source material, along with the accounts of travelers and newly dis-

---

[10] A detailed discussion of Siberian historiography may be found in A. N. Pypin, *Istoriya russkoy etnografii,* IV, Pt. 2; also in V. I. Ogorodnikov, *Ocherk istorii Sibiri* [A Study of the History of Siberia], 1-92. See also V. I. Mezhov, *Sibirskaya bibliografiya* [Siberian Bibliography].

[11] See G. F. Pekarsky, *Istoriya Akademii Nauk,* I, 366-68, 427.

[12] G. F. Müller, *Opisaniye sibirskogo tsarstva* [A Description of the Siberian Kingdom], St. Petersburg, 1750; 2nd ed., 1787; *Sammlung russischer Geschichte,* 9 vols., St. Petersburg, 1732-64. vol. X, Dorpat, 1816. Johann Eberhard Fischer (1697-1771), *Sibirische Geschichte von der Entdekkung Sibiriens bis auf die Eroberung dieses Lands durch die russischen Waffen. . . . ,* 2 vols., St. Petersburg, 1768.

covered Siberian chronicles (the Stroganov, Yesipov, and part of the Cherepanov chronicles). It was not until the middle of the nineteenth century that P. A. Slovtsov, whom the local patriots came to regard as the "Siberian Karamzin," took up the work of Müller in a more able manner. Slovtsov stressed the internal forces of colonization rather than those emanating from the central administrative authority of Moscow.[13]

In spite of certain faults, questionable methodology, and ponderous style, the merit of Slovtsov's work lies in the fact that for the first time the old idea of presenting a strictly chronological narration was abandoned. Even at that the author was very much handicapped, for to him Siberia was merely the "Russian backdoor to Asia and America" and therefore only an annex to the Empire. This accounts for the considerable space he still devoted to administrative measures by central and local authorities. An additional difficulty, which in the end was bound to defeat Slovtsov's scheme, was the fact that the government was still reluctant to open many of its archives. Nonetheless Slovtsov succeeded in compiling two volumes of documents: one covering the period of 1585-1742; a second, the years 1742-1765. These contain accounts of the conquest of Siberia, the character of the new administration, and of government policy pertaining to the aborigines, trade, commerce, and industry. In attempting to integrate this mass of information, however, Slovtsov demonstrated his inability to dissociate authentic from fictitious material, being apparently unaware that any such confusion existed.

The intensive publication of documents in western Russia by the Archeographic Commission and the Russian Geographical Society, the latter with branches in Siberia, stimulated

[13] P. A. Slovtsov, *Istoricheskoye obozreniye Sibiri* [An Historical Survey of Siberia], 2 vols., St. Petersburg, 1838-44.

further interest in the eastern domain, as did the growing local press and the activities of publicists like N. M. Yadrintsev. G. Yudin, I. Kuznetsov, and A. I. Sibiryakov, among others, also aided Siberian research considerably. The new type of student was best represented by Shchapov, of whom mention has been made previously. Here it may only be said that, among all his works, his essay on the ethnological development of the Siberian population remains to the present day a significant contribution.

A second writer to whom Siberian historiography is much indebted, a contemporary of Shchapov, is Serafim Serafimovich Shashkov (1841-1882). Shashkov, a pupil of Shchapov at the University of Kazan, was author of a number of monographs, notably on Siberian slavery and on the causes of social unrest in Irkutsk from 1758 to 1760. His writings were published posthumously in two volumes entitled *Historical Studies* (*Istoricheskiye etyudy*) and *Historical Sketches* (*Istoricheskiye Ocherki*). Shashkov's studies present admirable accounts of the family status among the Siberian aborigines, of the place of church and clergy in Siberian society, and of the moral decline among the natives, and bring to light the sorrowful exploitation of the aborigines by the administration as well as by individual entrepreneurs who sought quick gains and amassed fortunes. The study brings to mind the remarkable similarity between the American Indian and the Siberian aborigine, whether with respect to economics, politics, or social conflict between native and invading population.

Two other historians in the general field of Siberian history merit mention. One is N. M. Yadrintsev (1842-1894), who published two studies: *Siberia as a Colony* (*Sibir kak koloniya*) and *Siberian Aborigines, Their Conditions and Present Status* (*Sibirskiye inorodtsy, ikh byt i sovremennoye polozheniye*).

Both studies contain much that retains importance to this day. The other historian is A. A. Titov, author of a monograph on *Siberia in the XVII Century* (*Sibir v XVII veke*), a competent account of the formative period in Siberian history.

For those who search for general chronological information, the compilation of data by I. V. Shcheglov will prove most useful.[14] Similar material about administrative measures and various statistical data will be found in the writings of Major-General V. K. Andriyevich, based mainly on the complete code of laws published by the government in the reign of Nicholas I.[15] A much more important methodological study was made by P. N. Butsinsky (1853-1917), who in a series of monographs stressed the further need for archival investigation, without which he considered the writing of Siberian history completely inadequate.[16] Butsinsky's research in the field of eastern colonization was instrumental in arousing scholarly interest in the field of Siberian historiography. Analyzing more carefully the various means of Siberian colonization, Butsinsky included three main ones: two involving official action, declaratory law and forcible exile; the third, voluntary migration. Though the author failed by far to exhaust the subject, his study had a salutary effect upon later research; a considerable portion of his published work was based on archival materials from the Ministry of Justice and the Foreign Office. These two important depositories were hardly explored until Butsinsky

---

[14] I. V. Shcheglov, *Khronologichesky perechen vazhneyshikh dannykh iz istorii Sibiri (1032-1882)* [A Chronological List of Most Important Data in the History of Siberia, 1032-1882], Irkutsk, 1883.

[15] V. K. Andriyevich, *Istoriya Sibiri* [A History of Siberia], 5 vols. in 2, St. Petersburg, 1889.

[16] P. N. Butsinsky, *Zaseleniye Sibiri i byt pervykh eya naselnikov* [The Settlement of Siberia and the Life of the First Settlers], Kharkov, 1869; *K istorii Sibiri: Surgut, Narym i Ketsk do 1645 goda* [Notes on the History of Siberia: Surgut, Narym, and Ketsk to 1645], Kharkov, 1893; *Mangazeya i Mangazeysky uyezd (1601-1645 g.g.)* [Mangazeya and Mangazeysk District (1601-1645)], Kharkov, 1893.

focused the attention of scholars on the wealth of materials they contained. As to Siberian archives, they were barely explored by Butsinsky, a fact which the author himself regretfully acknowledged.

Other spade work was done by A. V. Oksenov, whose most notable contribution was on the relations between Great Novgorod and Yugria—or northern Siberia—and between Muscovy and Yugria; by A. A. Adrianov, who compiled valuable data concerning the province of Tomsk; and by P. M. Golovachev, who made a special investigation of the population of Siberia in the seventeenth and eighteenth centuries.[17] Even more valuable service to Siberian historiography was performed by N. N. Ogloblin, who compiled a most thorough catalogue of the sources in the Siberian *Prikaz* [Department], as well as of many documents pertaining to Siberia in other Russian archives. What Ikonnikov did for Russian historiography in general, Ogloblin accomplished for Siberia.[18] Equally important are the two works of V. I. Vaghin and S. M. Prutchenko on Speransky's administrative reforms in Siberia,[19] and I. P. Barsukov's two-volume work on the administration of Count Muravyev-Amursky.[20] Finally there should be noted the single account of the Russian-American Company by P. Tikhmenev and a more recent study of the same organization by S. B. Okun'.

---

[17] P. M. Golovachev, *Rossiya na Dalnem Vostoke* [Russia in the Far East], St. Petersburg, 1904; N. M. Yadrintsev, *Sibir kak koloniya* [Siberia as a Colony], St. Petersburg, 1892.

[18] N. N. Ogloblin, *Obozreniye stolbtsov i knig sibirskogo prikaza 1592-1768 g.g.* [A Survey of the Rolls and Books of the Siberian Department], 4 vols., Moscow, 1859-1900.

[19] V. I. Vaghin, *Istoricheskiye svedeniya o deyatelnosti gr. M. M. Speranskogo v Sibiri s 1819 po 1922 g.* [Historical Data on the Activities of Count M. M. Speransky in Siberia from 1819 to 1822], 2 vols., St. Petersburg, 1872; S. M. Prutchenko, *Sibirskiye okrainy* [Siberian Borderlands], 2 vols., St. Petersburg, 1899.

[20] I. P. Barsukov, *Graf N. N. Muravyev-Amursky* [Count N. N. Muravyev-Amursky], 2 vols., Moscow, 1891.

The history of the Russian-American Company constitutes part of the drama of eastern expansion that climaxed in Russia's colonial establishments in Alaska and California.[21]

A general survey of Siberian historiography in the nineteenth century plainly shows that virgin soil was broken but that little else was done. The first attempt to write a general social and economic history of Siberia was that of Professor N. N. Firsov. It stemmed from the course he offered at the University of Kazan and at the Moscow Archeological Institute.[22] Though a secondary account, Firsov's work represents an advance in the development of Siberian historiography, a transition from the merely compilatory and monographic to the more general and synthesized method of writing.

Of the more recent historians, the foremost students in the field are S. V. Bakhrushin and V. I. Ogorodnikov. The two complement each other's writings: Bakhrushin's interest centered chiefly on the general subject of colonization; the latter's study stresses the Siberian aborigines in relation to the incoming tide of Russian settlers and the development of the new administration.[23] Both authors endeavored rather successfully to in-

[21] P. Tikhmenev, *Istoricheskoye obozreniye obrazovaniya Rossiysko-amerikanskoy kompanii i deystvy eya do nastoyashchego vremeni* [An Historical Survey of the Formation of the Russian-American Company and its Activities to the Present], 2 vols,. St. Petersburg, 1861-63. S. B. Okun', *The Russian-American Company,* tr. by Carl Ginsburg, Cambridge, Mass., 1951.

[22] N. N. Firsov, *Chteniya po istorii Sibiri* [Readings in the History of Siberia], 2 vols., Moscow, 1920-21; *Polozheniye inorodtsev severo-vostochnoy Rossii v Moskovskom gosudarstve* (Position of the Natives of Northeastern Russia in the Muscovite State], Kazan, 1866.

[23] S. V. Bakhrushin, *Kazaki na Amure* [Amur Cossacks], Leningrad, 1925; *Ocherki po istorii Sibiri XVI i XVII v.v.* [Studies of the History of Siberian History of the XVI and XVII Centuries], Moscow, 1927; *Pokruta na sobolinnykh promyslakh semnadtsatogo vyeka* [Contracts in the Sable Trade in the Seventeenth Century], N.p., n.d.; "Sibirskiye sluzhiliye tatary v XVII veke [Siberian Tartar Vassals in the XVII Century]," *Istoricheskiye zapiski,* (Moscow), I, 1937, 55-80.

V. I. Ogorodnikov, *Ocherk istorii Sibiri do nachala XIX stoletiya. Vvedeniye. Istoriya do russkoy Sibiri* [An Outline of Siberian History to the Nineteenth Century. Introduction. History to the Russian Conquest], Irkutsk, 1920; *Zavoevaniye russkimi*

corporate earlier historical writings and present an over-all picture of Russian eastward expansion. The increased economic and political importance of Siberia in recent years has led to a steadily rising interest in her past. The long-neglected field is beginning to assume an important place in Russian historiography.

## OTHER HISTORIANS OF THE PERIOD

### *Shakhmatov* (1864-1920)

The study of Russian sources continued during the entire nineteenth century, culminating in the investigations of Aleksey Aleksandrovich Shakhmatov, a most remarkable linguist and one of the greatest authorities on the language of the chronicles. Shakhmatov's work illustrates the assistance that philology can render the historian, especially the student of the early periods.[24] His persistent analyses of the chronicles resulted in a series of monographs and books, some of which have been lauded by Slavists the world over. Yet his general deductions met with doubt and criticism. Slavists like Alexander Brückner, Reinold Trautmann, and Samuel H. Cross were skeptical of Shakhmatov's methodology. Others criticized his conclusion that the Great Russian, Ukrainian, and White Russian languages, though stemming from a common Old Slavic tongue, developed independently; extreme nationalists among the Great

---

*Sibiri* [The Russian Conquest of Siberia], Vladivostok, 1924; *Russkaya gosudarstvennaya vlast i Sibirskiye inorodtsy v XVI-XVII v.v.* [Russian State Authority and Siberian Aborigines in XVI-XVII Centuries], Irkutsk, 1920; *Iz istorii pokoreniya Sibiri. Pokoreniye Yukagirskoy zemli* [From the Story of the Conquest of Siberia—The Conquest of the Yukagir Territory], Chita, 1922; *Tuzemnoye i russkoye zemledeliye na Amure v XVIII vyeke* [Native and Russian Agriculture in the Amur District in the XVIII Century], Vladivostok, 1927.

[24] *Russky istorichesky zhurnal*, VII, 1921, 114-20.

Russians bitterly censured Shakhmatov for admitting the very existence of independent languages.

Schlözer's method was to restore by means of textual criticism and scholarly scrutiny the original text of the Nestor Chronicle. This involved a laborious "peeling off" process; that is, by eliminating all detected apocryphal additions and alterations of later writers, he hoped to arrive at the original text. The same method was applied by later students of Russian history, such as Bestuzhev-Ryumin and, notably, Pogodin. Shakhmatov handled the problem by employing historical rather than textual criticism. He began by examining each component of the chronicle as a product of certain historical circumstances. Each examined part was then considered a reflection of the environment in which it must have been recorded. Each detected textual change or new "layer" of later date served as *zeitgebunden* evidence of period and place. By assiduously dissecting and then reconstructing each part, Shakhmatov set the entire problem in a new light. Each textual part of a later date came to reveal the nature of local history or of the time when it had been incorporated by the chronicler.[25]

Philology was only one of the instruments with which

[25] Volume XXV (1922) of the *Izvestiya otdeleniya russkogo yazyka i slovesnosti Rossiyskoy Akademii Nauk* includes an excellent collection of essays on Shakhmatov. See also *A. A. Shakhmatov, 1864-1920. Biografiya*, Leningrad, Academy of Sciences, 1930.

Among the most notable works of Shakhmatov may be mentioned the following: *Rozyskaniya o drevneyshikh letopisnykh svodakh* [Investigations Concerning the Earliest Chronicles], St. Petersburg, 1903; *O yazyke novgorodskikh gramot* [The Language of the Novgorodian Charters], St. Petersburg, 1885; *Issledovaniye o Dvinskikh gramotakh* [A Study of the Dvinsk Charters], St. Petersburg, 1903; *Neskolko zametok o yazyke Pskovskikh pamyatnikov* [A Few Notes Concerning the Language of the Pskov Records], St. Petersburg, 1909; *Ocherk drevneyshogo perioda istorii russkogo literaturnogo yazyka* [A Study of the Modern Russian Literary Language], St. Petersburg, 1915; *Vvedeniye v kurs istorii russkogo yazyka* [Introduction to the History of the Russian Language], Petrograd, 1916; *Drevneyshiye sud'by russkogo plemeni* [Concerning the History of the Earliest Russian Tribe], Petrograd, 1919.

Shakhmatov attacked the problem. The primary weapon he employed was a carefully deduced historical narrative. It is particularly for these reasons that Shakhmatov can be rightly considered both as an eminent philologist and historian. Each of his investigations resulted in a critical essay, based on a particular source, which essentially represented a study of a given period. This process involved minute analyses of political, religious, social, economic, or military conditions of a particular locality. At times the method resulted in startling revelations of the relations between the principalities. Philology thereby became wedded to history and was later employed most effectively by scholars like N. Ya. Marr and A. E. Presnyakov.

Shakhmatov's greatest contribution was in the field of chronology with respect to the chronicles. With considerable ingenuity and scholarly care he undertook to determine on a linguistic basis the approximate dates of the various sources: the Kievan, Novgorodian, and other chronicles. Thanks to his extraordinary linguistic erudition, Shakhmatov was able to disclose the interdependence of these sources, particularly in the matter of style. In his study of the Primary Chronicle, *Povest' vremennykh lyet,* published by the Archeographic Commission in 1916, he accomplished what neither Tatishchev nor Schlözer, nor even Abbot Joseph Dobrovsky—who in 1812 first suggested the method later employed by Shakhmatov—had succeeded in doing, because they lacked sufficient material for comparative study. Shakhmatov's task was to discover "the most complete and most accurate, authentic" Nestor Chronicle. By a masterful comparison of the chronicles he established conclusively not only the dates of the various documents but also the origin, place, and nature of the environment in which each document was produced, and the motives of their authors. All this was a genuine revelation to many historians because it threw light upon several important moments in the course of Russian history, reclaiming, as it were, the outlook of contemporaries of these periods upon their own time as well as upon the past. Of course many aspects of the chronicles remained obscure; some reconstructions of the past were based on sheer hypotheses, and Shakhmatov himself seemed to have accepted them with misgivings. Yet, notwithstanding some of his unfortunate assumptions, Shakhmatov advanced the study of the chronicles to a point never dreamed of by historians of previous centuries.

## *Ikonnikov* (1841-1923)

In the field of Russian historiography the name of Vladimir Stepanovich Ikonnikov is eminent. His four-volume work entitled *A Study of Russian Historiography* stands not only as a unique achievement in scholarship but also as a rare demonstration of phenomenal knowledge and of an amazing capacity to combine quantity of output with a high degree of accuracy.[26] Of his other works, there must be mentioned his extensive monograph on Count N. S. Mordvinov, a study of the economic and political life of Russia in the early nineteenth century, and the annotated publication of documents pertaining to the peasant movement following the Decembrist uprising in 1825.

## *Pavlov-Silvansky* (1869-1908)

In connection with Russian works of broad historical synthesis by earlier writers like Karamzin, Solovyev, Klyuchevsky, or Milyukov, the name of Nikolay Pavlovich Pavlov-Silvansky

[26] V. S. Ikonnikov, *Opyt russkoy istoriografii* [A Study of Russian Historiography], 2 vols. in 4, Kiev, 1891-1908; *Graf N. S. Mordvinov* [Count N. S. Mordvinov], St. Petersburg, 1873; "Krestyanskoye dvizheniye v Kiyevskoy gubernii v 1826-27 g.g. v svyazi s sobytiyami togo vremeni [The Peasant Movement in the Kiev Gubernia in 1826-27 in Connection with the Events of that Time]," *Sbornik Statey, Posvyashchennykh V. I. Lamanskomu*, St. Petersburg, 1908, Part 2, 657-742.

must not be overlooked. By his assertion that the institution of feudalism, which had been formerly associated with western Europe only, had also existed in Russia, he started a lively debate among historians and forced many to revise their former views. Today, except for some modifications, the basic contentions of Pavlov-Silvansky have been generally accepted by the majority of students of Russian history.[27]

For many years Pavlov-Silvansky worked with the national archives. His association with university life began rather late and proved of less than a year's duration: his promising academic career ended in death when the thirty-nine year old scholar contracted cholera. As a student at the University of St. Petersburg he became keenly interested in Russian feudalism, a subject he studied until the end of his life. A pupil of Sergeyevich, he was deeply impressed by this illustrious teacher and eminent representative of the "juridical school." Later Pavlov-Silvansky came to admire Solovyev's writings even more, in which he discovered a unity of historical forces previously unnoticed. He familiarized himself with the works of Guizot and studied with interest his views on the development of feudalism. He was fascinated also by Klyuchevsky's theories concerning the origin and development of serfdom. It was under this combined influence of teachers and authors that Pavlov-Silvansky decided to undertake a comparison of medieval institutions in Russia and in the Romano-Germanic countries.

In 1907 Pavlov-Silvansky published his first book, entitled *Feudalism in Medieval Russia*. The basic problem was to prove the absence of any "uniqueness" in the social structure of medieval Russia, which was similar to that which prevailed in medieval feudal Europe. This book was soon followed by an-

[27] See G. Vernadsky, "Feudalism in Russia," *Speculum, XIV,* 1939, 300-23.

other, *Feudalism in Appanage Russia,* published posthumously though never completed by the author. The main thesis, sufficiently clear nevertheless, pursued the thematic problem a step further, to comparative investigation of feudal and legal institutions between the thirteenth and sixteenth centuries. Pavlov-Silvansky firmly believed that Russian feudalism developed long before it had been formulated by political authority; the latter only sanctioned what had already become a well-established institution. The medieval structure of society, whether in Russia or in the Romano-Germanic countries, was not imposed from without but was brought about by internal conditions, by social and economic strife between the large landowning classes and the peasantry. This in turn led to forcible seizure of land by the former and the suppression and gradual economic enslavement of the latter. As state servants the privileged military class managed to defeat the peasants, and eventually their trumph became a legalized institution within the state.

The pattern of historical development as presented by Pavlov-Silvansky can be outlined thus:

*First period, 1169-1565.* Characterized by communal land ownership which prevailed within society.

*Second period, 1565-1760.* Noticeable shift of balance of political and economic power in favor of the rising aristocracy; eclipse of the communal system and defeat of peasant claims to the land.

*Third period, 1760-1825.* Ascendancy of the state, sanctioning the claims of the privileged classes. The merging of state and privileged class interests at the expense of the peasantry.

*Fourth period, 1825-1861.* Emergence of libertarian views followed by gradual emancipation and triumphant assertions of the rights of the masses.

The reign of Peter I was regarded by Pavlov-Silvansky, not as a unique era, but rather as the continuation in accelerated form of social, political, and economic forces that had been in operation prior to the ascendancy of this rebel in purple, and that continued to operate for many decades after his departure from the scene. The distinguishing characteristic of the Petrine era was merely the tempo with which national development kept forging ahead: whereas formerly these changes were creeping, now they were galloping. Attention may be called to the fourth period, which Pavlov-Silvansky traced to the beginning of the nineteenth century. The Decembrists, including such of their ideological predecessors as A. Radishchev, marked the dawn of the fourth period, when libertarian ideas from the West entered as the new factor in Russian society. This era, signalized by the Decembrist revolt, initiated an effective opposition by the opressed masses to the wedded interests of the state and privileged aristocratic classes. This period carried with it the ideas of the Era of Enlightenment and the slogans of the French Revolution. The year 1825 in Russian history, according to Pavlov-Silvansky, corresponds to the year 1789 in France.

By a parallel study of western and Russian society, and by tracing identical institutional developments in both, Pavlov-Silvansky arrived at a new historical synthesis. The similarity is particularly noticeable when the legal aspects are analyzed. By his masterful constructive ability and undeniable originality Pavlov-Silvansky set later historians to revising many of their formerly-held views of Russia's historical uniqueness. He exploded once and for all the theory that Russian medieval society, with its institution of serfdom, was characterized by peculiarly humanitarian and presumably Christian socialist qualities not to be found anywhere in the West. Later other writers, notably B. D. Grekov, broadened the thesis pioneered by Pavlov-Silvansky. The Marxian writers enthusiastically accepted the thesis and expanded it to include its economic as well as political and social aspects. Pavlov-Silvansky, stated Pokrovsky, definitely proved that five hundred years ago Russia marched politically in step with Romano-Germanic society, and what was destined to die in western Europe would do likewise in eastern Europe; the only difference between the two was one of tempo.[28]

### "Legal" Marxists

During the last decades of the nineteenth century the Russian Empire witnessed a noticeable industrial advancement. Railroad construction and extensive foreign investments in industrial enterprises served as harbingers of an encroaching era of industrial revolution with all its familiar attributes: shifts of population, depopulation in certain rural areas, and congestion in others. This caused a disturbance in prices, a fall in market prices in depleted areas, and a rise in the newly formed urban centers. Western capital—lured by prospects of fat returns, abundant resources, cheap labor, and protective government policy—began to flow eastward. The number of factories climbed, the ranks of workers in the cities swelled, Western technology advanced, and markets expanded, while the homecraft industry began to show symptoms of decline. The nation came to face the well-known implications of the transi-

[28] N. P. Pavlov-Silvansky, *Feodalizm v drevney Rusi* [Feudalism in Early Russia], St. Petersburg, 1907; *Feodalizm v udelnoy Rusi* [Feudalism in Appanage Russia], St. Petersburg, 1910; *Gosudarevy-sluzhiliye lyudi: proiskhozhdeniye russkogo dvoryanstva* [The Sovereign's Servant-men: the Origin of the Russian Nobility], St. Petersburg, 1898; *Dekabrist Pestel pred verkhovnym ugolovnym sudom* [The Decembrist Pestel Before the Supreme Criminal Court], Rostov, 1907.

See also B. D. Grekov, *Feodalniye otnosheniya v Kievskom gosudastve* [Feudal Relations in the Kievan State], Moscow, 1935.

tional period when a backward economy had to yield to an incoming technological revolution.

Opinions as to how the critical period should be faced were by no means unanimous. While some observers enthusiastically predicted national prosperity and material blessings which would assure mass contentment, thereby hoping to reduce the chances of appeal to mass violence, others felt far less optimistic about the turn of events. There was feeling that industrial development would bring with it all the evils of Western society —a restless proletariat and an entrenched bourgeois class clamoring for a more favorable position in government; it held out the prospects of grim economic crises accompanied by unemployment and social disturbance which in the end might imperil the entire social order. Fear of such sorrowful consequences was professed by the agrarian classes, for reasons too obvious to elucidate. There were similar misgivings in the Populist Party, whose motivations were not without self-interest. The Populists watched with alarm the economic changes that spelled the end of the "uniqueness" of national development upon which they based their entire philosophy. The new order would destroy their revered institution of the village commune, the peasant system of communal landownership to which they were sentimentally attached, and then, they predicted, all the grievious consequences of what had taken place elsewhere would be repeated in Russia.

The interesting feature was the anomaly of the role of government in this industrial development. The government became the owner of an expanded system of railways, mines, and industrial plants; it shared in the benefits which industry came to enjoy. The official attitude, it may be said, was a divided one: while on the one hand it actively supported the industrial revolution, on the other it professed hesitance as to the potential threat to the existing political and social order. If on one hand the imperial government became a partner in or outright owner of numerous industrial establishments and means of transportation, on the other it remained the owner of large estates and by virture of that fact could not but share the fears of the privileged class that sulkily looked down upon the economic innovations.

It was in the midst of this critical turn of events that we find what might be defined as a Marxist reflection in bourgeois historiography, which in turn led to a school of Marxist interpretation of Russian history. It began with the so-called "Legal" Marxists who presumably accepted the Marxist economic theory, even though refuting its political tenets or implications. They brushed aside the views of the orthodox Marxists and their doctrines pertaining to class struggle or to the predestined role of the proletariat. The "Legal" Marxists did accept collectivism and state ownership as a sign of a national evolutionary process in modern society that did not necessarily invite social revolution.

## Struve (1870-1944)

One of the first economic historians to formulate the "Legal" Marxist views was Peter Berngardovich Struve. In 1894 he published his *Critical Notes on the Question of Economic Development of Russia*.[29] The main purpose of the *Notes* was to demolish the contention of the Populists, and the censor saw no harm in this occupation. With the appearance of Struve's book

---

[29] P. B. Struve, *Kriticheskiye zametki k voprosu ob ekonomicheskom razvitii Rossii* [Critical Notes on the Question of Economic Development of Russia], St. Petersburg, 1894; *Krepostnoye khozyaistvo: issledovaniya po ekonomicheskoy istorii Rossii v XVIII i XIX v.v.* [Serfdom: a Study of Economic History of Russia of the 18th and 19th Centuries], Moscow, 1913.

"Legal" Marxism made its maiden appearance in Russia. It was perfectly "legal" from the official point of view to question the validity of the Populists' contentions concerning the economic role of the village commune; it was equally acceptable to the office of the censor to insist that capitalism in Russia was an established fact or a desirable development as long as there was no reference to labor problems, nor a call for improvement of the workingmen's lot by means of violence, nor a subtle attack upon the institution of private property. In short, "Legal" Marxism was tolerated and its thematic content admissible in print as long as it was stripped of revolutionary allusion.

Analyzing the general economic state of affairs, Struve first pointed out the extreme backwardness that prevailed throughout the country and advocated that Russia learn from Western capitalism. This was an immediate challenge to the Populists, who staked their entire philosophy upon the "distinct" development of Russian rural economy and social institutions. Pursuing his thesis further, Struve then came to arouse the wrath of the orthodox Marxists when he arrived at the cardinal point of his theme—that the appearance of capitalism in Russia carried with it a sign of permament progress. Struve departed from the view that capitalism necessarily implied an inevitable social cataclysm and maintained instead that it held out peaceful means to transform the old order. It was not by revolution but by evolutionary reforms that an advanced economic system could be secured.

Struve thus rejected the Marxian thesis that hoary capitalism signified a transitory period, at the end of which it was bound to dig its own grave to make way for a higher social order to be attained by revolution. According to Struve, capitalist society does not constitute a stepping stone to an advanced society built on bourgeois ruins, but carries with it a stamp of finality.

Capitalism, he believed, represents a natural advanced stage from which eventually all classes would derive some blessings. He denied the belief of the Marxists that capitalism was bound to disintegrate and to augur nothing but class antagonism within society. Whereas the one endeavored to dissociate political developments from economic evolution, the others professed the two to be absolutely inseparable.

Pointing to the changes that had already taken place in Russia, such as the considerable growth of a commodity economy and the expansion of markets, transportation, and industrial output, Struve concluded that capitalism in Russia was no longer a question of acceptance or denial; capitalism was already the established economy. By virtue of this fact, he declared, the nation could henceforth anticipate not class strife but general welfare; not conflict but peaceful coexistence between the old and the newly established economy. He firmly opposed an interference in its natural development and the notion that the old and new were destined to work at cross purposes; on the contrary, both were bound to aspire to a common goal—national welfare. Following the same line of thought, Struve later published another study of serfdom in which he endeavored to show that the old agrarian economy coexisted with encroaching capitalism. Occasional conflicts between the two were arbitrated by the state until the old and the new merged into a single economic force that operated for the common good.

The "Legal" Marxists thus came to believe that the new capitalist economy could advance despite the presence of a backward rural economy, provided the government extended its protective wings over the former either by protective tariffs or by actual partnership in a collectivist form. Backward rural conditions would be no impediment to modern technology; on the other hand, technocracy would stimulate the rise of agrarian standards through improved means of transportation and similar developments. The sharper the contrast between the legacy of serfdom and technological advancement, the stronger the "Legal" Marxists believed would be the country's realization of the need for capitalist expansion. Adjustments, however, should not be enforced from above, since these might result in an artificially imposed superstructure; there must be no interference with the natural course of economic development.

The turbulent events of 1905-1906, however, caused a serious revision of views among the "Legal" Marxists. The consternation and panic which the revolution produced in the midst of their camp compelled them to retreat from their position and sharply move to the right. Whereas formerly they looked upon the state as the unpartisan arbitrator instrumental in preventing conflicts of interests, now they ran to the state to secure protection against the rebellious masses. In addition to benevolent economic assistance, they now appealed for more extensive aid against the perilous mass fury displayed in recent years. Strangely enough, their haunting fear and desperate search for protection against revolution brought them ideologically much closer to the now-faded "juridical school." The state, Struve now philosophized, could not be considered as either good or evil, but as an indispensable agency singly capable of taming the rebellious elements within the nation, regardless of whether those be eighteenth-century Cossacks or twentieth-century intellectuals. He saw in both nothing but the seeds of anarchy and irreligiosity sown by a minority that severed itself from the body of the state. Struve was therefore now willing to assign to the state a primary role and grant it unrestrained freedom for the purpose of suppressing the ever-present spirit of elemental social rebelliousness.

## *Tugan-Baranovsky* (1865-1919)

The same line of thought was taken by Michael I. Tugan-Baranovsky, another "Legal" Marxist, in his study of the Russian factory during the past century.[30] Basically the thesis of Tugan-Baranovsky followed closely that of Struve. Peter the Great, according to Tugan-Baranovsky, was the sovereign who introduced capitalism into Russia. There was no conflict between the feudal and capitalist economies—the two functioned side by side harmoniously; friction stemmed rather from tension at the top, where minor leading groups strove for influence. Whatever other antagonism was present could be traced largely to the aspirations of labor to shake off its feudal bonds. The state played a decisive part in settling such social or economic unrest; it was to capitalism that the state assigned the task of combatting national backwardness and raising the cultural level of the working masses engaged in industry.

Peter I had dealt with the problem when he came to recognize industry as a vital branch of the national economy and relegated power to the middle classes. Capitalism, according to Tugan-Baranovsky, was now destined to pursue the same aims originally perceived by this monarch, securing economic and cultural progress within the state. Therefore, he concluded, Populist fear that capitalism must destroy Russian "uniqueness" or that it was bound to lead to inevitable class warfare had been historically disproved. He firmly believed that continued legislation favoring industrial development was the best assurance of national progress. Furthermore, although the state must render benevolent support or participate wherever necessary, nonethe-

[30] M. I. Tugan-Baranovsky, *Russkaya fabrika v proshlom i nastoyashchem. Istoricheskoye razvitiye fabriki v XIX v.* [The Russian Factory in the Past and Present. Historical Development of the Russian Factory in the XIX Century], 7th ed., Moscow, 1938.

less it must follow a strict policy of *laissez faire* and allow a free play to economic forces for the good of all concerned. As in the case of Struve, under the impact of revolutionary developments Tugan-Baranovsky gradually altered his former views, shifting slowly but surely into the camp of the extreme right. "Legal" Marxism passed, as one writer well summarizes, "from demonstration of the inevitability and progressiveness of capitalism in Russia to apologetics and glorification; from a bowdlerized Marxism cut to measure for the censor as a matter of reluctant necessity, to a castrated Marxism robbed of its revolutionary vigor; and finally, to open opposition to Marxism." [31]

[31] Bertram D. Wolfe, *Three Who Made a Revolution*, 122.

# Marxist Historians

*Plekhanov* (1856-1918)

*THE APPLICATION* of Marxian dialectics to Russian historical writing was pioneered by Georgy Valentinovich Plekhanov. In a series of studies, largely of a monographic nature, written while he was a political *émigré* abroad, Plekhanov championed the Marxist interpretation. In his later years he made a noble effort to synthesize his vast amount of information when he undertook to write a *History of Russian Social Thought.*[1] Numerous adversities seriously impeded his progress, and Plekhanov never completed his projected work. Severed from Russian archives, he was compelled to draw information largely from the writings of Solovyev, Klyuchevsky, Milyukov, and other secondary sources. Archival materials being inaccessible to him, his work assumed the nature of reflections upon the subject of social development in Russia. Nonetheless Plekhanov's three-volume *History* demonstrates an astonishing familiarity with Western philosophy. His wide philosophical knowledge, spiced with dialectical materialism, he ably wove into the pattern of Russian social history. To this day it represents an interesting attempt at a philosophical interpretation of Russian history, though it falls short of accomplishing the goal at which the author had originally aimed.

[1] G. G. Plekhanov, *Istoriya russkoy obshchestvennoy mysli* [A History of Russian Social Thought], 3 vols., Moscow, 1925. Also in his *Collected Works*, Vols. XX-XXII, Moscow, 1923-27.

## Rozhkov (1868-1927)

In the case of Nikolay Aleksandrovich Rozhkov we find more of the "professional" historian who, particularly during the later period of his life, endeavored to formulate a Marxist historical view in a general survey of Russian history.[2] However his bulky study has failed to leave any lasting impression upon historical writing; today the voluminous work is half-forgotten, marking perhaps only the birth pangs of Marxist interpretation of Russian history. One senses throughout Rozhkov's history a Marxist doctrine artificially mounted upon an otherwise colorless, orthodox narrative of bygone events. The reader discerns far more the influence of Spencer's positivism upon Rozhkov than the dialectical materialism of Marx.

In his periodization of Russian history he displayed neither originality nor consistency. His earlier monographic studies of such subjects as the sixteenth-century Muscovite state, the role of town and country in the history of Russia, or the origin of Russian absolutism, demonstrated a more profound scholarly accomplishment. One of the reasons for this fact is most likely the influence which his teacher, V. O. Klyuchevsky, must have had upon him. As one compares Rozhkov's earlier writings with those of later date, one can detect a certain duality in the author's dominating theme. On one hand Rozhkov displays parts of the best traditions of Russian liberalism of the end of the last century, while on the other he betrays a sign of surrender to the politically triumphant ideology of the November Revolution. Seizing wholly on neither, he pitifully falls between the two.

[2] N. A. Rozhkov, *Selskoye khozyaystvo moskovskoy Rusi v XVI veke* [Agrarian Economy in Muscovite Russia in the XVI Century], Moscow, 1899; *Gorod i Derevnya v russkoy istorii* [Town and Country in Russian History], Moscow, 1904; *Proiskhozhdeniye samoderzhaviya v Rossii* [The Origin of Absolutism in Russia], Moscow, 1906; *Russkaya istoriya* [Russian History], 12 vols., Moscow, 1919-26.

## *Pokrovsky* (1868-1932)

Among the early Marxists who came to leave a formidable influence upon Russian historiography was Mikhail Nikolayevich Pokrovsky. He pioneered a reinterpretation of the entire course of Russian history at a time when Marxist influence upon historical writing was still in an inchoate state. The case of Pokrovsky is entirely different from that of Rozhkov, since his break with "Menshevism" was much more drastic, even though posthumously he ended just as sadly. The reason is not difficult to discover: whereas Rozhkov remained a lonely figure, Pokrovsky, on the other hand, left behind him an entire school of Soviet historians, a legion of disciples with whom the Party later had to deal most harshly. As a graduate of the University of Moscow in 1891, Pokrovsky had been bred in the best traditions of that institution: he was the pupil of such eminent teachers as Klyuchevsky and Paul G. Vinogradov, the distinguished scholar in the field of Western feudalism. Klyuchevsky's "economism" and Struve's "Legal Marxism" were already current topics when Pokrovsky entered his most formative years.

Originally Pokrovsky started in the field of medieval European history. He soon shifted his interest and initiated the thesis, later advanced in more detailed form by Pavlov-Silvansky, of the similarity between Russian and Western feudal institutions and medieval structures of society. While feeling his way, he associated himself with liberal groups who professed Marxist proclivities. The years 1905-1910 represent a period of soul-searching among many intellectuals and Pokrovsky was no exception, shifting from one Marxist grouping to another. It was during this period of vacillations that Pokrovsky commenced his extensive writings.

Among his more noted works may be mentioned first his

*Russian History from the Earliest Times* in four volumes, leading up to the nineteenth century, and a two-volume *History of Russian Culture.*[3] The first was supposed to supplement Klyuchevsky's *Course;* the second, Milyukov's *Outlines of Russian Culture.* Both failed to demolish the works at which Pokrovsky aimed his lances; he only formulated a brand of Marxist interpretation which the Marxists themselves later refuted. Contributing to a collective work on the nineteenth-century history of Russia, he later published his own chapters separately under the title of *Diplomacy and Wars of Tsarist Russia in the Nineteenth Century.* This represented a novel attempt to demonstrate the relationship between domestic and foreign policies in Russian history.

The fundamental idea that runs throughout all of the writings of Pokrovsky may be formulated thus: material needs are at the bottom of all human activity and of all history. This simple formula became the keynote, the all-encompassing explanation of every historical phenomenon. Under its domination history became the record of an inevitable process which left little or no room for the role of leadership or of cultural determinants. Nationalism was eschewed as a bourgeois device, and no trace of national glorification can be found in any of his writings. This mechanical interpretation of history was laid down in topical form, so that the chronology of events was difficult to follow. Even the admiring Lenin was constrained to suggest

[3] M. N. Pokrovsky, *Russkaya istoriya s drevneyshikh vremyen* [Russian History from the Earliest Times], 4 vols., Moscow, 1913-14; later ed., Moscow, 1932-33; *History of Russia,* tr. by J. D. Clarkson, New York, 1931; *Diplomatiya i voyny tsarskoy Rossii v XIX stolyetii* [Diplomacy and Wars of Tsarist Russia in the 19th Century], Moscow, 1923; *Ocherki russkogo revolyutsionnogo dvizheniya XIX-XX v.v.* [Essays on the Russian Revolutionary movement of the 19th-20th Centuries], Moscow, 1924; *Ocherk istorii russkoy kultury* [A Study of the History of Russian Culture], 2 vols., Petrograd, 1923; *Istoricheskaya nauka i borba klassov* [Historical Science and Class Struggle], Moscow, 1933; Rubinstein, *op. cit.,* 575-99. For a complete list of Pokrovsky's works see *Istorik-Marksist,* I-II, 1932, 216-48.

that a chronological table be appended to Pokrovsky's *Brief History*. Nor can one fail to notice his disregard for national groups within the multilingual Russian Empire, except the fortuitous reference he was compelled to make to the Ukrainian people. The predominant role in history seems to be ascribed to the Great Russian people as surely by Pokrovsky as by the "bourgeois" historians whom he so severely took to task.

After Lenin read the *Brief History* of Pokrovsky, he praised the author for displaying originality in approach to the subject and in making it readable. Yet the praise was extended with some reservations when he suggested: "To make it a textbook (and this it must become), it must be supplemented with a chronological index. This is, roughly, what I am suggesting: first column, chronology; second column, bourgeois view (briefly); third column, your view, Marxian, indicating the pages in your book. The student must know both your book and the index so that there should be no skimming, so that they should retain the facts, and so that they should learn to compare the old science and the new." In 1924 Pokrovsky published his *Essays on the Russian Revolutionary Movement of the XIX-XX Centuries*. During the same year Pokrovsky's essays on historiography, entitled *Historical Science and Class Struggle,* also appeared. It consisted largely of the lectures he delivered at the Communist University at Moscow. Aside from the above works one must also refer to the numerous articles he contributed to various papers and magazines, not to mention the virulent debates in which he frequently engaged with his opponents.

To Pokrovsky the Revolution was the hour of *a verbis ad verbera*. As a full-fledged member of the Communist Party he saw his star ascend with particular speed after November, 1917. He began as head of the Moscow Soviet and shortly afterward became Assistant Commissar of Education and chief of the historical section. By his order the Institute of History was placed under the Academy of Sciences of the USSR. A Society of Marxist Historians, with chapters in the chief towns of the Soviet Union, was established in 1925 for the purpose of training a new generation of historians free from the influence of the older generation. He was editor of the various collections of archival materials pertaining to the Pugachev rebellion and to the Decembrist movement, and of the well-known periodical, *Krasnyi Arkhiv*, devoted to the publication of documentary sources. He was founder of the militant Marxist Historical Society and of its publication, *Istorik-Marksist*, the aims of which were (1) the maintenance of a united front of all Marxists engaged in historical research, (2) the study of Marxian methodology, (3) the combating of all anti-Marxist bourgeois distortions in historical writings, (4) the establishment of a Marxian critical literature, (5) assistance to its members in matters of research, and, finally, (6) the popularization of the Marxian historical view.[4] During the later years Pokrovsky was also engaged in an elaborate publication of sources concerning Russian foreign policy since 1878.[5]

Clio, according to Pokrovsky, was no meek goddess; any historian who dared to digress from the righteous path of Marxian tenets risked invoking the wrath of his authority. As the official judge of historical literature he saw to it that historians recognized the set Marxian canon or face the consequences. A harsh critic, he spared no one, not even his colleagues, if they happened to be "class enemies" or their allies. His acrid style made him a dangerous opponent: after the Revolution many

[4] *Istorik-Marksist*, I, 1926, 320.
[5] *Mezhdunaroniye otnosheniya v epokhu imperializma, 1878-1917* [International Relations During the Era of Imperialism], Moscow, 1931- (the set remains incomplete to date).

historians—some of them eminent figures such as Platonov, Lyubavsky, and Tarlé—suffered from the lash of his tongue, his piercing pen, and, most of all, his powerful political influence. Upon him rests a heavy moral responsibility for the utter routing of the older school and for the physical suffering inflicted upon its representatives, among whom were the most eminent members of the historical profession.[6]

Oddly enough, the position of Pokrovsky in the Communist Party was that of a relative newcomer and not of the old guard; he was not always in harmony with the "party line." On this account from time to time he had been given notice of perilous "deviations," and on as many occasions he would "admit" his ideological errors. Nevertheless Pokrovsky remained until the end of life in good standing within the ranks of the Party, wielding enormous power. In history he saw an effective political weapon, and with unusual vigor he undertook the task of transforming history from an "obscure literary form into a real, living, concrete fact." To Pokrovsky, Marxism was a means, not a dogma; an omnipotent instrument, not an inflexible pattern; while he used the field of history as a battleground on which to meet his political foes. Scarcely any other writer has ever equaled Pokrovsky's skill in subordinating history to politics. "History," he once said, "is politics fitted to the past." Whether or not one agrees with Pokrovsky's presentation, his erudition and his talent cannot be denied. As one writer put it, "No

---

[6] See the list of imprisoned and exiled scholars in the *Slavonic Review*, April, 1933, 711-13. On the early controversies within the ranks of the Society of Marxist Historians and the sorrowful lot that befell some of the men see R. Stuart Tompkins, "Communist Historical Thought," *Slavonic Review*, January, 1935, 298 ff.

On the persecution and continuous nagging of eminent scholars by some of the stump-historians see G. Zaidel, and M. Tsvibak, *Klassoviy vrag na istoricheskom fronte. Tarlé i Platonov i ikh shkoly* [The Class Enemy on the Historical Front. Tarlé and Platonov and Their Schools], Moscow-Leningrad, 1931.

future student of Russian history will be able to dispense with his works or to find complete satisfaction in them."

In general terms the periodization of Russian history as developed by Pokrovsky is sound, even if definitions of terms employed are not always lucid or convincing. He divides the past into two main periods: feudal and capitalist. The first he defines as a type of society where a natural economy, a large landholding system, a pyramid social structure, and a ruling landlord class prevail. While dealing with the Russian feudal period, Pokrovsky follows closely the thesis developed by Pavlov-Silvansky, whom, incidentally, he regarded most highly and lauded publicly. Pokrovsky refuted the old methodology that started with the shift of population to the northeast and thereby originated the national state in Russia. Nor did he accept the view that ascribed decisive effects upon the state to the Mongolian period. He regarded the development of a natural economy not necessarily as a contributing factor, as formerly believed, since, as he rightly argued, the Kievan period had already witnessed a similar development. Likewise he challenged the method of dividing history according to political institutions; he suggested instead that the past be divided according to the evolution of the material culture, the development of trade, and the appearance of a money economy. This was a departure from former methods of periodization, and many historians subsequently have followed Pokrovsky without acknowledging it. Thus far Pokrovsky stood on firm ground.

When, however, Pokrovsky undertook to analyze the era of imperialism, his interpretation proved more shaky. The origin of imperialism he ascribed to the introduction of protective trade policies leading to the formation of national monopolies within the state; these in turn, motivated by schemes of expansion beyond national frontiers, were bound to carry with them the imperialistic policies that led to inevitable conflicts. This was precisely the shape of developments that led Russia to war in the Far East in 1904 and subsequent wars elsewhere. The entire architectonic system of Pokrovsky is somewhat flimsily mechanistic and served to expose him eventually to violent criticism even from Party members themselves. Though criticizing bourgeois historians, he based his antithesis on the very errors for which he derided his opponents. His economic Marxism did not depart basically from Klyuchevsky's "economism." His effort to demonstrate dialectic unity throughout the entire course of history was overshadowed by his accounts of the socio-economic formations. By lumping all social developments into a single narrative he naively believed that he would be able to achieve an elucidating synthesis which was bound to explain the underlying forces of history.

Pokrovsky either failed to see or neglected to mention the fact that at various periods the state was closely related to the form of production which he himself considered vital for the understanding of history. Though employing dialectical materialism, he never succeeded in proving the social implications of this relationship; once stripped of the presentation Pokrovsky's entire thesis was robbed of its essence and bound to become a lifeless mechanical process, a mere account of an exchange of commodities and purposeless play of economic factors. The picture was thereby oversimplified: in the absence of commodity exchange, society is defined as feudal; when commodity exchange and trade capital make their entrance, society becomes capitalist. The pattern fits even less when Pokrovsky initiates the subject of class formation and class struggle. These he saw in terms of the international struggle and not as national phenomena. Except for the peasant rebellions, which

Pokrovsky treated as a local development, he presented the labor movement as an inseparable part of a global class struggle. The entire interpretation left many questions unanswered while a number of the answers raised only more queries.

In summary, what were Pokrovsky's ideas about history? Primarily that history is an effective branch of politics, or, as he phrased it, "history is politics projected into the past." Thus Pokrovsky explicitly believed that the frame of reference from which history is written is of far greater importance in determining its validity than the actual research. In his view bourgeois historians were in honest error, for they knew of no other frame of reference than their own. Their "scientific history" was nothing more or less than a defense of the bourgeois system. Since history, according to Pokrovsky, is fundamentally an account of all human activity and since the latter is motivated exclusively by material needs, the result was quite obvious: history became a record of an inevitable process with little or no room for the role of leadership or of cultural determinants, as was pointed out previously.

This is important to bear in mind, for Pokrovsky's views led his followers into endless embarrassments after his death and caused violent criticism of his writings. It is well to note also that, though the bourgeois are censured, no antiforeign sentiments appear in Pokrovsky's work. The teaching of history in the schools during the Pokrovsky era serves to throw some light upon the subject. In 1923 the People's Commissar for Education forbade any teaching which might stimulate nationalism or encourage imitation of the past; historical science must not tolerate such bourgeois anachronisms as patriotism and nationalism. Russian political and literary history were discontinued as subjects in the schools.

The rigors of writing history in the Pokrovsky era were somewhat mitigated during the period of the New Economic Policy (NEP), 1921-1928. In those years Soviet historians went so far as to attend a number of meetings of the World Conference of Historians. The general course of the meetings was uneventful, with the exception of the somewhat tense relations between the Bolshevik and the *émigré* historians. This policy of diffident co-operation with bourgeois historians was, however, short-lived and broke down completely under the strains engendered by the split between Leon Trotsky and Joseph Stalin, the inauguration of the Five-Year Plan (1928), and the great depression, which revived hopes for a world revolution.

The tightening of party lines for a renewed struggle was made apparent in several ways. Beginning in 1930, a new drive against bourgeois historians both at home and abroad was initiated in the pages of the *Istorik Marksist*. Eugene Tarlé a non-party-member of the Society of Marxist Historians and a prominent historian of the French Revolution, was criticized by Pokrovsky as a bourgeois historian. Tarlé was banished from the capital and sent east in 1931. His principal errors were the identification of the foreign policy of the USSR with that of tsarist Russia and of assigning to Germany a major share of guilt for the First World War. The latter opinion ran directly counter to the Pokrovsky concept of economic pressures as the sole explanatory factor in history.

In March, 1931, the Society of Marxist Historians began publication of the journal *Class Warfare* (*Borba klassov*), which was to be devoted to the study of the postwar period, especially in the USSR. Its object was announced as the "militant education of the masses." The appearance of this journal marked the height of Pokrovsky's influence, but his triumph rested upon shifting sands. A number of factors caused a radical change. Among these may be mentioned first the increased aspiration for national autonomy best manifested among the intellectual groups of Ukraine, Georgia, and Kazakstan, and the purges of their respective Academies of Science.

During the revolution the Bolsheviks had gained the support of the various national component groups of Russia by the promise of complete autonomy. The pledge to support the various national cultures of the USSR gradually became a source of serious embarrassment. Especially was this true in the case of the Ukrainians, whose historians, under the leadership of Hrushevsky and others, devoted themselves with intensified fervor to Ukrainian nationalism rather than to Marxist tasks. Other contributing factors were the rising military threat of Germany and Japan, the repercussions of the widening chasm between the Stalinist and Trotskyite factions, and the growing disillusionment with the meager results obtained by Soviet historians in the field of education. A survey of schools as early as 1929 had revealed an appalling ignorance of history, a low intellectual level, and the absence of any originality of thought among the pupils.[7]

The first definite sign of the anticipated changes was given by Stalin in his speech in 1931, in which he complained that within intellectual circles theory lagged behind practice. Shortly thereafter a decree of the Central Committee of the Communist Party called for a complete overhaul of study and research in all fields. Early in 1932 Stalin spoke again upon the same subject. To these stimuli the Society of Marxist Historians responded with several soul-searching reports denouncing many of their members for backwardness. The same year the *Istorik Marksist,* after being temporarily suspended, reappeared in new form. The incident not only was significant of change but was

---

[7] L. Mamet, "Istoriya i obshchestvenno-politicheskoye vospitaniye [History and Socio-Political Education]," *Istorik-Marksist,* XIV, 1929, 159 ff.

portentous, in that Pokrovsky was editor-in-chief of the journal. Equally significant was the abandonment of the study of foreign history and the concentration upon the home front.

## After Pokrovsky

A complete *volte-face* in Soviet historiography occurred during the 'thirties. Changes followed one another swiftly and assumed many different forms. Pokrovsky became the principal victim, but it was his personal good fortune to die in 1932, before his work was completely condemned. It gradually became the custom to denounce Pokrovsky's work as unsound "schematic sociology" and "mechanical economism." By the middle of 1934 the sweeping nature of the oncoming changes became quite evident.

The most important and conclusive evidence of the shift in policy was the realization that the plan of communist indoctrination by way of history had been a failure. This view was basic in the joint decrees of the Council of People's Commissars of the USSR and the Central Committee of the All-Union Communist Party (Bolsheviks) of May 16, 1934. They pronounced government disapproval of all former abstract and formal history textbooks and teaching as conducted to date. They ordered that history be taught in chronological sequence and that the students be required to memorize the more important dates and events. The "bourgeois deviationist" and enemy of Pokrovsky, Eugene Tarlé, was summoned back to Moscow from his place of banishment. Momentarily the old-time history textbook and time-tested method of teaching made its reappearance. The decree of May 16th is of such historic importance that its full citation is justified. It reads:[8]

[8] *Izvestiya,* May 16, 1934.

DECREE OF THE COUNCIL OF PEOPLE'S COM-
MISSARS OF THE U.S.S.R. AND THE CENTRAL
COMMITTEE OF THE ALL-UNION COMMU-
NIST PARTY (BOLSHEVIKS)

CONCERNING THE TEACHING OF CIVIC HISTORY
IN THE SCHOOLS OF THE U.S.S.R.

---

The Council of People's Commissars and the Central Committee
of the All-Union Communist Party (Bolsheviks) state that the
teaching of history in the schools of the U.S.S.R. is not administered
satisfactorily. Textbooks and even the teaching are of an abstract,
schematic nature. Instead of teaching civic history in a lively manner, narrating in their chronological sequence the most important
events and facts accompanied by characterizations of historical
figures, the students are given abstract definitions of social-economic
structures, thus substituting obscure schemes for the coherent narration of civic history.

An essential requirement for the thorough mastery of history is
the observance of a chronological sequence in the presentation of
historical facts, personalities, and chronological dates. Only such a
course of history can assure the student accessibility to, and clarity
and concreteness in, historical records; on this basis alone can correct
analysis and synthesis of historical events be arrived at, which will
guide the student to a Marxist understanding of history.

In accordance with this, the Council of People's Commissars of
the U.S.S.R. and the Central Committee of the All-Union Communist Party (Bolsheviks) decree:

1. By June, 1935, the following new textbooks shall be prepared:
(*a*) a history of the ancient world; (*b*) a history of the Middle
Ages; (*c*) a modern history; (*d*) a history of the U.S.S.R.; (*e*) a
modern history of dependent and colonial countries.

2. Approval of the following list of members of groups entrusted

with compiling the new historical textbooks shall be confirmed: [there follows the list of names] . . .

3. In order to train qualified specialists in history, the faculties of history at the Universities of Moscow and Leningrad shall be restored on September 1, 1934, with a contingent of students to be admitted in the autumn of one hundred and fifty for each of the faculties, the term of training to be five years.

Chairman of the Council of People's Commissars of the U.S.S.R.

(signed) V. Molotov

Secretary of the Central Committee of the All-Union Communist Party (Bolsheviks),

(signed) J. Stalin

The order of the day was now history textbooks with less stress upon sociological deductions and generalities and more upon facts; they must include descriptive biographies of historical personages and follow a chronological order in telling the story of the past. Historical writing was expected to be scholarly and based on first-hand data, although what constituted scholarship or scientific method was not quite clear. This was defined as best as could be by one prominent Soviet historian, A. Pankratova, thus: "To produce a scientific history textbook is to create a Bolshevik science. The problem in preparing a Bolshevik history textbook of any period is to demonstrate history in the light of our own grandiose epoch and the historical struggle of the laboring class for a proletarian dictatorship and socialism in the entire world." [9]

This decree hardly augured well for scholarship. From Pankratova's elucidation it is evident that basically little had changed, since political motivation still remained the dominat-

---

[9] A. Pankratova, "Za bolshevistskoye preobrazovaniye istorii [For a Bolshevik Reorganization of History Teaching]," *Bolshevik*, XXIII, 1934, 40.

ing factor in the writing of history. The scheme recommended by government officials as to the organization of the accumulated "scientific data" is not without interest. As an illustration, Stalin had outlined the pattern for modern history as follows: (1) rise of modern capitalism, 1789-1871; (2) decay and defeat of capitalism, 1871-1918; (3) postwar imperialism and economic crisis: Fascism and the struggle for colonies in western Europe; planned economy and triumphant socialist construction in the USSR.

The response to this order from above was soon to follow. The demand for a better knowledge of the ancient world was the first to be met. In July, 1937, the first quarterly publication appeared under the title, *Messenger of Ancient History* (*Vyestnik drevney istorii*), which included the writings not only of Soviet historians but of recognized foreign authorities as well. Even here, Soviet patriotism triumphed, as can be judged by the following announcement of the editors: "Since the history of the peoples of the USSR will always constitute an essential part of general history, we shall consider it our duty to study the problems of ancient history primarily as they relate to our motherland." [10] The new publication proclaimed that its main purpose would be a systematic study of the formerly oppressed peoples of the USSR, and for this purpose the editorial committee made an appeal to students of the Ukraine, White Russia, Uzbekistan, Kazakstan, Georgia, Armenia, Azerbeydzhan, and other parts of the Union to co-operate in the enterprise.

Simultaneously with the condemnation of the older textbooks and teaching methods, criticism was levied against the founder of the Marxist school, Pokrovsky, who in an atmosphere of acrimonious charges was denounced as the man responsible for the vulgarization of history. It was pointed out that Pokrovsky

[10] *Izvestiya*, July 22, 1937, 4.

began to write at the beginning of the twentieth century, at a time when "Marxism in Russia was quite widespread not only among the working class but also among the petty bourgeois and even in bourgeois circles of the intelligentsia." It was also a time when opportunism flourished, giving rise to the "Legal Marxists," who were condemned by Lenin himself. Pokrovsky, it was recalled, was closely associated with this apostate group.[11] Under the party baton a chorus of protests rose against his historical method, and soon there followed a wholesale denunciation of the entire school which Pokrovsky had so painstakingly built up. Marxist writers suddenly threw overboard a ballast which only recently had been considered imperative for smooth sailing in Soviet waters; the impregnable truth of yesterday became the unfortunate error of today. The man who had been hailed as the "most devout and unswerving Communist, disciple of Lenin, consecrating all his powers to the struggle for the proletariat," [12] the person who had been proclaimed in dithyrambic terms the greatest historian and student of philosophy, who had rebelled against schematism in historical study, who had combatted "the vulgarization of dialectic materialism," and who had always been mindful of his Communist affiliations[13]—this man was now brought to post-mortem trial and found guilty of the very heresies which he had formerly ascribed to his opponents.

Pokrovsky was now charged with advocating a too subjective conception of Marxism and held responsible for its infiltration into the writings of others; he was blamed for the arbitrary attributions of modern social and economic ideas to bygone generations utterly ignorant of them; ululations were raised against

[11] F. Gorokhov, "An Anti-Marxist Theory of History," *International Literature*, IX, 1937, 73.

[12] *Izvestiya akademii nauk, O.O.N.,* Ser. VII, Vol. IX, 1932, 782.

[13] *Vyestnik kommunisticheskoy akademii*, IV, 1933, 33, 48.

his doctrine that Communism needed no objective science; he was ridiculed for forcing the course of history into a Procrustean bed of materialism; and, finally, he was charged with the advocacy of a rigid conception of Imperial Russia now regarded as the worst historical blunder of them all.[14] "He saw Tsarism as a static instrument of trade and capital, not as did Lenin, who saw in Tsarism, too, movement and development," wrote one critic. The Central Committee of the Communist Party specifically censured the "vulgar, sociological views" of this former leader of the Marxian school, declaring that "bourgeois subjectivism can only be defeated by a sufficient accumulation of objective knowledge."[15]

The campaign against Pokrovsky soon followed the violent purges of the Trotskyite heresy. The two issues were soon identified as belonging to one heretical sect, or, as one observer remarked, "both were allowed to be lost in the lampless depths of historical mystery." The persecution of Trotskyism reached deep into the ranks of the historians. A vicious campaign was begun against numerous prominent Soviet historians: writers like Piontkovsky, Vanag, Friedland, Oksman, M. Lurye, and a host of others were suddenly discovered to be "agents of Trotsky" or "smugglers" of Pokrovsky's ideas. Strangely enough, Trotsky himself never accepted Pokrovsky as the master of

[14] M. Kammari, "Teoreticheskiye korni oshibochnykh vzglyadov M. N. Pokrovskogo [Theoretical Basis of the Fallacious Historical Views of M. N. Pokrovsky]," *Pod znamenem marksizma*, IV, 1936, 5-6.

[15] N. Bukharin, "Nuzhna li nam marksistskaya istoricheskaya nauka? [Do We Need a Marxist Historical Science?]," *Izvestiya*, January 27, 1936, 3-4; *Moscow News*, September 1, 1937. See also Pankratova, *op. cit.*, 32-51.

Stalin's view concerning the writing of history was presented in the *Istorik-Marksist*, II, 1937, 29-31, and in *Krasniy Arkhiv*, III (82), 1937, 3-5. It is perhaps appropriate to recall the letter from Lenin to Pokrovsky, the first paragraph of which reads: "I congratulate you very heartily on your success; I like your new book, *Brief History of Russia*, immensely. The construction and the narrative are original. It reads with tremendous interest. It should, in my opinion, be translated into the European languages." See M. N. Pokrovsky, *A Brief History of Russia*, tr. by D. S. Mirsky, I, 5.

Marxism. "While taking due cognizance of the erudition, con-
scientiousness, and talent of the deceased scholar," he writes,
"it is impossible not to state that Pokrovsky failed to master the
method of Marxism, and instead of providing an analysis of
the continued interaction of all the elements in the historical
process, he provided for each occasion mechanistic constructions
*ad hoc,* without bothering about their dialectic interconnection."

Since "Soviet patriotism" had now regained its respect in the
current vocabulary, demands were also made for a nationalistic
interpretation of history, with greater reverence for the nation's
past. This tendency was aptly demonstrated by an incident in
November, 1936, when the government suddenly suppressed the
comic opera *Knights* (*Bogatyri*), on the ground that the
libretto, though written by the eminent Communist writer,
Demyan Byednyiy, was not only historically incorrect but was
also "a grossly disrespectful misrepresentation of the country's
history." The official decree banning the luxuriously staged performance is illuminating, and the official stand, as announced
in the press, is worth citing. It reads, in part, as follows:[16]

It is well know that the Christianization of Russia was one of
the principal factors in the *rapprochement* of the backward Russian
people with the people of Byzantium and, later, with the people of
higher culture. It is also well known how important was the part
that clergymen, particularly Greek clergymen, played in promoting
literacy in the Russia of the Kievan period.

Marxists are not admirers of feudalism, and still less of capitalism.
But Marx, Engels, Lenin, and Stalin many times noted in their
works that at certain historical stages feudalism and, later, capitalism
were instruments of progress in human history, promoting the
productivity of labor and fostering culture and science. Thus,
Byednyiy's libretto reveals not only an anti-Marxist but also a light-

[16] *Za kommunisticheskoye prosveshcheniye,* May 16, 1937.

minded attitude toward history and a cheapening of the history of our people.

The instructions to teachers of Russian history that followed the episode required that they explode the fascist theories of racial superiority and repudiate the humble role in the progress of humanity that had been ascribed to the Slavs. The same instructions requested teachers to present the official adoption of Christianity in 988 by Prince Vladimir as "an act of progress in the history of the Russian people"; the growth of Imperial Russia should be interpreted not only as a result of the imperialistic gluttony of the Muscovite princes but also as a natural, progressive, national development; the leaders in the struggle against Poland in 1612, Minin and Pozharsky, had now become true sons of the people, a statement supported by a reference to no other than N. Polevoy.[17] The war of 1812 against Napoleon had to be shown as an act of elevated mass emotion—a united people rising against foreign occupation and in defense of national freedom. Finally, Peter I was to be introduced as a great statesman and a colorful historical figure.[18] No longer was Peter to be looked upon as a willful despot, but rather as a leader who conceived profound reforms and by his tireless activity awakened a dormant nation, a man whose conduct others must imitate in order to advance Western civilization and culture.[19] Not only did historical figures of the "Socialist Fatherland" undergo a drastic face-lifting, but even historical dramas and operas had to answer the recent ebullient call to national

[17] *Izvestiya*, September 15, 1937. On the latest interpretation of the adoption of Christianity in Kievan Russia and the correction of the "pseudoscientific views of Pokrovsky's school," see S. Bakrushin, "K voprosu o kreshchenii Kievskoy Rusi," *Istorik-Marksist*, II, 1937, 40, 63.

[18] See *Za kommunisticheskoye prosvyeshcheniye*, February 14, 1937. Note also *Izvestiya*, August 22 and 24, 1937; *Bolshevik*, XVIII, 1937, 39 ff.

[19] *Izvestiya*, August 24, 1937, 2. Cf. M. Pokrovsky, *Russkaya istoriya* (1933 ed.), II, 236 ff., 300-02.

colors. For example, Glinka's opera, *A Life for the Tsar,* was revised and performed under the name of *Ivan Susanin.* Instead of the former chorus song,

> Glorify thyself, glorify thyself, Holy Russia!
> Upon the Russian throne ascends
> Our Russian legitimate Tsar!
> He comes to us in glory,
> Our Orthodox Sovereign-Tsar!

the new version was:

> Glorify thyself, native soil.
> Glorify thyself, my native land.
> May forever and to eternity be strong
> Our beloved native land.

On August 22, 1937, the judges composing a special government commission announced the awarding of the second prize (75,000 rubles) for the most satisfactory textbook on the history of the USSR.[20] The first prize had not been awarded. For the benefit of future writers the decision was accompanied by critical comments which constitute an illuminating document on the subject.[21] Omitting some of the most slanted annotations,

---

[20] *Kratky kurs istorii SSSR* [A Brief Course of the History of the USSR], ed. by Professor A. V. Shestakov, Moscow, 1937.

The opening paragraph of this textbook reads as follows: "The USSR is the land of socialism. There is only one socialist country on the globe—it is our motherland." And the closing paragraph of the Introduction chants: "We love our motherland and we must know her wonderful history well. Whoever knows history will better understand current life, will fight the enemies of our country better, and will consolidate socialism."

[21] The complete text of the decision may be found in *Izvestiya,* August 22, 1937, 2. Also P. Drozdov, " 'Istoricheskaya shkola' Pokrovskogo [The 'Historical School' of Pkrovsky]," *Pravda,* March 28, 1937, 2-3.

such as those that pertain to the process of the Russian Revolution, the role played by the Communist Party, or the importance of the Stalin constitution, one finds others which point to a more constructive approach to historical writing, based, however, on a strictly national interpretation. The judges directed the attention of those who might in future strive for similar awards to blunders committed by previous contestants. The fact must be recognized that Christianity marked a step forward; its introduction brought in certain elements of the higher Byzantine culture and helped to spread literacy among the Slavs. Contestants must also not overlook the progressive role the monasteries played during the early days in Russia after Christianity had been officially adopted, when they were indeed valuable agencies for the promotion of literacy and colonial advancement. Future writers must be able to discern in Bohdan Khmelnitsky's struggle against Poland and Turkey not only violence but also a constructive national conflict for emancipation from foreign occupation. Similarly, the incorporation of the Ukraine and of Georgia into Russia should be interpreted not as an act of imperialism, but as a circumstance dictated by historical forces. Georgia, for instance, faced but two alternatives: either absorption by Persia and Turkey or the protectorateship of Russia. Exactly the same sort of alternative confronted the Ukraine, which was forced to choose between Poland and Turkey on the one hand and Moscow on the other. Moscow was the more logical choice, since it seemed a lesser evil both to Georgia and to the Ukraine.[22] Thus began the ingenious *lesser evil* interpretation of Russian expansion.

The jury also cautioned contestants against overidealizing

[22] Cf. Pokrovsky's interpretations in *Russkaya istoriya* (1933 ed.), II, 153-54, 160, 168. See also *Diplomatiya i voyny tsarskoy Rossii v XIX stolyetii* [The Diplomacy and Wars of Tsarist Russia in the 19th Century], *passim*.

earlier revolts, including such distinctly reactionary uprisings as those of the *Stryeltsy* (the Moscow garrison) against the reforms of Peter I. The final criticism of particular interest was a strictly "dated" bit of historical wisdom for German enlightenment. The judges directed attention to the fact that many of the contestants inadequately interpreted the significance of a number of past events, for example, the historical battle between the Novgorodians and the Teutonic Knights on Lake Chudskoye (Peipus) in 1242. That battle, which ended in a fiasco for the Teutonic Knights, marked the earliest defeat of German plans for eastward colonization. The lesson to be derived from that in Berlin should have been clear enough!

University professors were now specifically forbidden to make arbitrary interpretations of history, to minimize the functions of the state, or to neglect the distinction between just and unjust wars. A complete revision in the teaching of history was called for. The textbooks used throughout the Soviet Union, written by Pokrovsky and his disciples, were jointly condemned by Joseph Stalin, Sergey Kirov, and Andrey Zhdanov. They deplored the treatment of the Russian people as remote from the culture of the West. The trio also scored historians for neglecting Western democratic and socialist movements and their effects upon the social development of Russia. Finally, the influence of Western ideas was not to be ignored. These instructions became fundamental to the new "line" but were destined also to become from the date of their issue a source of unending grief to historians.[23]

Under a shower of new directions historians were ordered to rediscover the past of Russia. Ivan IV was rehabilitated and became an eminent statesman, a "people's ruler and great

[23] *Bolshevik,* No. 3, 1936, 60-66; No. 5, 1936, 53-68; No. 8, 1936, 32-42; No. 9, 1937, 8-10.

patriot." [24] "His reforms assured Russia order within and effective security against aggression from without. His policy was warmly supported by the Russian people." The reforms of 1861 were reinterpreted as the beginning of the bourgeois epoch rather than as a defensive feint of autocracy. Tarlé, recently restored to grace and spurred by the new official declarations, commenced works in which the careers of Alexander Suvorov, Mikhail Kutuzov, and Pyotr Bagration reappeared in full glory. The war of 1812 was interpreted as a people's war won by the mighty exertions of the Russian masses under the inspired and skillful leadership of the rediscovered military heroes.

A fitting illustration of historical interpretation to accommodate the new orientation may be found in Tarlé's *Bonaparte* (1937):[25]

Never did Napoleon, or his marshals, or their companions in arms, speak of the war of 1812 as a "national" war, in the same sense that they spoke of the Spanish guerrilla war as a "national" war. Nor could they compare the two phenomena. The war in Russia lasted six months. Of these six months, the first three saw Napoleon constantly victorious as he advanced along a direct line from Kovno to Vilna to Smolensk to Moscow, interrupted by battles and petty skirmishes with the regular Russian army. There was, however, not a single national mass revolt against the French— neither then nor after Napoleon's entry into Moscow. Indeed, there were occurrences of quite a contrary nature, as when the peasants of Smolensk complained to the French authorities that their master, the landowner, Engelhardt, had been guilty of betraying the French.

[24] P. Yu. Vipper, *Ivan Grozniy*, Moscow, 1944, 57; S. B. Bakhrushin, *Nauchniye trudy*, Moscow, 1945, Vol. II, 355.

See also N. K. Cherkasov, *Zapiski sovetskogo aktyora* [Memoirs of a Soviet Actor], Moscow, 1953, 380-82. Cf. S. M. Dubrovsky, "Protiv idealizatsii deyatelnosti Ivana IV [Against the Idealization of Ivan IV]," *Voprosy istorii*, VIII, 1956, 121-29.

[25] Eugene Tarlé, *Bonaparte*, New York, 1937, 302-03.

... The peasants as a group took no part in these activities. ... It is clear that if the Spanish guerrilla warfare might justifiably be called a national war, it would be impossible to apply this term to any Russian movement in the war of 1812. People began to regard even the burning of Smolensk and Moscow and the firing of villages as manifestations of "national war," overlooking the fact that these were systematic acts of the Russian army in its retreat to Moscow.

For this interpretation Professor Tarlé was sternly rebuked. No more than a year later, in his following book, the author took into consideration the admonishing reviews and none too subtle warnings, and changed his thesis completely. In his new book, *The Invasion of Russia by Napoleon,* Tarlé now presented the following picture:[26]

The guerrilla movement that began immediately after the battle of Borodino, as we shall see further, could have attained success only by means of the most active voluntary aid sedulously rendered by the Russian peasantry. This insatiable hatred toward the usurpers, marauders, and oppressors, ignorant of whence they came, was expressed by the way in which the Russian peasants joined the army of 1812 and how they fought. The national character of this war could express itself immediately in the organized form—the army. ... Further, in describing the retreat of the Grand Army, I refer in detail to the guerrilla warfare, to the participation in it of the peasants. ... According to the unanimous opinion of the French, absolutely nowhere except in Spain did the peasants in the villages show such desperate resistance as in Russia. "Each village was transformed at our approach into either a bonfire or a fortress," so the French wrote afterwards. ... It was precisely the

---

[26] Eugene Tarlé, *Nashestviye Napoleona na Rossiyu, 1812 goda* [Napoleon's Invasion of Russia, 1812], Moscow, 1938.

peasant who destroyed the magnificent cavalry of Murat, first in the world, under whose victorious onslaught all European armies ran; it was this very army that the Russian peasant destroyed. . . . One cannot write in the history of 1812 a separate chapter on "The National War." The *entire* war against the invading Napoleon was solidly a national war. Napoleon counted in his strategy the number of his troops and the troops of Alexander, but he had to fight with the Russian people, whom Napoleon had forgotten. It was the people's arm that inflicted upon the greatest commander in world's history the fatal blow.

The order of the day was to extol Russia's past and glorify national pride. Some historians went at it with a vengeance!

By 1937 the teaching of Soviet patriotism had overshadowed former internationalism and "mechanical economism"; the term "people's democracy" as different from "bourgeois democracy" found its acceptance in Soviet parlance. The role of the leader both in tsarist and in Soviet Russia was stressed. The struggle for Communism was given relatively little space. The reliable barometer of trends in the world of history, namely, the professional journals, reacted strongly. In January, 1937, *Class Warfare* (*Borba klassov*) was renamed *Historical Journal* (*Istorichesky zhurnal*).

The growing menace of Nazi Germany inspired the relative neglect of internationalism, stimulated Soviet patriotism, and necessitated great stress upon Western democracy with the possible benefits that the USSR might derive therefrom. The new campaign was aimed at a cultivation of greater faith in Soviet leadership (later to be derided as the "cult of the individual"), and the eschewal of the theory of class struggle, as well as the doctrine of the disparate nature of the Soviet peoples—a thesis formerly prominent in most of the historical writings. In no uncertain terms Tarlé later explained the fallacious views of the Pokrovsky school thus:[27]

What went on, in essence, was the moral disarmament of the Russian people. If a nation consists only of drunkards, sluggards, and idlers, of Oblomovs, is such a nation worth much? Is it possible that the "fair-skinned Aryans" are really right in committing their atrocities? Is General Reichenau right in saying that there are no cultural values in Russia? Many who showed this tendency in their historical work did not think of these consequences and might have been horrified if they had seen them. But objectively their work was harmful.

The Second World War caused even greater emphasis upon the foregoing tendencies in the historical writings of the USSR. The movement went to such an extreme that A. M. Pankratova, in an essay entitled "Twenty-five Years of Soviet Historical Science," claimed S. M. Solovyev and V. O. Klyuchevsky as part of a proud tradition.[28] A year later Tarlé extolled Solovyev as the exceptional prerevolutionary historian for having traced the course of Russia's foreign relations; he indicated that Klyuchevsky, Pokrovsky, and others had dismally failed the Russian people in this respect and had not acquainted them with the long tradition of a German desire for the annihilation of Russia.

The end of the war meant further departure from the former interpretation, which was bound to affect historical writing profoundly. The historical profession was seized by a cult of patriotic tribalism. Control by the party and the government over

[27] E. V. Tarlé, "Soviet Historical Research," *Science and Society,* VII, 1943, 230-31.

[28] V. P. Volgin, E. V. Tarlé, and A. M. Pankratova (editors), *Dvadtsat-pyat lyet istoricheskoy nauki v SSSR* [Twenty-Five Years of Historical Science in the USSR], Moscow, 1942, 7-8.

historians was intensified; survivors of the Pokrovsky school found themselves in the unenviable position of either revising their former interpretation or being labeled as vagrant cosmopolites. The observer, in endeavoring to discover trends which have been dominant since 1945, is forced to accept one of three conclusions: (1) that the party has not followed a consistent policy and that under the pressure of foreign and domestic problems it has oscillated between several different objectives, with the result that confusion and sorrow have characterized the efforts of the faithful; (2) that two or more schools of historians have engaged in internecine war for the mastery of the profession; or (3) that the party has indicated its new policies in so slovenly a manner that historians have been confused and have not understood the "line."

Probably elements of all three have been present. Taken singly, the first possibility appears to be the most plausible. As has been seen, Party discipline over historians has been good, and, as will be later shown, Stalin had taken a very active interest in the writing of history. The quarrels among historians were important only in revealing Party policy and not as determining policy itself. Because inefficiency in ideological warfare has not usually been characteristic of the Party, the third possibility in large measure can be ruled out.

It is almost superfluous to indicate that the appearance of confusion or indecisiveness in Party policy may have been not only the result of external pressures but also evidence of the existence of factions contending for control. It is not feasible to examine the latter possibility, for there is no convincing evidence to support any conclusions. Furthermore, so long as Stalin held the Party reins in firm hands, the probability of a serious struggle within the Party can only be judged by later events, as after the famous speech of N. Khrushchev at the Twentieth Congress of the Communist Party on February 25, 1956.

## Postwar Historical Writing

In June, 1945, the first indication of a new shift in the "line" was a ruling of the Central Committee of the Communist Party notifying subscribers to *Istorichesky zhurnal* that publication of the periodical had been suspended and that a new leading journal would be initiated in its place. The new publication, *Problems of History* (*Voprosy istorii*), was to have a different board of editors to replace the old group, which had failed to carry out its assignments.

The name of the new journal indicated a desire to give more attention to theoretical questions. Its announced objective was to act as a progressive influence on research outside as well as inside the USSR. It was to be a "militant organ of the Marxist-Leninist historical school" and was to apply dialectical materialism to the past. This announcement seemed to have indicated at least a partial reversion to the historical principles of the pre-1934 period and was probably designed to counteract the narrowly nationalistic fervor produced by the war.

On February 9, 1946, Stalin delivered a speech in which he made it quite clear that a major shift in the "line" was either taking place or was about to occur. As a candidate for the Supreme Soviet of the Union, he declared that the people must prepare themselves for the wars which would be inevitable as long as the capitalist system endured. Stalin voiced his confidence that Soviet scientists could overtake and surpass their fellows abroad in the coming struggle. The speech appears to have been the signal and command for new developments and projects in all phases of cultural and scientific work. In the field of history great activity soon followed. The Institute of History of the Academy of Sciences evolved a five-year plan. A twelve-volume collective *History of the USSR,* designed to provide a Marxist interpretation of Russian history from the earliest times, was projected. Special studies of the towns, peasantry, proletariat, domestic markets, and diplomatic, foreign, and military affairs were planned.

Before the plans of the Institute of History were formally launched, Colonel-General Zhdanov, secretary of the Central Committee of the Communist Party, in a speech delivered before the Committee in September, 1946, rapped the "cultural front." [29] Zhdanov made more specific what Stalin had earlier only alluded to—the necessity of uprooting the still lingering obsequiousness to the contemporary bourgeois culture of the West. The antiforeign theme was clear and unequivocal; the primary thesis was that both feudalism and the later bourgeois system created art and literature which asserted the superiority of their respective system. This being the case, and because the socialist system embodies all the best in the history of human civilization and culture, it is capable of creating the most advanced literature. The creation of a socialist literature, Zhdanov maintained, is the obligation of all Soviet writers in order to rebuff the "hideous slanders and attacks against Soviet culture." A further task was to expose and attack bourgeois culture, to show its decadent nature and prevent its disintegrating effects upon Soviet art.

Zhdanov's speech might be interpreted as a phase of a new campaign for world revolution. A drift in this direction was rapidly occurring. At the same time, the stress of postwar foreign affairs either augmented or was concomitant with a surging nationalism. Definite efforts were to be made to reconcile

[29] *Bolshevik,* Nos. 17-18, 1946, 4-19.

the internationalism of communism with the nationalist fervor of Russia. The words of Zhdanov in practice could be interpreted either way.

Apparently the historians, in creating their five-year plan, had not anticipated accurately the magnitude of the shift in policy, for on November 30, 1946, their program was denounced in the pages of *Culture and Life* (*Kultura i zhizn*), the official organ of the board for propaganda and agitation of the Central Committee of the Communist Party. The plan of the historians was criticized for neglecting the following subjects: the history of America and Asia in the age of imperialism, colonial exploitation, revolutionary parties and movements abroad, Moscow's role of leadership in world revolutionary movements, the influence exerted by the Russian people upon the historical growth of the nationalities of the Soviet Union, and the period after 1920.

Zhdanov's attack upon the West may have been in some measure the reaction to an official desire to eradicate the fairly friendly attitude toward the countries of the West which had risen under the necessity of war. The attack was intensified, and Marxist scholars were notified that "academic" and "objective" research was unworthy of them. All "subservience" to Western culture was to be terminated. Real objectivity was to be found in the class interests of the proletariat, which are identical with the objective course of historical development. So historians once again endeavored to bring their work into conformity with the policies of the party. The textbook, *History of the USSR* (1939), was revised in 1947, this time giving greater emphasis to foreign affairs and accentuating the important role of the Great Russian people in the history of the fatherland. The latter change indicated that the old problem of separatism still plagued the Party.

The revision failed, however, to win the praise of the Party. In November, 1947, *Bolshevik*, official magazine of the Central Committee, suggested that historians should once again toil over a textbook. The specific criticism in this case was that the text produced was too "factual" and that it demonstrated inadequate attention to the question of "theoretical generalization." This interesting criticism must have bewildered the profession completely, for the last major pronouncement upon the subject had been that of Stalin in 1934, denouncing schematic sociological approaches and advocating a factual, chronological survey of history. Pokrovsky had long since been denounced and his writings declared heretical, but his basic approach (not his specific idea) was again finding favor. Moreover, to this was now added an intense sentiment of cultural chauvinism which manifested itself in every publication. "The feeling of Soviet national pride," declared *Bolshevik*, "is based on the understanding of the great and unequaled superiority of Soviet culture, ideology, science, and morals." [30]

Thus far the only evidence was of a shift in policy, but there had been no evidence of reactions. N. L. Rubinstein, author of a notable work on Russian historiography, which was written during the years 1936-1939 and published in 1941, held a high place in the ranks of the historical profession. [31] In 1948 Rubinstein began to sense the importance of the changes; anticipating the oncoming storm, he opened a campaign against his own book, denouncing its thesis by characterizing it as "formal, objective, and academic." Other grievous faults which he con-

[30] P. Vyshinsky, "Sovietsky patriotizm i ego velikaya sila [Soviet Patriotism and its Great Strength]," *Bolshevik*, No. 18, 1947, 28-29. See also G. F. Aleksandrov, "Kosmopolitizm—ideologiya imperialisticheskoy burzhuazii [Cosmopolitanism—the Ideology of Imperialist Bourgeoisie]," *Voprosy filosofii*, No. 3, 1948, 174 ff; *Bolshevik*, No. 22, 1947, 26 ff.

[31] N. L. Rubinstein, *Russkaya istoriografiya* [Russian Historiography], Moscow, 1941.

fessed were his failure to cast off the traditional point of view of prerevolutionary writers, to adopt a military Party spirit, and to appreciate the theories of Lenin and Stalin as establishing an entirely new science of history rather than as the outcome of previously existing thought. Rubinstein's confession and self-chastisement were quickly followed by the attacks of his colleagues.

During 1948 the ideological struggle was further intensified. Deputy Premier G. M. Malenkov called for the encouragement of Soviet patriotism and for the eradication of Western bourgeois culture, which in his opinion made Soviet citizens easy prey to the "agents of American and British imperialism." It is important to note the use of the expression "Soviet patriotism," for an ingenious distinction was to be made between bourgeois nationalism of Western countries and the Soviet patriotism of the USSR. Not all historians were to be able to write their works in accord with a rather subtle and not always readily discernible distinction.

This brief indication of trends since 1945 serves as a background for the developments that were yet to follow when the writers of history and the members of the party desperately set out in search of a *modus operandi*. If some historians endeavored to regain a measure of independence, their efforts are not recorded. The intense struggle for professional survival among historians began in 1948. Whether that contest can be considered another closed chapter in the chequered story of Soviet historiography or projects itself into the post-Stalin era, is not quite clear.

During the course of the combat since 1948, many terms, which frequently degenerated into clichés, were employed. The most prominent among them is "cosmopolitanism." Presumably it had general reference to the "one-world" concept found in the Western world, and was apparently employed to designate a possible rival to the form of internationalism sponsored by the Communist Party. In a more restricted sense "cosmopolitanism" had reference to the Atlantic community of nations which under the leadership of the United States had become a rival of those nations led by the Soviet Union. Any vestige of foreign influence in the writings of Soviet historians was quickly identified with the interests of the competitors of the USSR and labeled "cosmopolitanism."

Officially, "cosmopolitanism" came to be regarded as a bourgeoise influence and as a tool of the United States to break the nationalism of countries under the sway of its economic imperialism. It was a spurious form of internationalism, for it only served to conceal American chauvinism directed against the Soviet Union. "Cosmopolitanism" thus became the reverse side of bourgeois nationalism and therefore a reactionary ideology disguised by lofty phrases that paid tribute to mankind and world culture.[32] Further, it was in direct conflict with the doctrine of Stalin that international culture had to be necessarily antinational. Soviet patriotism, which was the antithesis of American "cosmopolitanism," was capable of embracing both love of one's country and respect for internationalism.[33] The two must not be confused, for they are different ideological weapons employed by each hostile camp in this divided world.

Another term of reprobation commonly employed during these years was "bourgeois objectivism." This carried a stigma not easily or accurately defined; in general, it designated the school which the historians of the Western world rather fondly refer to as "scientific." In Soviet parlance it came to refer more

---

[32] See editorial, "Protiv burzhuaznoy ideologii kosmopolitizma [Against the Bourgeois Ideology of Cosmopolitanism]," *Voprosy filosofii*, No. 2, 1948, 14-29.
[33] *Pravda*, April 7, 1949.

precisely to the acceptance of acts and events as interpreted by Western historians and especially to the failure to bring the events of history into accord with Marxist-Leninist doctrine.[34] Then there was the tag "social reformism" or "socio-reformism," which denoted a rather comprehensive but relatively simple idea. It indicated such movements as the American New Freedom, New Deal, Fair Deal, and other movements of social and economic reform in the nations of the Western world. All such movements were represented as devices of the bourgeoisie to deceive the proletariat and to make the members of the latter class believe that they were objects of the solicitude of their respective states. None of these movements could be accepted by the acolyte of Marxism-Leninism as a manifestation of the growing power of labor in other countries. There was, of course, enough truth in the Soviet contention to give it a specious validity. If the real power of the proletariat in some countries were recognized by the Party, it would be difficult to explain why, once in power, the proletariat had failed to emulate the Soviet example.

The ideological offensive, as usual, brought home to historians grave issues and devastating attacks. Some of these attacks assumed a virulent antiforeign character and deserve mention, for they illustrate the existing schism in Soviet historiography as well as the application of the "line" to historical writing. The Institute of History was criticized for publishing in 1947 the *History of the USSR* because the work deprecated the value and independent significance of Russian culture. Another work, the four-volume *General History of the State and Law* (*Vseobshchaya istoriya gosudarstva i prava*), published by the All-Union Institute of Juridical Sciences, was especially censured for tracing the development of law in Western states and for

[34] *Voprosy filosofii*, No. 2, 1948, 14-15, 17.

altogether neglecting the corresponding development in Russia.[35]

These attacks reflected the objective of eliminating any reference to foreign influence in the growth of Russian culture. Departures from this somewhat unusual approach were regarded as belittling Russian culture. The specific task of writers dealing with national history had become the popularization and explanation of native cultures. It was considered inadvisable to use anything except Russian sources in such studies. The preeminence of Russian scientists—a fact hitherto jealously concealed by bourgeois historians—had to be demonstrated, and the "national" qualities of science were to be stressed in particular. The principal argument for the validity of these narrowly nationalistic doctrines was that Stalin studied Russian sources to secure the growth and formation of his knowledge and wisdom. Presumably the argument was conclusive.[36]

In May, 1949, two eminent Soviet historians came under fire. N. Rubinstein, who has already been referred to, continued to be periodically chastised. I. Mints, member of the editorial board of Voprosy istorii and a prominent member of the Academy of Sciences, was now attacked. Mints was described as a "national nihilist," that is, an advocate of "cosmopolitanism." His heresies were twofold. In the first place, he had committed an unpardonable offense by claiming that he was the originator of modern Russian ideas of history. This honor had been reserved exclusively for Stalin. Second, Mints failed to perceive the role of the Great Russians as the most advanced nation of the Soviet Union.

Accolades, often including the Stalin prize, showered upon a number of works which were in accord with the current ideas

[35] Voprosy filosofii, No. 2, 1948, 18-19.
[36] Ibid., 28-29.

of elucidating the purity and virtual primacy of Russian culture. B. A. Rybakov's *The Handicraft of Early Russia* (*Remeslo drevney Rusi*) allegedly proved that in the tenth to twelfth centuries Russia possessed a culture more highly developed than the national cultures of western Europe.[37] This theory ran directly counter to that which many former eminent historians had expounded. Scholars recently lauded had maintained that precisely during the period which Rybakov treated, Kievan Russia received cultural as well as economic stimuli from the Scandinavians in the north and the Byzantines in the south; now these historians fell under the shadow of suspicion as "bourgeois falsifiers." Another work, P. Lyashchenko's *History of the National Economy of the USSR* (*Istoriya narodnogo khozyaistva SSSR*), emphasized the material and cultural development of the eastern Slavs by contending that the Kievan state existed long before the arrival of the Varangians and that the evils in Russian society—for example, tsarism, aristocracy, and capitalism—were importations brought in by the invaders.[38]

The journal *Voprosy istorii* itself was savagely attacked in April by several writers. For reasons none too clear at first the journal was suspended for a period of four months. The mysterious interruption was cleared up after its reappearance, when it was revealed that nine out of the former thirteen members of the editorial board had been "purged" during the four months' lapse. The following names had been deleted: V. P. Volgin, M. N. Tikhomirov, A. M. Pankratova, V. M. Khvostov, E. N. Gorodetsky, E. A. Kozminsky, I. A. Kudryavtsev, I. I. Mints, and Z. V. Mosina. As one examines the list of those purged on the ground of "cosmopolitanism," it becomes evident that the campaign was not entirely free of anti-Semitic bias. Suffice

[37] *Pravda,* April 9, 1949.
[38] *Pravda,* May 7, 1949.

it to list a few of the purged of the "cosmopolites": A. M. Gurevich, N. L. Rubinstein, O. L. Weinstein, I. I. Mints, and A. M. Deborin.

Rubinstein and Mints were singled out particularly and denounced as "homeless cosmopolites," whose unforgivable errors consisted of "national nihilism" and "fawning before foreign things." Mints was characterized as a national nihilist who neglected the writings of Lenin and Stalin, thereby retarding the advancement of Soviet historical science, and as a man who was ignorant of the fact that the duty of an historian was "the cultivation of Soviet patriotism." Rubinstein was guilty of even greater crimes: he praised such German "racist" historians as Schlözer and Bayer, those falsifiers of history who believed in "the Norman theory that Varangians and not Slavs had founded Russia." Such harmful, false theory, concluded the author, "such kowtowing to German adventurers and fawning before the Prussians, is an ideological justification of the bandit slogan of the German annexationists—*Der Drang nach Osten*." [39]

The history journal *Voprosy istorii* was severely panned by A. Mitin and A. Likhomat for having neglected consideration of the fields suggested for study earlier (in 1946). The journal, they asserted, had failed to publish significant articles dealing with Soviet history after 1920. There was a readily understandable reluctance among Soviet historians to commit themselves with regard to the period after that date—it was not healthy. Parenthetically it might be observed that many Soviet historians had attempted to escape the perils of following the "line" by devoting themselves to the study of ancient and medieval history; however, party demands for a reinterpretation of the cultural history of Russia soon closed that avenue of escape.

In the field of foreign history, according to the prosecuting

[39] *Bolshevik*, No. 7, 1949, 46-47.

attorneys, the editors of *Voprosy istorii* had committed a fla-grant error by publishing articles which implicitly accepted the doctrine of "socio-reformism." As an illustration, the case of L. Zaktreger was cited. While reviewing Thomas A. Bailey's *Woodrow Wilson and the Great Betrayal,* he accepted the thesis that Wilson was a reformer and a liberal.[40] Another contributor, L. Zubok, blundered by failing to point out that the Mexican presidents, Alvaro Obregón and P. E. Calles, were agents of American imperialism.[41] The mounting tension with the United States was clearly reflected in a series of attacks made upon *Voprosy istorii.* Soviet historians were advised to minimize Russian imperialism in the past and stress instead the aggressive, expansionist policies of the United States and other Western powers. The antiforeign in general and the anti-American trend in particular were also indicated by the approval given to a number of works devoted to denouncing foreign affairs and foreign history. Two instances may suffice.

E. V. Tarlé's *Talleyrand,* a recent publication, was praised as a superb biography of the "prince of lies." The principal thesis of Tarlé's work was the importance of Talleyrand in the triumph of the bourgeoisie and of his work in establishing bour-geois diplomacy in France.[42] The real importance of Tarlé's contribution was its "usefulness"; that is, it demonstrated that the bourgeoisie of today emulate the methods of Talleyrand and served to explain to Soviet citizens the nature of Western diplomacy.

Another work, by V. V. Tarasov, on the Allied intervention in Murmansk in 1918-1920, received fulsome praise as demon-strating conclusively that the Allies employed their customary

[40] *Voprosy istorii,* No. 3, 1947, 135 ff.
[41] *Kultura i zhizn,* April 21, 1949.
[42] *Voprosy istorii,* No. 10, 1948, 157-60.

brutal methods in an effort to bring Russia within the orbit
of their respective colonial dominations. Russia was saved
from that fate by the gallant stand the Soviet government took
under the leadership of the ubiquitous Stalin. The sole de-
ficiency of Tarasov's study, it was pointed out, was his failure
to devote attention to the brigandage and cruelty of the Ameri-
cans.[43]

The generous praise lavished upon Tarlé for his biography of
Talleyrand by no means spared him from being punished for
past sins. In August, 1951, the magazine *Bolshevik* renewed
its attack on the aged scholar for a work that had appeared
almost a decade before, *Napoleon's Invasion of Russia.*
Throughout the 'forties the book was regarded as the definitive
work on the subject, and many young writers had at least referred to it, if not citing it copiously. As was pointed out previously, Tarlé himself on one occasion had hastened to alter
his thesis in order to toe the party line. Now suddenly it was
revealed that even the new interpretation was in error when the
author assumed that Napoleon's defeat was due principally to
space and weather rather than the superior strategy and valor
of the Russians. The critical analysis of Tarlé was spread over
no less than fifteen pages, through which marched his multitude of sins.

The French army, according to the critic, was not defeated
by vast spaces, hunger, Moscow fires, or unfavorable climatic
conditions, but by the superior strategy of Field Marshal M. I.
Kutuzov; not by the campaign exhaustion of the French, but
by the gallantry of the Russian army supported by the people.
Tarlé was given to understand that he was entirely wrong when
he ascribed the burning of the city of Moscow to the Russians.
There is definite proof, insisted the writer, that the fire was

[43] *Pravda,* September 7, 1949.

caused by the "barbaric army of Napoleon," which prevented the Russians from fighting it. Tarlé as well as others were given warning in precise terms to cease relying on "alien sources" and "bourgeois falsifications." He was advised to undertake a revision of the book.

The author of this new critical essay either was ignorant or had deliberately overlooked the fact that Western scholars have never taken the weather legend too seriously. Credit has been given on many occasions for the admirable fighting qualities of the Russian soldier and for the superb generalship demonstrated by Field Marshal Kutuzov. It has also been pointed out that the winter of 1812 was not exceptionally cold; the sagging morale during the retreat had a far more adverse effect upon the outcome of the campaign than did the seasonal temperature. Yet all these oft-mentioned facts were of no account to the Stalinist Torquemadas.

It may be of interest to note that, while the cultural and national uniqueness of the USSR was being trumpeted, at least one significant exception was made. The seventh congress of Polish historians meeting in 1948 at Wrocław was criticized principally for writing history from a nationalist point of view and for contrasting Russian and Polish cultures rather than emphasizing their fundamental similarity.[44] The motivation for this criticism was not difficult to discern; yet, falling out of the pattern of the "line" as it does, it neatly demonstrates the tie between political problems and historiography.

The subordination of the Soviet historian to the state and to the Party, or the correlation between political problems and the writing of history, was further evidenced by the directions given historians during the middle of 1949. For the sake of convenience, these directions could be classified as covering the

[44] *Slavyane*, No. II, 1948. See article by P. Tretyakov.

following subjects: methodology; Russian history (early, modern, and recent); problems of periodization; foreign history; and prominent figures among professional Soviet historians.

In the field of methodology, denunciations of cosmopolitanism, objectivism, bourgeois tendencies, and foreign ideas were encountered. "Scientific" writing was demanded of Soviet historians, and the bases of the science were defined in several documents, namely, Stalin's treatise, *Concerning Several Problems of the History of Bolshevism* (*O nekotorykh voprosakh istorii bolshevizma*), which appeared in the journal *Proletarian Revolution;*[45] the decrees of the Council of Commissars and the Central Committee in 1934; various commentaries of Stalin, Kirov, and Zhdanov; Stalin's *History of the Communist Party* (1938);[46] decrees of the Central Committee on ideological matters; and the speeches of Stalin delivered on various occasions.[47]

On the basis of the foregoing documents and with the use of great caution (for the documents in 1949 already contained several outdated views), the Soviet historian was to wage ideological warfare on the bourgeois historians of the West. Soviet historians were expected to devote themselves to vital tasks and to tolerate no ideological distortions. They were to refrain from merely cataloguing facts and materials. The latter rule cut off another avenue of escape which Soviet historians had formerly used to circumvent the hazards of ideological interpretation.

---

[45] *Proletarskaya revolyutsiya*, No. 6, 1931, 3-12.

[46] See the speech of N. Khrushchev concerning the "Cult of the Individual," Delivered at the Twentieth Congress of the Communist Party of the Soviet Union, February 25, 1956. In the *Anti-Stalin Campaign and International Communism. A Selection of Documents*, ed. by the Russian Institute, Columbia University, New York, 1956, 72.

[47] See editorial, "O zadachakh sovetskikh istorikov v borbe s proyavleniyami burzhuaznoy ideologii [Concerning the Tasks of Soviet Historians in the Combat with Manifestations of Bourgeois Ideology]," *Voprosy istorii*, No. 2, 1949, 3-13.

Themes without scientific importance—that is, subjects not politically recommended—were also discouraged.[48]

Specifically, Soviet historians had to realize that Stalin, in furnishing them with the theory of "historical materialism," had established history as an exact science "capable of making use of the laws of societal development for practical purposes." Stalin had supplied a definition of the basic content of history. All historical phenomena were to be given a class analysis; otherwise, historians might be in grave danger of slipping into bourgeois objectivism.[49]

The policy of methodology, by no means a settled problem in the Soviet Union and heatedly debated perennially, might be summed up thus: it was necessary (and still is!) for the Soviet historian to familiarize himself carefully with the Party directives and then write in conformity with those directives. Lest it be assumed that this requirement reduced the historian to a mere hack, it must be constantly borne in mind that it required no little skill to depart from the pattern indicated in the party directives. The task became most bedeviling when certain parts of the directives were no longer applicable to the current "line." For instance, the decrees of 1934, which though still recommended, contained totally unacceptable propositions regarding the West.

With respect to the period of Russian history before the First World War, some of the directions and criticisms are not without our interest. One of the first things the historian had to remember and stress was the independent nature of Russian culture. In this respect the publication *Byzantine Journal* (*Vizantiysky vremennik*) was excoriated for attempting to cooperate with

[48] *Kultura i zhizn,* April 21, 1949.

[49] See editorial, "Protiv ob'yektivizma v istoricheskoy nauke [Against Objectivism in Historical Science]," *Voprosy istorii,* No. 12, 1948, 3-12.

Byzantine scholars outside the Soviet Union.[50] Eurasian and Normanist interpretations were specifically singled out for criticism and rejection. The class and international significance of Russian culture had to be shown. The primacy of the Great Russians in furnishing leadership to the peoples of the former Empire was to be accentuated. For this purpose historians were assigned to write a collective work, entitled *History of Russian Culture*. It was to demonstrate the role of the Great Russian people in the development of mankind's culture and prove the superiority of Soviet science and culture.[51]

Another assignment, and one by no means of less significance, was to show which of Russia's wars were just, for the acquisition of territory held by the USSR could be effectively condemned as an imperialistic process. An example of the latest "line" was Stalin's rejection of Friedrich Engel's contention that in the late nineteenth century, tsarist Russia was, of all states, the greatest menace to world peace. Stalin denied, too, that Russia was the last bastion of reaction. A further document which no student could afford to overlook as he delved into the history of imperialism was the letter which Stalin had written in 1930 to Maxim Gorky. In this open letter he said quite succinctly: "We are not against any war. We are against the imperialist war, as being a counterrevolutionary war. But we are for the emancipational, anti-imperialist revolutionary war, despite the fact that such a war, as is well known, is not free from the 'horrors of bloodshedding,' but rather is full of them." [52]

The history of Russian foreign relations—a field hitherto

---

[50] See editorial, "Zadachi sovetskikh istorikov v oblasti novoy i noveyshey istorii" [Problems of Soviet Historians in the Field of Modern and Recent History], *Voprosy istorii*, No. 3, 1949, 3-13.

[51] *Ibid.*

[52] J. Stalin, *Sochineniya* [Collected Works], Moscow, 1946-49, XII, 176.

much neglected by both prerevolutionary and Soviet historians —was now ordered to be thoroughly explored. In addition, historians were to devote themselves to many studies ignored by "scientific historians" (Soviet version). Among these subjects were the peasantry, foreign capital, the role of the proletariat, the menace and effects of the use of foreign capital, domestic revolutions, revolutionary parties, and foreign relations with specific nations. In the field of recent Russian history, more urgent problems were encountered. The most formidable of these was the constantly lamented reluctance of Soviet historians to work upon the October Revolution and the years after 1918. The Institute of History, the journal *Voprosy istorii,* and individual historians have been rebuked for this defect. In large measure, official prodding has been to no effect. The apparent diffidence of Soviet historians in undertaking a consideration of this field requires no explanation. As long as the writing of history must depend upon the "line," which is neither constant nor consistent, the historian will prefer to deal with the Stone Age rather than the Stalin Age.

What subjects were to be considered in this field, and how were they to be treated? The October Revolution must be analyzed and its socialist character presented. The role of the Russian people in building a socialist society and their primacy in defeating Germany had to be shown.[53] Yet when the historian I. M. Razgon undertook to write on the period of the civil war, he was castigated for presenting a purely factual narrative and for having failed "to expose the laws of development of the Soviet period." No less important tasks were the histories of the Communist Party, of the process of transition from capitalism to Communism, of the growth of people's democ-

---

[53] *Voprosy istorii,* No. 2, 1949, 11-12.

racies, of relations with the United States and Great Britain, of the work of the Soviet Union in behalf of world peace, of the peculiarities of Soviet economic development, of the class and political relationships within the USSR, of the national liberation movement, and of culture and ideas.[54] In like measure industrialization, collectivization, the five-year plans, development of cultural and national construction of the USSR, foreign policy of the Soviet state, and the military history of the USSR remain subjects not to be tampered with despite all the prodding from the authorities.

The rigid application of Party definitions to history and the demand that a class approach be followed consistently have made necessary a new periodization of Russian and world history. Only the former has been essayed, and that on a rather weak and tentative basis. In April, 1949, *Voprosy istorii* reported that members of the Institute of History had discussed the problem of periodization and that two papers on the subject had been read. Although the details of the problem of periodization are far from settled even as these lines are written, some of the reactions they evoked from the very start call for comment. S. V. Bakhrushin approached the problem by employing two general concepts: (1) socio-economic phenomena and (2) superstructural, political phenomena. Bakhrusin limited himself to a consideration of the so-called "feudal" period. He found the great eras to be those of the clans, of feudalism, of the growth of landownership, and of political unification and division of labor. This approach provoked severe criticism because it ignored the existence of a Russian prefeudal state. The party was adamant in its insistence that such a state be discovered. The plan was considered weak, since it did not employ a single criterion of periodization and be-

[54] *Ibid.*, No. 3, 1949, 9-10.

cause it was based upon a scheme of economic materialism—the old Pokrovsky concept.[55]

N. M. Druzhinin attempted to periodize the capitalist era of Russian history. He also employed two basic criteria: (1) stages in the decay of capitalism and (2) phases of the class struggle. In general, Druzhinin's report was well received. Only a few carping suggestions were made, and they did not fall within the realm of his study. He silenced the opposition by citing Lenin's opinions on periodization.[56] The periodization of Russian history before the eighteenth century remains officially inchoate. That of the later period remains unsettled. No evidence exists of attempts to periodize the history of the USSR since the Revolution.

The suggestion for subjects to be considered and conclusions to be reached are most prolific in the field of foreign history. These demands reflect far more accurately the problems of Soviet diplomacy than do the other demands reflect Soviet domestic problems. The seemingly better correlation may be only the result of the impossibility of clearly ascertaining the nature of the domestic problems of the Soviet Union.

In the history of the Great Patriotic War (The Second World War) the plots of Germany, Italy, Japan, Great Britain, France, and the United States against the Soviet Union must be shown as a primary cause for the war. In the prosecution of the war itself, the nobility of Soviet war aims must be contrasted with the selfish and imperialistic objectives of the United States and Great Britain. Needless to say, the great role of the Russian armies was to be presented in invidious comparison to the minor part played by the Anglo-American armed forces.[57]

[55] *Voprosy istorii*, No. 4, 1949, 149-52.
[56] *Ibid.*, No. 4, 1949, 7-8.
[57] *Bolshevik*, No. 22, 1947, 36-37.

For a guide, historians were referred to an historical reference work published by the Soviet Information Bureau, entitled *Falsifiers of History*. It has been cited as an excellent example of militant Bolshevist treatment of questions concerning the Great Patriotic War. Incidentally, *Falsifiers of History* warns Soviet students of history against distortions of the past deliberately presented by writers abroad, including White Russian *émigrés* such as Struve, Vernadsky, Karpovich, and others. Struve has been accused of falsification in the Russian section of the Cambridge history, while Vernadsky and Karpovich came under indictment for their Eurasian concept of Russian history. According to the accusation from Moscow, Eurasian philosophy was designed to prove the absence of native national roots of Russian culture—an obvious bourgeois aim. It should be pointed out that Karpovich has never adhered to the Eurasian school and on occasion even criticized its historical views.

The course for Soviet historians to take in respect to the Orient was not less specific. An interesting and significant editorial appeared in the April issue of *Voprosy istorii,* outlining tasks in the field. Historians were reminded that the Soviet East and the foreign East are fundamentally different in that they are subject to different political systems. One represents the international unity of peoples, the other the "capitalist principle" of oppression and exploitation of colonial peoples. This condition imposed upon Soviet historians the primary duty of portraying the struggle of "democratic" forces to terminate oppression in the Orient. *Voprosy istorii* outlined the great need for both general works and monographs in this hitherto neglected field.

What were the projected studies to demonstrate? They must show, first of all, the influence of the October Revolution in China, former French Indo-China, and Korea. They must explode the false theory of bourgeois historians that the conquest of the Orient by the European powers was inevitable or that they delivered any blessings of a new civilization to the Asian peoples. Soviet historians were also to demonstrate the bourgeois reactionary role of leaders like Mohandas Gandhi, the retarding influence of the colonial system, and the untruth of the claim that independence can be achieved within the colonial system of Western states. They must reveal British tyranny in India and discuss the mass movement of the Oriental peasantry and the workingmen employed in industry; they must dispel the bourgeois myth that the USSR has played an imperialist role in the Orient; they should treat in detail the history of United States expansionist policies in the Pacific, including the annexation of the Hawaiian Islands, the sinister suppression of the Philippine insurrection led by Emilio Aguinaldo, and the anti-Russian diplomacy of the Russo-Japanese War.[58]

It may be noted that almost every major field of conflict between the Soviet Union and the Western bloc of states was assigned to historians for study. Ordinarily, not only were assignments made but the conclusions and theses were supplied as well. This condition should occasion no surprise, for from the party point of view history must serve to instruct and to make the present intelligible. The harsh epithet "propaganda" could well be a reflection of a Western attitude. Obviously, historical research and writing have nothing to do with finding truth but only of corroborating it. Unfortunately, the truth has not been constant.

In no way has the inconsistency of the "truth" been more apparent than in the rise and fall of historians. First, the giant Pokrovsky fell, and his most prominent opponent, Tarlé, re-

[58] *Voprosy istorii,* No. 4, 1949, 7.

turned to grace. Tarlé retained that enviable position until his
death, despite occasional niggling criticism. The promising
student of history, N. L. Rubinstein (1910-1952), lost his footing in the shift after the war and remained an object lesson in
bad judgment. I. I. Mints had to face a heavy barrage of criticism for his alleged poor management of the journal *Voprosy
istorii* and for claiming to have originated modern historical
science. Many other historians have fallen since 1945. Among
their number may be mentioned A. A. Andreyev, who credited
the reforms of Peter the Great to English influence;[59] S. N.
Valk, who praised the Petersburg historical school;[60] G. A. Deborin, who accepted the United States on an "objective" basis;[61]
I. M. Razgon, who made a factual survey of the October Revolution in the Caucasus without presenting any "laws of conduct"; and a legion of others.[62] "Falsifiers of history" have been
detected and fiery accusations leveled at such men as L. I. Zubok,
O. L. Weinstein, and D. Lam. Death removed some of the
older members from the ranks of the profession: E. Tarlé,
S. V. Bakhrushin, N. D. Grekov; a few of the old names, such
as P. I. Lyashchenko or S. D. Skazkin, appear from time to
time in the press. More often one is apt to meet the names of
M. N. Tikhomirov, A. M. Pankratova, M. Nechkina, A. Mitin,
N. M. Druzhinin, V. V. Tarasov, A. S. Yerusalimsky, N. A.
Smirnov, B. E. Shtein, Y. Borisov, A. Likhomat, A. D. Udaltsov,
I. Koloskov, and others. These men appear either as authors of
accepted studies or as critics of fallen historians. One can never
tell whether they speak out of conviction or merely ride the
pendulum to power.

One must never envy the historian who may temporarily

[59] *Voprosy istorii*, No. 12, 1948, 7.
[60] *Ibid.*, No. 12, 1948, 9-10.
[61] *Kultura i zhizn*, August 21, 1949; *Voprosy istorii*, No. 12, 1948, 9-10.
[62] *Voprosy istorii*, No. 1949, 6-7.

find himself at the helm of power. To follow the "line" is precarious and involves hazards for the historian. The application of the "line" to specific studies is too often most difficult in terms of the complexity and subtlety of the Marxist-Leninist ideology. When the "line" shifts abruptly, the career of the professional historian is gravely threatened. The Party will acknowledge, upon occasion, errors in performance but never in ideas; thus the historian must bear the blame for yesterday's truth which has become today's error. Conversely, the writing of history and official statements in respect to the historical profession are excellent indexes to the nature of and shifts in the "line." The historian can be certain that the "line" will never change one thing, which is that the USSR has achieved socialism and is destined triumphantly to achieve Communism. The historian can also rest assured that he will always be regarded as the educator. As such he is bound to advocate Soviet patriotism and "show the leading role of the Party in the history of the Soviet state and in the building of Communism in the world." There has not been the slightest deviation on this score before, during, or after Stalin. This remains the official position, and its dictates constitute law for the student of history.

## ÉMIGRÉ HISTORIANS

Something must be said, if very briefly, about those students of Russian history who through political circumstances found themselves on foreign soil. The lives of the majority of these men were by no means enviable: material want, lack of library facilities, the necessity for cultural readjustment, sometimes a callous environment accompanied by tense nationalism—all this was not conducive to the inspiration of the Russian scholar abroad. And yet, despite the cold foreign wind that threatened to extinguish the flickering lamp of scholarship, it has been kept burning at the price of enormous hardships ever since the year of the exodus, 1921. Throughout the years of this modern Diaspora an impressive number of works—including books, monographs, and articles—have appeared in about ten different languages. The articles, for obvious reasons, are the predominant form of writing, since they involve the least financial outlay.[63] Though handicapped by distance and by political feuds, some *émigrés* succeeded during the 'twenties and 'thirties in organizing historical societies. Among these may be noted the now defunct Russian Archeological Society in Yugoslavia, and the Kondakov Institute and Russian Historical Society, both in Czechoslovakia. The latter accumulated an extensive library and amassed source material of the Civil War, including the Denikin archive, all of which had been removed after 1945 to Moscow. Needless to say, the existence of these associations was precarious. Herculean efforts had to be exerted to keep them intellectually alive. The Second World War extinguished most of them.

The subjects of study by the *émigré* historians varied widely. Men who found shelter in the Slavic countries seemed to concentrate upon early Russian history; among these were A. L. Pogodin, A. V. Florovsky, and L. G. Bagrov. M. V. Shakhmatov and E. Y. Perfetsky were engaged in a revaluation of the chronicles; I. I. Lappo published a capital work on the Lithuanian statute of 1588; M. I. Rostovtsev completed his well-known monographs on southern Russian archeology;[64] D. N.

[63] See an early account of *émigré* publications discussed in *Russkaya zarubezhnaya kniga* [Russian Books Abroad], Praha, 1924, I, 66-95.

[64] M. I. Rostovtsev, *Iranians and Greeks in South Russia*, Oxford, 1922; *Skythien und der Bosporus*, Berlin, 1931; *Sredinnaya Aziya, Rossiya, Kitai i zveriniy stil* [Central Asia, Russia, China, and the Animal Style], Prague, Seminarium Kondakovium, 1929.

Odinets and V. A. Myakotin took up respectively the annexation and the social history of the Ukraine. P. B. Struve proceeded with his research on the economic and social history of
Russia, but the work was interrupted by his death. Incomplete,
it was published posthumously in Paris.[65] S. G. Svatikov made
a pioneering investigation of the Don Cossacks and their relations with Moscow, and another of the history of Siberian administration in the nineteenth century. P. N. Milyukov made
an extensive revision of his *Outlines of Russian Culture*; Baron
Nolde wrote on the formation of the Russian Empire.[66] G. V.
Vernadsky published a detailed account of Novosiltsov's constitutional project of 1820 and has been successfully working on
an ambitious scheme of rewriting Russian history.[67] Professor
Vernadsky represents the Eurasian school, a school which war-
rants attention even though in brief form.

### *The Eurasian School*

The Eurasian school emerged amidst the political chaos of
the *émigré* life of the Russian intelligentsia in Yugoslavia in
1921. The school embraces various outlooks upon national
life—political, social, economic, religious, philosophical, and
historical. The present discussion, by the very nature of the
general study concerned, must limit the subject exclusively to

[65] P. B. Struve, *Sotsialnaya i ekonomicheskaya istoriya Rossii s drevneyshikh
vremyen to nashego, v svyazi s razvitiyem russkoy kultury i rostom gosudarstvennosti*
[A Social and Economic History of Russia in Relation to the Cultural Development
and the Growth of the Russian State from the Earliest Times to the Present], Paris,
1952.

[66] B. Nolde, *La formation de l'Empire russe*, Paris, 1952, I.

[67] G. V. Vernadsky, *La Charte constitutionelle de l'empire russe de l'an 1820*, Paris,
1933; *Ancient Russia*, I, New Haven, 1943; *Kievan Russia*, II, New Haven, 1948;
*The Mongols and Russia*, New Haven, 1953.

its historical aspect.[68] The conception of history held by the Eurasians is somewhat as follows.

Former writers seem to have accepted the national growth of the Russian Empire as an organic, uninterrupted, single process, modified in some measure, of course, by influences from East and West. These influences were considered but casual factors, however, and regardless of them Russia would have flourished in all her imperial glory; they never deeply penetrated the national core; they left few visible marks on the national character or the political body.

Prior to 1917 the courses in history were usually divided into Russian and Western history, two entirely separate subjects; the western border of the Empire was a sort of Chinese wall separating two different worlds. The Westerners of the nineteenth century were the first to raise their voices in favor of Russia's inseparable bond with western Europe, though that "bond" was hardly ever formulated clearly. They referred to the Russian people as a European nation which had passed through stages of development similar to those of nations on the Continent; yet on Russia's part the dividing line remained —"We and the West." The situation was not much different with respect to the opposite, eastern border of the Empire. If the West represented to Russians a world by itself, a living body, the eastern borderland, on the other hand, was considered by Russian historians as simply a void space, a "geographical expression" that was little heeded except by Orientalists like Bartold.[69] When former writers, including Solovyev, Klyuchev-

---

[68] The mouthpiece of the Eurasian philosophy is Prince N. S. Troubetskoy, whose earliest work, *Evropa i Chelovechestvo* [Europe and Mankind], Sofia, 1920, was the warning flash on the *émigré* intellectual horizon.

[69] V. V. Bartold, *Istoriya izucheniya Vostoka v Evrope i Rossii* [A History of the Study of the East in Europe and in Russia], 2nd ed., Leningrad, 1925. See I. Y. Krachkovsky, "V. V. Bartold v istorii islamovedeniya [V. V. Bartold in the History of Islamic Study]," *Izvestiya Akademii Nauk O.O.N.*, Ser. VII, Vol. I, 1934, 5-18.

sky, and Milyukov in the earlier editions of his *Outlines of Russian Culture,* referred to the geographic foundations of the Russian state, they had in mind chiefly the so-called "European" or "west of the Ural Mountains" Russia. The dominance of the Mongols was scarcely mentioned, not even by Klyuchevsky in his monumental *Course of Russian History*; and others referred to the Mongolian invasion as a mere episode, a raid of ferocious hordes who descended from Asia, like a beast of prey, and began to consume the vitality of the state. This plague (some refer to it as a "yoke") lasted for some two centuries; then came a realization of the situation, which led to the expulsion of the detested Mongols, and Russia breathed freely once again.

Just as American scholars have in recent years endeavored to correct the outlived parochialism of United States history in the light of what they call Euro-American development, so the Eurasian school is making an effort to reinterpret Russia in a Euro-Asian light. It attempts to correct the manifest error of interpreting the eastern border as a void space by showing it to be a present factor in the life of the nation, and is thus presenting a new concept of the Russian historical process. The very essence of this process, it maintains, is the fact that the former Empire—the present USSR—constitutes, in itself, an historic-geographic world. Such an interpretation coincides with that of individual students, for example P. N. Savitsky, who presents a similar conception with emphasis upon its geographic aspect.[70] Though Moscow began to colonize the territories beyond the Urals only at the end of the sixteenth

---

[70] P. N. Savitsky (Savickij), "Evraziyskaya kontseptsiya russkoy geografii [The Eurasian Conception of Russian Geography]," *Zbornik radova na III Kongresu slovenskih geografa i etnografu v Yugoslavji,* 1930, 13-14.

century, even from the earliest times the fate of the Russian tribes has been closely knit with that of the other peoples of Eurasia: for in those very early centuries they came in contact with the Iranian, Finnish, and Turco-Mongolian tribes, and thus formed, through this interrelationship, the backbone of the later vast Empire.

In his book, *Nachertaniye russkoy istorii* [An Outline of Russian History], and the one that followed, *Zvenya russkoy kultury*[71] [Links in Russian Culture], Professor Vernadsky, a member of the Eurasian school, brought to the attention of the general reader the following interrelated facts: that Asia is as much a part of Russia as the West is, if not more so; that central Asia played an extremely significant role in the past of the people; that from the earliest days until Moscow established her autocratic form of government, the people of the south-western plains and of the north were in continuous communication with the eastern tribes; and, lastly, that the Gargantuan territorial appetite of Genghis Khan gave rise to the imperial designs of the tsars, and that these have lately become also the policy of the USSR. All these things really represent a series of traditional acts in a single historical drama.[72] Both the century-long westward expansion of the Mongols and the later eastward expansion of the Russians, Vernadsky maintained, were dictated by "geopolitical" conditions and a common striving for the realization of one and the same idea—a Eurasian

---

[71] G. V. Vernadsky, *Nachertaniye russkoy istorii* [An Outline of Russian History], Prague, 1927; *Opyt istorii Yevrazii s poloviny VI vyeka do nastoyashchego vremeni* [Essay on the History of Eurasia from the Middle of the 6th Century to the Present], Berlin, 1934; *Zvenya russkoy kultury* [Links in Russian Culture], n.p., 1938; other works were previously referred to.

[72] See I. R——, *Naslediye Chingiskhana* [The Legacy of Genghis Khan], Berlin, 1925. It may be noted that the views of the Eurasians coincide with those of Pokrovsky in some respects. See Pokrovsky, *Istoricheskaya nauka i borba klassov* [Historical Science and the Class Struggle], II, 307.

state.[73] Reasonable as this theory may seem, it lay dormant until the Eurasian school made it the alpha and omega of Russian history, and to men like Vernadsky and Savitsky belongs the honor due to pioneers.[74] They came out as advocates of a new presentation of the dreaded Mongolians—formerly the symbol of, if anything, destruction—now to be considered a mighty, constructive factor in molding Imperial Russia.

When the Eurasian school refers to the "Russian people," it has in mind not only the Great Russian but also the Ukrainians and White Russians, each of whom represents a cultural branch of the Eastern Slavs, though politically they stand together. Moreover, in the history of Eurasia these peoples occupy only a segment of an entire "geopolitical unit." The merit of such a conception is that it compels the three-fold study—social, economic, and cultural—of all parts of this "sixth of the world," rather than a study of the political center alone, a view which coincides with that of Dragomanov, Antonovich, Shchapov, and other students of the above-mentioned "federal school." Furthermore, by acknowledging cultural debts in both eastern and western directions, the Eurasians believed they were bound to advance historical science far beyond the reach of their predecessors, the Slavophiles and the Westerners.

To conclude, Vernadsky and Savitsky maintained that, in the future, Russia must be considered a "geopolitical unit" on

---

[73] Vernadsky, *Opyt istorii Evrazii* [Essay on the History of Eurasia], 7-8.

[74] P. N. Savitsky (Savickij), *Geograficheiye osobennosti Rossii* [Geographical Characteristics of Russia], Prague, 1927; *Rossiya osobiy geografichesky mir* [Russia as a Distinct Geographical Entity], Prague, 1927; *Šestina světa* [A Sixth of the World], Prague, 1933.

Other important Eurasian literature: Prince N. S. Troubetskoy, *K probleme russkogo samopoznaniya* [Contributions to the Problem of Russian Self-Realization], Paris, 1931; P. O. Yakobson, *K Kharakteristike evraziyskogo soyuza* [Descriptive Notes on the Eurasian Linguistic Union], Paris, 1931; N. N. Alekseyev, *Teoriya gosudarstva* [The Theory of the State], Paris, 1931.

a Euro-Asiatic scale and that its past must be presented not only in chronological but also in "spatial" form. Geography therefore must play a significant part, and the growth of the nation must parallel the geographic factors involved—hence, Vernadsky's coined term, *myestorazvitiye*, best rendered into English as "place-development," subsequently accepted even by his strong opponent, Milyukov.[75] Here, however, the Eurasian school revealed its Achillean heel: the "geopolitical" aspect of the historical development of Russia—the "Eurasian idiographic singleness"—remained an obscure postulate; it was what one caustic critic of the Eurasians called "geopolitical mysticism." Nor did the Eurasians succeed in presenting with sufficient lucidity the underlying forces in the political make-up of Eurasia: psychological similarity alone is hardly enough to bring one sixth of the globe under a single flag. Other forces as well— the economic, for instance—have driven this immense number of peoples into a political family. Finally, the overemphasis upon the uniqueness of Eurasian civilization and on special qualities of the "Turanian" peoples leads one to fear that the earlier blunders of the Slavophiles repeat themselves.[76] Yet despite certain shortcomings and sharp criticism from almost every political camp, the Eurasians contributed undeniably to historical research in one respect: they broadened the field of Russian history to dimensions of intercontinental nature. It is still too early to pass final judgment as to their place in Russian historiography. One thing, however, remains clear: the future student will be unable to disregard the Eurasian

[75] Milyukov, *Ocherki po istorii russkoy kultury,* rev. ed., Paris, 1937, Vol. I, Part 1, 35-36.

[76] The Eurasian school has been subjected to severe criticism by Professor Milyukov. See particularly his essay, "Eurasianism and Europeanism in Russian History," *Festschrift Th. G. Masaryk zum 80. Geburtstage* (Supplement to *Der russische Gedanke*), Bonn, 1930, Vol. I, 225-36.

school entirely; fertile ground has been broken by these men, a new seed sown, and there is good reason to believe that a richer harvest is bound to follow.[77]

## AFTER STALIN

The death of Stalin marked the end of the "Cult of Personality." There followed for almost three years a transitional period during which a noticeable relaxation of state controls was evident. The revision of the teaching of history became inevitable. "The general history curriculum," it was announced euphemistically, "has been made in accord with the new data of Soviet historical science. Particular attention has been paid to the decisive role of the masses as the maker of history [and not to one man—Stalin]." An extensive list of history textbooks was prepared for revision. Then came the Twentieth Congress of the Communist Party at which the Secretary, N. Khrushchev, delivered on February 25, 1956, his now well-known, blistering attack on the "Cult of the Individual." He discussed the sorrowful story of how the "Cult of the person of Stalin has been gradually growing, the cult which became at a certain specific stage the source of a whole series of exceedingly serious and grave perversions of Party principles, of Party democracy, of revolutionary legality."

Mr. Khrushchev touched the subject of historical writing only inadvertently, though the allusion exposed, as he said, the "shameful facts" concerning the field. As in every other field the "cult" expressed itself in anti-Marxian "loathsome adulation" of the leader and resulted in distortion of history. His illustration of how history had been written during the era of

[77] For further exposition of the Eurasian philosophy and its conception of state, church, and nation, see the admirable summary by D. S. Mirsky, "The Eurasian Movement," *Slavonic Review,* December, 1927, 311-19; "Histoire d'une émancipation," *Nouvelle Revue Française,* September, 1931, 384-97.

Stalin aptly demonstrates the situation and may well be cited. He recalled that a group of authors was designated to write a history of the Communist Party. However, in the official biography of Stalin the assignment was described thus:

A Commission of the Central Committee, All-Union Communist Party (Bolsheviks), under the direction of Comrade Stalin and with his most active personal participation, has prepared a *Short Course of the History of the All-Union Communist Party (Bolsheviks)*.

When the manuscript was presented to Stalin for approval, he did not like the phraseology, which he corrected to read:

In 1938 appeared the book, *History of the All-Union Communist Party (Bolsheviks)*, *Short Course,* written by Comrade Stalin and approved by a commission of the Central Committee, All-Union Communist Party (Bolsheviks).

"Can one add anything more?" asked Mr. Khrushchev. The minor episode casts sufficient light upon the vulgarization of historical writing that characterizes the period. Khrushchev ended with an appeal to correct the widespread errors in the sphere of history and pointed out that it was especially necessary to compile a serious textbook of the history of the party in accordance with "scientific Marxist objectivism, a textbook of the history of Soviet society, a book pertaining to the events of the Civil War and the Great Patriotic War." And so begins the story all over again!

Pokrovsky still remained the erring Marxist, but he was now credited with what was due him: he remained the father of Marxist historical interpretation. Names of other historians who recently had been anathema to the profession gradually regained the right to grace the honorary rolls of eminence. Epithets such as "homeless nihilists," "cosmopolites," and "bourgeois objectivists" lost their former stigma. The tribal patriotic fervor, with its juvenile boasts of "original discoveries," now began to subside or was allowed to pass into oblivion. Foreign influence upon Russia once again became permissible to discuss in historical literature; former tsarist imperialism ceased to be interpreted as exclusively "defensive wars." A number of personalities who only recently had been appointed to the halls of fame in Russian history were once more reduced to their actual size and reassigned to more deserving places in history.

These were all welcome signs, even though occasionally accompanied by harassing warnings that freedom of expression in Soviet historical writing is by no means an accomplished fact. Thus in the middle of June, 1957, the Communist Party reminded Soviet historians that it had no intention of tolerating "liberal interpretations." The Party ordered a shake-up of the editorial board of *Voprosy istorii,* dismissed the editor—the leading critic of Stalin—and placed this monthly publication under the stricter surveillance of its sponsor, the Academy of Sciences. Of the eleven board members only four survived. The newly appointed board accused the preceding members of being too charitable toward "revisionism and nationalism"; of insufficiently exposing the true "aggressive character of American imperialism"; of besmirching Stalin's record of achievement and of "idealizing" Menshevism, questioning the "negative evaluation of Trotsky" and not scurrilously mentioning Kamenev and Zinoviev. The chief errant member was E. N. Burdzhalov, first deputy editor of the magazine and author of several articles in which he "reappraised" Stalin during the preceding year, "blackened his activities," depicted him as an opportunist, and denied opponents space in the magazine for rebuttal. The latest version is that although Stalin had committed many errors, he was still "a great Marxist, a great fighter for communism."

The new editorial board began with a self-chastised announcement for the too-liberal interpretation of the cult of the individual, for failing to expose the latest revisionist tendencies in Yugoslavia and Poland. The recently named editor pledged to make amends in the future by incorporating correct content. The former editor, the eminent Soviet historian Anna M. Pankratova, died in good time, on May 21, 1957, to escape the humiliating experience of being purged. The entire episode demonstrated one irrefutable fact: the proverbial monolithic unity among the historians was a myth. Individual members adamantly continue to refuse conformity even in the face of grave danger. The historians' opposition evidently is by no means an entirely "liquidated matter." Whether the recent sacking of the editorial board means a revival of Stalinism is not clear. Nor can the continuous presence of a refractory element among the ranks of Marxist historians be considered as necessarily the arrival of a new era of genuine freedom. The future is still dim and unpredictable, while the present bids for patient hope that objective writing and honest errors be tolerated and genuine truth in the end be found.

## In Retrospect

In a review of the accomplishments of Russian historiography during the last two centuries or so, what can be said are the most notable features, and what are the immediate prospects for the future? It remains indisputable that the nineteenth century and the prerevolutionary period of the twentieth century showed amazing progress both in the publication of sources

and in the writing of history. Formed with the direct encouragement of the government and of private individuals, special societies commenced publishing activities on a gigantic scale.
The most notable of these organizations is the Archeographic
Commission, which managed to publish a staggering amount
of source material. Simultaneously with this feverish activity
the art of paleography progressed, as did the study of chronicles, which culminated in investigations by scholars like A. A.
Shakhmatov. Equally impressive results were obtained in the
study of special periods by men like Platonov, Lyubavsky, and
Presnyakov. In the field of monographic subjects, legal and
agrarian history, and the Petrine epoch, a number of students
were no less distinguished: suffice it to recall the names of
Sergeyevich, Semevsky, and Bogoslovsky. In the realm of "federal" interpretation of Russian history such names as Shchapov,
Kostomarov, and Hrushevsky stand out prominently; and,
finally, in the work of historical synthesis solid foundations have
been laid by Klyuchevsky, Milyukov, Pokrovsky, and Vernadsky—divergent, indeed, in views, scope, and methods of approach, yet suggestive, stimulating, and capping the efforts of
many preceding generations.

A closer analysis, however, of the entire field of Russian
historiography also reveals a lack of monographic treatment of
certain periods and aspects of Russian history. The reason was
largely the somewhat uneven development of historical writing
in Russia both before and after the Revolution. Before the Revolution, the typical work of the majority of Russian historians
was a one-sided concentration on the problems of Russia's
internal development; consequently, the country's foreign relations were given little attention. This situation has not been
remedied since 1917. To be sure, a few monographs on diplomatic history have been added to the arid field, such as those

of Tarlé on the Crimean War, Skazkin on the Three Emperors' League, and Romanov on Russian diplomatic history in the Far East at the beginning of the present century.[78] Yet the fact remains that when one searches for treatment of more important and broader phases of Russian diplomatic history, one must look to the research done by foreign scholars, such as P. E. Mosely's on Russia's Near Eastern policy in the 1830's; B. H. Sumner's outstanding volume on the Balkan policy of Russia in the 1870's; W. L. Langer's monograph on the Franco-Russian Alliance; or R. P. Churchill's on the Anglo-Russian Convention of 1907.[79] These do not by any means fill all the gaps in the field of Russian diplomatic history. The history of Russia's foreign relations still remains to be written.

There are certain neglected phases in the field of domestic history, for the reason that prior to 1917 the majority of Russian historians limited their attention to certain aspects of the problem at the expense of others. Thus, problems of institutional history during the first half of the nineteenth century and problems of social and economic history—with particular emphasis on agrarian relations—during the second half of the nineteenth and first half of the twentieth century have been studied extensively. But in the field of history of Imperial Russia three subjects remain inadequately covered. One is expansion and colonization. Important contributions were made

[78] E. V. Tarlé, *Krymskaya voyna* [The Crimean War], 2 vols., Moscow, 1950; B. A. Romanov, *Rossiya v Mandzhurii. Ocherki po istorii vnyeshney politiki samoderzhaviya v epokhu imperializma* [Russia in Manchuria. A Study of Russian Foreign Policy During the Age of Imperialism], Leningrad, 1928; *Ocherki diplomaticheskoy istorii russko-yaponskoy voyniy, 1895-1907* [A Study of the Diplomatic History of the Russo-Japanese War, 1895-1907], Moscow, 1947.

[79] Philip E. Mosely, *Russian Diplomacy and the Opening of the Eastern Question,* Cambridge, Harvard University Press, 1934; B. H. Sumner, *Russia and the Balkans, 1870-1880,* Oxford, 1937; William L. Langer, *The Franco-Russian Alliance, 1890-1894,* Cambridge, Harvard University Press, 1929; Roger P. Churchill, *The Anglo-Russian Convention of 1907,* Cedar Rapids, Ia., 1939.

before the Revolution and more has been done since 1917, particularly in regard to Siberia and the Pacific area by writers like Ogorodnikov, Bakhrushin, and Okun. In the United States, Professor Frank A. Golder contributed a considerable share to the subject.[80] Still, Russian historical literature on this subject compares very unfavorably with the wealth of American historical literature on the westward movement or on regional history ("sectionalism").

Another aspect of Imperial Russian history that calls for more intensive study is imperial administration and imperial policies. Here is indeed almost a virgin field. There are very few monographs in Russian historical literature which could be compared with G. V. Lantzeff's work on Siberian administration in the seventeenth century.[81] The contrast with the wealth of English literature on the history of the British Empire is striking.

Thirdly, regional histories and histories of national minorities have only lately begun to make substantial gains. Prior to 1917, except for the works of the "federal" school, mainly by Hrushevsky, or in the realm of western regionalism by Lyubavsky, there is a conspicuous absence of notable contributions.

Turning to the field of economic history Russian and Soviet historiography shows a more favorable record. Substantial contributions have been made to agrarian relations, industrial development—especially in the eighteenth century—and Russian labor problems. But there is a great lack of monographic works in the field of Russian trade such as that of Raymond H. Fisher

[80] Frank A. Golder, *Russian Expansion on the Pacific, 1641-1850,* Cleveland, 1914; *Bering's Voyage; an Account of the Efforts of the Russians to Determine the Relation of Asia and America,* 2 vols., New York, American Geographical Society, 1922-25.
[81] George V. Lantzeff, *Siberia in the Seventeenth Century. A Study of Colonial Administration,* Berkeley, University of California Press, 1943.

on the Russian fur trade in the sixteenth and seventeenth centuries.[82]

As to the field of historical biography the situation is most unsatisfactory. There are a large number of eminent historical figures whose biographies would be illuminating to history. To mention only a few: Nikon and Avvakum among religious leaders; Catherine II, Alexander I, and Alexander II, among the sovereigns; Potyomkin, Speransky,[83] Gorchakov, the Milyutin brothers, Pobedonostsev, Witte, and Stolypin, among statesmen; Yermolov, Kaufman, Muraviev-Amursky, and Skobelev, among the empire builders; and a host of others in various other fields of national life.

There is also a great need for scholarly study of the two decades preceding the Revolution. Except for the outstanding political account of this period by Sir Bernard Pares, there is virtually little else on the subject.[84] The Revolution of 1905, the struggle for constitutional government, the establishment and function of the Duma are still subjects that await scholarly exploration. And although much has appeared lately on the Russian Revolution of 1905 in Soviet historical literature, its one-sidedness is such that the problem cannot be considered entirely answered. Nor is there a satisfactory history of Russian political parties. The forthcoming history of the Socialist-Revolutionary Party by Oliver H. Radkey is perhaps a pioneering effort in Russian historiography.[85] A history of Russian liberalism and liberal parties is badly needed. For this very reason

[82] Raymond H. Fisher, *The Russian Fur Trade, 1550-1700*, Berkeley, University of California Press, 1943.
[83] Marc Raeff has recently contributed an admirable study on Speransky. See Marc Raeff, *Michael Speransky—Statesman of Imperial Russia*, The Hague, Nijhoff, 1957.
[84] Sir Bernard Pares, *The Fall of the Russian Monarchy*, New York, 1939.
[85] The first volume recently appeared. See Oliver H. Radkey, *The Agrarian Foes of Bolshevism*, Columbia University Press, 1958.

there is no outstanding scholarly treatment of the short-lived though significant period of the Provisional Government between March and November, 1917.

Finally, to the list of neglected subjects in Russian historiography must be added those of cultural, religious, and intellectual history, as well as the history of religious sectarianism. Despite the outstanding studies of church and state prior to the Revolution, by J. S. Curtiss, and in the Kievan period, by G. Fedotov, much is left unsaid and undone.[86]

As time goes on, one cannot escape the realization that the legacy of Russian historiography opens avenues for wider interpretations; that freshly unearthed sources, steadily growing in amount, require analysis in the light of recent events; and that a "revaluation of many old values" is becoming urgent. The Revolution has temporarily allowed the blustering orator to dominate the footlights. Soviet historiography reached the crossroads during the early 'thirties while demolishing the Pokrovsky school; it drove itself into a giddy orbit during the Stalin era; it has endeavored to extricate itself since 1953. The stark aspect of the post-Stalin period remains: whichever road historical writing decides to take, the haunting shadow of political interference with objective scholarship seems ever present.

As the years go by, it is the hope of the historian that the pendulum will swing back, indicating a return at least to sanity if not to complete objectivity in re-examining the past. A number of conditions, both internal and external, make it imperative to restore, overhaul, and eventually revise the rich past of the nation. As for the history of the present turbulent

[86] John S. Curtiss, *Church and State in Russia, 1907-1917*, New York, 1940; *The Russian Church and the Soviet State, 1917-1950*, Boston, 1953; George Fedotov. *The Religious Mind. Kievan Christianity*, Cambridge, Harvard University Press, 1946.

time, it is definitely a subject for writers of the future. Attempts to write the history of the Russian Revolution have proved unsuccessful even for mature scholars of the caliber of Milyukov or Pokrovsky, who sadly failed in their endeavor to give an historical account of this latest Russian drama. The entire epoch is still too near to permit sufficient perspective and therefore precludes the detachment necessary for scholarship. Practically everything written on the Revolution is so strongly partisan that it will be of little value to the future historian except as it may serve to display the opinions of contemporaries in the various political camps, or of mere onlookers who could not withstand the temptation to narrate their dramatic experiences. In this respect we who are contemporary observers can aid the future historian in his task of interpreting our own complex, confused, and perplexing era by assuming the more humble role of the *Geschichtssammler,* the famulus of the later *Geschichtsmaler.* Thus, in one field at least, we, too, begin at the same point as did the historian of the eighteenth century.

# General Bibliography

## BOOKS

Bestuzhev-Ryumin, K. N. *Biografii i kharakteristiki* [Biographical Essays]. St. Petersburg, 1882.

Black, Cyril E. (Ed.). *Rewriting Russian History; Soviet Interpretations of Russia's Past*. New York, 1956.

Doroshenko, D. *Oglyad ukrainskoy istoriografii* [A Survey of Ukrainian Historiography]. Prague, 1923.

Dovnar-Zapolsky, M. *Iz istorii obshchestvennykh techeny v Rossii* [A History of Social Movements in Russia]. Kiev, 1905 (see pp. 232-67).

*Entsiklopedichesky Slovar* [Russian Encyclopedia]. 41 vols. St. Petersburg, Brockhaus-Efron, 1890-1904.

Gapanovich, I. *Russian Historiography Outside of Russia*. Peiping, 1935.

Hecker, Julius F. *Russian Sociology*. New York, 1934.

*Histoire et historiens depuis cinquante ans: méthodes, organisation et résultats du travail historique de 1876 à 1926*. Paris, Bibliothèque de la Revue Historique, 1927 (see Vol. I, pp. 341-70).

Ikonnikov, V. S. *Opyt russkoy istoriografii* [A Study of Russian Historiography]. 2 vols. in 4. Kiev, 1891-1908.

Klyuchevsky, V. O. [In memoriam]. *Kharakteristiki i vospominaniya* [Essays and Recollections]. Moscow, 1912.

Klyuchevsky, V. O. *Ocherki i ryechi* [Studies and Addresses]. Second Collection of Articles. Moscow, n. d.

Koyalovich, M. I. *Istoriya russkogo samosoznaniya* [History of Russian Self-Realization]. St. Petersburg, 1893.

Masaryk, T. G. *The Spirit of Russia*. 2 vols. New York, 1919.

Milyukov, P. N. *Glavniye techeniya russkoy istoricheskoy mysli* [Main Currents in Russian Historical Thought]. Moscow, 1898.

Milyukov, P. N. *Le mouvement intellectuel russe*. Paris, 1918.

Petrovich, Michael Boro. *The Emergence of Russian Panslavism, 1856-1870*. New York, 1956.

Picheta, V. I. *Vvedeniye v Russkuyu istoriyu. Istochniki i istoriografiya* [An Introduction to Russian History. Sources and Historiography]. Moscow, 1922.

Platonov, F. S. *Lektsii po russkoy istorii* [Lectures on Russian History]. St. Petersburg, 1915 (see introductory chapter).

Pokrovsky, M. N. *Borba klassov i russkaya istoricheskaya literatura* [The Class Struggle in Russian Historical Literature]. Petrograd, 1923.

252

Pokrovsky, M. N. *Russkaya istoricheskaya literatura v klassovom osvyeshchenii* [Class Interpretation of Russian Historical literature]. 2 vols. Moscow, 1927-30.

Pypin, A. N. *Istoriya russkoy etnografii* [History of Russian Ethnography]. 4 vols. St. Petersburg, 1890-92.

Rubinstein, N. L. *Russkaya istoriografiya* [Russian Historiography]. Moscow, 1941.

Shakhnazarov, I. D. *Russkoye revolyutsionnoye prosvyeshcheniye v borbe s burzhuazno-dvoryanskoy istoriografiey* [Russian Revolutionary Education in its Conflict with Bourgeois-Gentry Historiography]. Leningrad, Academy of Sciences, 1934. Also in *Problemy Marksizma*, V, 1933, 48-73.

Tikhomirov, M. N. (Ed.). *Ocherki istorii istoricheskoy nauki v SSSR* [Studies of the History of Historical Science in the USSR], Moscow, 1955, Vol. I. Published by the Institute of History of the Academy of Sciences.

Zharikov, D. A. *I. N. Boltin, kak istorik* [I. N. Boltin as an Historian]. Samarkand, 1941.

## Articles

"Arkhiv Semevskogo [The Archive of Semevsky]." *Literaturnoye naslyedstvo,* VII-VIII, 418-30.

Azadovsky, M. "Zadachi Sibirskoy bibliografii [Problems of Siberian Bibliography]." *Sibirskiye zapiski,* VI, 1919.

Bakhrushin, S. B. "Müller kak istorik Sibiri [Müller as an Historian of Siberia]." In Müller's latest edition of *Istoriya Sibiri* [History of Siberia], published in 1937 by the Academy of Sciences, 5-55.

Bidlo, Jaroslav. "Remarques à la défense de ma conception de l'histoire de l'orient Européen et le l'histoire des peuples slaves." *Bulletin d'Information des Sciences Historiques en Europe Orientale,* VI, fasc. 3-4. Varsovie, 1934. Cf. Derzhavin, N. "Iz itogov VII mezhdunarodnogo kongressa istoricheskikh nauk v Varshave [Observations on the 7th International Congress of Historical Sciences in Warsaw]." *Trudy instituta slavyanovedeniya Akademii Nauk SSSR,* II, 1934, 475-82.

Epstein, F. "Die marxistische Geschichtswissenschaft in der Sovjetunion seit 1927." *Jahrbücher für Kultur und Geschichte der Slaven,* VI, I, 1930.

Fedotov, G. "Rossiya Klyuchevskogo [Klyuchevsky's Russia]." *Sovremenniye zapiski,* Vol. L, 1932, 340-62.

Florovsky, A. "La littérature historique russe-émigration." *Bulletin d'Information des Sciences Historiques en Europe Orientale* (Varsovie). I, 82-121; III, 25-79.

Florovsky, A. "Russkaya istoricheskaya nauka v emigratsii [Russian Historical Science in Emigration]." *Trudy V-go S'yezda russkikh akademicheskikh organizatsy za-granitsey* (Belgrade), I, 1931.

Florovsky, A. "The Works of Russian Emigrés in History (1921-1927)." *Slavonic Review,* VII, 1928, 216-19.

Gautier, G. "Histoire de Russie: publications des années 1917-1927." *Revue Historique,* CLVII, 1928, 93-123.

Golubtsov, S. A. "Teoreticheskiye vzglyady V. O. Klyuchevskogo [Theoretical views of Klyuchevsky]." *Russky istorichesky zhurnal,* VIII, 1922, 178-202.

Gorin, P. "M. N. Pokrovsky—bolshevik-istorik [M. N. Pokrovsky—Bolshevik Historian]." *Vyestnik kommunisticheskoy akademii,* IV, 1933, 42-48.

Gurko-Kryazhin, B. "M. N. Pokrovsky i izucheniye istorii Vostoka [M. N. Pokrovsky and the Study of the History of the Orient]." *Noviy vostok,* XXV, 1929, 29-46.

Hrushevsky (Grushevsky), M. S. "Ob ukrainskoy istoriografii XVIII vyeka. Neskolko soobrazheny [A Few Reflections on Ukrainian Historiography of the 18th Century]." *Izvestiya* akademii nauk, O. O. N., Ser. VII, Vol. III, 1934, 215-23.

Jonas, Hans. "Die Entwicklung der Geschichtsforschung in der Sovjet-Union seit dem Ausgang des Weltkrieges." *Zeitschrift für osteuropäische Geschichte,* V, 1931, 66-83; 386-96.

Karpovich, Michael. "Klyuchevsky and Recent Trends in Russian Historiography." *The Slavonic and East European Review,* XXI, 1943, 31-39.

Khodorov, A. E. "M. N. Pokrovsky i izucheniye Dalnego Vostoka [M. N. Pokrovsky and the Study of the Far East]." *Noviy vostok,* XXV, 1929, 1-28.

Kiesewetter (Kizevetter), A. "Histoire de Russia: travaux des savants russes émigrés (1918-1928)." *Revue Historique,* CLXIII, 1930, 160-83.

Korablev, V. N. "Akademik A. N. Pypin i slavyansky vopros [Academician A. N. Pypin and the Slav Question]." *Vyestnik akademii nauk SSSR,* VIII-IX, 1933, 67-78.

Lappo-Danilevsky, A. S. "The Development of Science and Learning in Russia." *Russian Realities and Problems,* ed. by J. D. Duff. Cambridge, 1917, 153-229.

Leppmann, W. "Die russische Geschichtswissenschaft in der Emigration." *Zeitschrift für osteuropäische Geschichte,* V, 1931, 215-48.

Lukin, N. M. "Akademik M. N. Pokrovsky [Academician M. N. Pokrovsky]." *Izvestiya akademii nauk SSSR, O.O.N.,* Ser. VII, Vol. IX, 1932, 773-82.

Maklakov, B. "Klyuchevsky." *Slavonic Review,* XIII, 1935, 320-29.

Mazour, Anatole G. "Modern Russian Historiography." *Journal of Modern History,* IX, 1937, 169-202.

Mazour, Anatole G. and Bateman, Herman E. "Recent Conflicts in Soviet Historiography." *Journal of Modern History,* March, 1951, 56-68.

Milyukov, P. "Eurasianism and Europeanism in Russian History." *Festschrift T. G. Masaryk zum 80. Geburtstage* (Supplement to *Der russische Gedanke,* Bonn), I, 1930, 225-36.

Milyukov, P. "Velichiye i padeniye M. N. Pokrovskogo [The Greatness and Decline of M. N. Pokrovsky]." *Sovremenniye zapiski* (Paris), LXV, 1937, 368-87.

"Neskolko dokumentov iz tsarskikh arkhivov o M. N. Pokrovskom [Several Documents from Tsarist Archives Concerning M. N. Pokrovsky]." *Krasniy Arkhiv,* III, 1932, 5-53.

Nevsky, V. M. "M. N. Pokrovsky—istorik oktyabrya [M. N. Pokrovsky—Historian of the October Revolution]." *Istoriya proletariata SSSR,* XII, 1932, 3-20.

Pfitzner, J. "Die Geschichte Osteuropas und die Geschichte des Slawentums als Forschungsprobleme." *Historische Zeitschrift,* Bd. 150, 1934, 21-85.

Piksanov, N. K. "Akademik A. N. Pypin [Academician A. N. Pypin]." *Vyestnik akademii nauk SSSR,* IV, 1933, 39-44.

Piontkovsky, S. "Velikoderzhavniye tendentsii v istoriografii Rossii [Autocratic Tendencies in Russian Historiography]." *Istorik-Marksist,* XVII, 1930, 21-26.

Piontkovsky, S. "Velikorusskaya burzhuaznaya istoriografiya poslednego desyatelitiya [Great-Russian Bourgeois Historiography of the Last Decade]." *Istorik-Marksist,* XVIII-XIX, 1930, 157-76.

Pokrovsky, M. N. " 'Noviye' techeniya v russkoy istoricheskoy literaturye ['New' Currents in Russian Historical Literature]." *Istorik-Marksist,* VII, 1928, 1-17.

Powell, A. "The Nationalist Trend in Soviet Historiography." *Soviet Studies,* April, 1951, 372-77.

Presnyakov, A. E. "V. O. Klyuchevsky." *Russky istorichesky zhurnal,* VIII, 1922, 203-24.

Rubinstein, N. "M. N. Pokrovsky—istorik vneshney politiki [M. N. Pokrovsky— Historian of Foreign Policy]." *Istorik-Marksist,* IX, 1928, 58-78.

Schlesinger, Rudolf. "Recent Discussions on the Periodization of History." *Soviet Studies,* October, 1952, 152-69.

Schlesinger, Rudolf. "Recent Soviet Historiography." *Soviet Studies,* April, 1950, 293-312; July, 1950, 3-21; October, 1950, 138-62; January, 1951, 265-88.

Shcheglov, A. "Metodologicheskiye istoki oshibok M. N. Pokrovskogo [Methodological Sources of the Errors of M. N. Pokrovsky]." *Pod znamenem marksizma,* V, 1936, 55-69.

Skubitsky, T. "Klassovaya borba v ukrainskoy istoricheskoy literaturye [The Class Struggle in Ukrainian Historical Literature]." *Istorik-Marksist,* XVII, 1930, 27-40.

Struve, P. "Ivan Aksakov." *Slavonic Review,* II, 1924, 514-18.

Sukhotin, L. M. "Kratky ocherk russkoy istoriografii [A Brief Outline of the Development of Russian Historiography]." *Sbornik arkhelogicheskogo obshcehestva* (Belgrade), 1927, 61-76.

Tompkins, Stuart R. "Trends in Communist Historical Thought." *Slavonic Review,* XIII, 1935, 294-319.

"Uebersicht der historischen Literatur Russlands für die Jahre 1860-1865." *Historische Zeitschrift,* XVI, 126-74.

Yugov, M. "Polozheniye i zadachi istoricheskogo fronta v Belorussii [The Situation and Problems Concerning the Historical Front in White Russia]." *Istorik-Marksist,* XVII, 41-50.

# Index